Following the Proceeds of Environmental Crime

Huge quantities of natural resources are illegally harvested and their proceeds laundered in the Asia-Pacific region, fostering corruption and undermining environmental governance. Most illegal exploitation and pollution occurs in countries with poor governance capacities, but much of the sale for profit and money laundering occurs in mature markets with well-developed governance capacities. Their asymmetrical enforcement capacities can complement each other.

This book explores ways to combat illegal fishing and logging in the Asia-Pacific region by the use of cooperative legal measures, particularly anti-money laundering and confiscation of proceeds techniques. Contributors to this volume cover themes including: the nature of transnational environmental crime; patterns in laundering of illicit fish and forest products; networks for distribution of illicit products; weaknesses in current systems for assurance of the legality of products; and international legal cooperation to enforce anti-money laundering laws in relation to illicit products. In considering these topics the book explores how the innovative use of anti-money laundering measures and the seizure of criminal proceeds can be utilized as policy options to combat transnational fishery and forestry crimes.

The book will be of keen interest to scholars and students of environmental law and criminal law, and excellent use to practitioners in natural resources conservation law.

Gregory Rose is Professor at the University of Wollongong, Australia.

Following the Proceeds of Environmental Crime

Forests, Fish and Filthy Lucre

**Edited by
Gregory Rose**

Routledge
Taylor & Francis Group

LONDON AND NEW YORK

First published 2014
by Routledge
2 Park Square, Milton Park, Abingdon, Oxon, OX14 4RN

and by Routledge
711 Third Avenue, New York, NY 10017

Routledge is an imprint of the Taylor & Francis Group, an informa business

British Library Cataloguing in Publication Data
A catalogue record for this book is available from the British Library

Library of Congress Cataloging-in-Publication Data
Following the proceeds of environmental crime : fish, forests and filthy lucre / edited by Gregory Rose.
    pages cm
    Includes bibliographical references and index.
    ISBN 978-0-415-53239-6 (hardback)—ISBN 978-0-203-70181-2 (ebk)
    1. Offenses against the environment.   2. Environmental law—Criminal provisions.   I. Rose, Gregory (Gregory Lawrence), 1960–editor of compilation.
    HV6401.F65 2014
    364.1'45—dc23   2013050055

ISBN: 978-0-415-53239-6 (hbk)
ISBN: 978-0-203-70181-2 (ebk)

Typeset in Baskerville
by Keystroke, Station Road, Codsall, Wolverhampton

MIX
Paper from
responsible sources
FSC
www.fsc.org   FSC® C013604

Printed and bound in Great Britain by
CPI Group (UK) Ltd, Croydon, CR0 4YY

Contents

Notes on contributors

Salwa Amira, Center for International Forestry Research, Jalan CIFOR, Situgede, Sindangbarang, Bogor Barat, Bogor 16115, Indonesia; Independent researcher, Jalan Tebet Barat Dalam VI K No.11, Jakarta Selatan, Indonesia.

Dr Kate Barclay, School of International Studies, Faculty of Arts and Social Sciences, University of Technology, Sydney, NSW, Australia.

Duncan Brack, independent environmental policy analyst and adviser, London, UK. Associate Fellow of Chatham House (Royal Institute of International Affairs), Associate of Green Alliance UK. From 2010 to 2012, special adviser at the UK Department of Energy and Climate Change. Before that he worked for Chatham House, and from 1998 to 2003 was head of its Sustainable Development Programme. He has worked extensively on issues of illegal logging, forest governance and the international trade in illegal timber.

Dr Samantha Bricknell, Deputy Research Manager and Principal Research Analyst, Australian Institute of Criminology, 74 Leichhardt Street, Griffith, ACT 2603, Australia.

Professor John Broome, Chairman at Grievance Authority of the Reserve Bank Australia, Director at Milgrove Consulting Group Pty Ltd. Previously, inaugural Co-Chair of the Asia-Pacific Group on Money Laundering, a senior representative of Australia at the Financial Action Task Force.

Ahmad Dermawan, Center for International Forestry Research, Forests and Governance program, Jalan CIFOR, Situgede, Sindangbarang, Bogor Barat, Bogor 16115, Indonesia.

Professor Lorraine Elliott, Department of International Relations, School of International Political and Strategic Studies, College of Asia and the Pacific, Australian National University.

Dr Yunus Husein, Staff Expert, Directorate of Human Resources, Bank Indonesia. Former Head of Bank of Indonesia Transaction Reports and Analysis Center (INTRAC/PPATK). Head of Public Governance Sub-Committee, National Committee of Governance (KNKG); Team Head for Drafting of Assets Forfeiture Act and Terrorism Funding Act.

Murray Johns, Senior Policy Adviser, Northern International Fisheries, Department of Agriculture Fisheries and Forestry, ACT, Australia.

James Lehane, Assistant Manager (Investigations), Australian Pesticides and Veterinary Medicines Authority, 18 Wormald Street, Symonston, ACT 2609, Australia.

Sofi Mardiah, Research Officer, Climate Change Mitigation, Center for International Forestry Research, Forests and Governance Program, Jalan CIFOR, Situgede, Sindangbarang, Bogor Barat, Bogor 16115, Indonesia.

Krystof Obidzinski, Principal Scientist, Globalised Trade and Investment, Center for International Forestry Research, Jalan CIFOR, Situgede, Sindanbarang, Bogor Barat, Bogor 16115, Indonesia.

Dr Mary Ann Palma-Robles, Senior Research Fellow, ANCORS – Australian National Centre for Ocean Resources and Security, School of Law, University of Wollongong, Northfields Avenue, NSW 2522, Australia.

Ian Parks, Director of Education and Enforcement, Fisheries Victoria, Department of Primary Industries, Melbourne, VIC, Australia.

Grant Pink, Director, Regulatory Capability and Assurance Section, Australian Government Department of Environment, Parkes, ACT, Australia, and PhD Candidate, University of New England.

Professor Gregory Rose, ANCORS – Australian National Centre for Ocean Resources and Security, School of Law, University of Wollongong, Northfields Avenue, NSW 2522, Australia.

Anna Christina Sinaga, Research Officer, Integrated Law Enforcement Approach Project, Forests and Governance, Center for International Forestry Research, Jalan CIFOR, Situgede, Sindangbarang, Bogor Barat, Bogor 16115, Indonesia.

Part I
Introduction

1   Forests, fish and filthy lucre

Gregory Rose

This book explores a new frontier in environmental law: the use of financial intelligence to prosecute environmental crime.

Studies of how to follow the proceeds of environmental crime can inform governmental efforts to manage natural resources by improving our understanding of links between environmental crime and associated corruption and money laundering. It is hoped that these insights will translate into practical applications to combat environmental crimes by using financial intelligence to track the profits back to the 'kingpins' of environmental crimes.

Anti-money laundering techniques appear to offer great promise to law enforcers seeking to block and punish the beneficiaries of organized crime. However, these techniques are still largely an esoteric area of specialist practitioners within the criminal justice system. Anti-money laundering techniques are yet to make inroads into other areas of governmental regulation, such as environmental management.

Anti-money laundering also has its critics, particularly among academic commentators (Sharman 2011). A major concern is the imbalance between the great expense of sophisticated infrastructure for financial surveillance and intelligence as compared with the poor returns on investment. Vast amounts of data, time-consuming and complicated sifting and protracted legal cases may nevertheless lead to a futile end. Notionally, the use of anti-money laundering techniques should be generically applicable across all types of crime for profit. They have been used with some success to seize the proceeds of illicit drug trafficking, although with less success to seize the proceeds of corruption. Common sense suggests that it may be simpler and more efficient to apply anti-money laundering techniques to some types of crimes than to others. Their use to combat organized transnational environmental crime is largely untested.

Environmental harm and its prohibition

The notion of environmental crime is not new, although the phenomenon is evolving with startling speed in response to the increasing opportunities provided by new technologies. Environmental crime is premised on two elemental factors: the act of causing environmental harm and the illegality of that causal act.

The acts of direct harm to the environment can be conceived of in two categories: damage to the living world and damage to the inanimate world. Criminal damage to the living world may typically be the result of illegal exploitation, such as poaching, harvesting beyond allowances or with improper equipment or in prohibited areas or at prohibited times, or the illegal introduction of biological pests. Criminal harms caused to the inanimate world may include improper waste disposal, illegal use of hazardous substances, accidental or deliberate pollution and illegal alteration of habitats. Acts causing environmental harm undergo continuous metamorphosis and take on many modern forms.

The criminalization of these acts causing environmental harm expands in tandem with the growing sphere of governmental regulation and its broadening over the range of activities considered illegal. Yet the range of acts causing environmental harm expands more quickly than the range of reactive regulations and law enforcement techniques introduced by governments to combat them. The lag in regulation and enforcement is especially prevalent in countries with poor capacities for natural resources governance and law enforcement, such as the less developed countries located in the Asia-Pacific region. Much of the existing regional law enforcement and regulatory infrastructure is inadequate to prevent environmental crimes.

Defining crime: a procedural problem

The meaning of crime is potentially broad and is narrowed here within manageable bounds, then contracted further to the area of overlap between the subcategories of environmental crime and transnational crime.

A crime occurs when there is an intersection of two factors: (1) non-compliance with law and (2) specification that such a breach is an offence against that law. Non-compliance that does not entail a penalty cannot be a crime. A breach of a standard of behavior is more than mere non-compliance when it entails a penalty.

Furthermore, even non-compliance that does incur a penalty is not necessarily a crime. Penalties may be administrative or civil, rather than criminal. As governmental regulation has burgeoned, so have the types of sanctions and processes for addressing breaches of regulations, the range and diversity of which seem limited only by the imagination. Types of sanctions include imprisonment, fines, fees and other financial penalties, confiscations, compensation, bans, deregistration, suspensions, community service, enforceable undertakings, injunctions, withheld benefits, negative publicity, apologies, and so on. Terminology used to describe the wide variety of sanctions for crimes is often confusing and is sometimes inconsistent. Environmental crimes are generally minor offences for which administrative or civil sanctions and processes apply. The characterization of a sanction as criminal, rather than as administrative or civil, therefore, is important within the context of international cooperation to combat environmental crime.

'Administrative sanctions' can be understood as penalties imposed by a regulator or some other enforcement body that is a government executive agency, 'without intervention by a court or tribunal' (Australian Law Reform Commission (Aust. LRC) 2002: 2.64). Given that administrative penalties generally result from the 'mechanical' or 'automatic' imposition of statutorily determined sanctions, and do not involve a judge at first instance, there are few procedural elements. They are defined in large part by the process of imposition. Notionally, these sanctions are intended to ensure the prevention of further damages rather than to penalize and abrogate rights (European Commission 2004: 6). They include fines, fees, taxes, infringement notices and orders to pay compensation, as well as loss of licenses, permits, allowances or privileges.

A 'civil penalty' is one 'imposed by courts applying civil rather than criminal processes' (Aust. LRC 2002: 2.45). Most commonly, civil sanctions consist of monetary fines, which can be imposed on both personal and corporate bodies, but can also extend beyond punishment to include imposition of corrective behavior activities and the payment of compensation.

In contrast, a crime is a breach of a law that incurs a criminal penalty. 'Criminal sanctions' are punishments imposed by courts for breaches of criminal law, such as by a fine or imprisonment, with imprisonment being within the exclusive juris-diction of criminal law and entailing the stigma of a criminal record. Criminal sanctions are distinguished by their enforcement procedures, which are relatively formal (Aust. LRC 2002: 2.71). For example, they are required to be heard before a court presided over by a judge and, depending on the offense and jurisdiction, a jury. In the common law adversarial system, a prosecutor must tender evi-dence that proves beyond reasonable doubt that the accused intended and did commit the prohibited conduct. Most importantly, criminal procedural rights benefit the accused, including the presumption of innocence, prohibition on self-incrimination, the right to silence and the right not to be tried twice for the same alleged crime or for a retrospective crime.

Thus, the differences between criminal, civil and administrative sanctions lie within the procedures used to implement them. The main feature distinguishing criminal from civil and administrative sanctions is arguably the unique nature of the criminal trial. The legal processes prior to non-criminal sanctions also differ greatly. Criminal sanctions require police authorities to investigate criminal behavior and gather evidence. Within administrative processes, the investigation of breaches occurs on a lower evidentiary standard, presumptions of innocence generally do not exist and, in the cases of corporations, regulations may require cooperation with competent authorities.

In relation to international criminal law, non-criminal sanctions have been defined as 'penalties for conduct proscribed under international criminal law, [but] which have been imposed by civil courts, administrative agencies of other law enforcement authorities outside of a criminal trial' (Meyer 2006: 552). Thus, the international criminal trial itself is the sole identifier for whether a sanction is criminal or not. In addition, a significant difference between administrative and criminal sanctions is that the presumption of innocence within criminal procedures is not found within case law regarding civil and administrative sanctions.

International and transnational environmental crime distinguished

International institutional and academic studies in the field of environmental crime peaked in the late 1980s and first half of the 1990s, and tended to be criminological, examining primarily the motivations, patterns and social structures characteristic of environmental crime with a view to controlling and reducing it (Edwards, Edwards and Fields 1996). Thus, the focus of attention was on the phenomenon of environmental crime under national and local laws. Interest subsided in the mid-1990s and has recently revived, taking on a transnational focus, as evidenced by the several publications of Rob White (2008, 2009, 2010, 2011). The United Nations Interregional Crime and Justice Research Institute (UNICRI), having produced a book concerning the role of criminal justice in environment protection in the 1990s (Alvazzi del Frate and Norberry 1993), has recently recommenced work in this area (UNICRI n.d.).

The majority of contemporary studies on the subject of environmental crime are produced by environmental advocacy organizations in civil society, such as the World Wide Fund for Nature (WWF), TRAFFIC and the Environment Investigation Agency, and by think tanks such as Chatham House. These studies focus on hot topics within environmental sub-sectors, particularly wildlife, logging, fishing, hazardous waste and ozone-depleting substances (Environment Investigation Agency 2008; WWF-UK 2003).

In an age of globalization, environmental crime has adapted quickly to international opportunities generated by efficient transport, internationally integrated markets and instant financial transfers and communications. Illegally harvested natural resources enter international markets, profits are transferred internationally and laundered in multiple foreign countries, and, hence, an integral feature of the criminal activity is its cross-border nature. This inherently transnational dimension features strongly because it is usually to the advantage of criminals. Historically, law enforcement efforts are concentrated within a country's national borders, with relatively weak arrangements for cross-jurisdictional cooperation. Therefore, a transnational dimension may be simple for organized crime to add to its activities but difficult for law enforcement authorities to respond to.

Consequently, the attention of intergovernmental institutions is gathering in this area, addressing its international dimensions. Since 2005, the Commission on Crime Prevention and Criminal Justice has undertaken a program of work focused on illegal logging and wildlife crime, and has since extended its work to address illegal wildlife trafficking. Illegal fishing has appeared on the agendas of the UN General Assembly, Economic and Social Commission, Food and Agricultural Organization. Also in 2013, the UN Environment Programme and INTERPOL convened a Summit on Environmental Crime and Compliance. This trend in intergovernmental activity has been considered likely to lead to overlapping institutional agendas and to the need for their coordination (Elliott 2007).

A distinction that needs be made in the context of the international institutional attention is between international and transnational environmental crime. International crimes are activities that offend against direct prohibitions upon them in international law. They are offences prescribed by the international community acting collectively, rather than by national governments. Clear-cut examples include the crime of genocide, war crimes and crimes against humanity, as set out in the Rome Statute of the International Criminal Court.

Despite the contention that states breaching international laws can be subjected to criminal penalties and be considered to commit international crimes, there are no environmental offences enacted under international law and directed against states. Nor are there environmental crimes prohibited by international law and directed against individuals.

Transnational crimes are those acts committed in breach of national laws in which the offences committed have elements that cross national borders. Transnational crimes do not offend against international law directly but offend against national laws, the commission of which has crossed national borders (Boister 2003).

The constitutive legal elements of transnational crime can vary widely, from physical acts, such as smuggling, to intangible acts, such as conspiring. The cross-border nature of these crimes ranges from simple movements across the border between two countries by a lone operator smuggling illegally harvested natural resources or prohibited species, such as illegally logged timber, to complex multi-layered transactions across multiple jurisdictions by organized criminal syndicates. The nature of fisheries crime, for example, is that it often involves a vessel that operates beyond the boundary of the flag state, is owned in another country, managed in yet another, uses officers and crew of diverse nationalities and lands its catch in the ports of yet other states. Intangible transnational elements can include organizing, financing, laundering or profiting outside the country in relation to an environmental crime committed partially inside it. Transnational environmental crime is among the categories of emerging transnational crimes identified by the United Nations (UN Office on Drugs and Crime n.d.).

The UN Convention on Transnational Organized Crime (CTOC) sets out a definition in Article 3.2:

> For the purpose of paragraph 1 of this article, an offence is transnational in nature if:
>
> (a) It is committed in more than one State;
> (b) It is committed in one State but a substantial part of its preparation, planning, direction or control takes place in another State;
> (c) It is committed in one State but involves an organized criminal group that engages in criminal activities in more than one State; or
> (d) It is committed in one State but has substantial effects in another State.

Forests and fisheries crimes in the Asia-Pacific

The Asia-Pacific region is rich in natural resources. Yet its relatively dense human population is often lacking in economic opportunities. Therefore, opportunistic, savvy or desperate entrepreneurs embark on the low-risk, high-return illegitimate ventures that depredate natural resources. Their short-term profits negatively impact on longer-term and more widely spread national opportunities for economic growth and poverty reduction (Dupont 2001).

Where fishing exports generate a large proportion of a country's income, ensuring there are enough fishing stocks for future generations of people is important for that country, especially for many island nations where fish are one of the primary sources of food. Prevention of illegal fishing will play an important part in ensuring fish stocks remain robust. In the tuna-rich waters of the western central Pacific, poor governance in fisheries licensing, in negotiating access for foreign fishers and in monitoring and surveillance of compliance causes significant revenue losses to Pacific island governments (Marine Resources Assessment Group 2005). There is substantial evidence of corruption as a factor contributing to the prevalence of illegal fishing in the Asia-Pacific region. Illicit payments made to officials are enabled by the lack of measures to ensure transparency in financial transactions and to combat money laundering. Therefore, illegal fishing and corruption both produce proceeds of crime that might be identified by the application of financial intelligence mechanisms.

Similarly, sound stewardship of forest resources promotes sustainable livelihoods for regional forest industries dependent upon timber resources and for the people who live in close proximity to forests and depend upon them for environmental and resource benefits. Preventing further illegal deforestation in the Asia-Pacific would positively impact on flood prevention, climate change mitigation and the utility of carbon credit systems that need reliable law enforcement on the ground to support their paper value. Additional negative impacts from illegal logging flow from its close links with corruption and bribery, as well as smuggling, fraud, bank offences and organized crime, which undermine the rule of law and the sustainable economic of regional countries (Setiono and Husein 2005).

Laundering the filthy lucre

At various stages of progress in the commission of illegal fishing and illegal logging crimes, 'crossover' offences may be committed, such as bribery and corruption, fraud and embezzlement and money laundering. The same complex of close association between organized criminal activity and environmental crime is present in the forest sector as in fisheries in the Asia-Pacific region. Bribery and corruption are more likely to occur upstream, at the source of illegally harvested natural resources, when securing, harvesting and transporting them. Downstream, during the recovery and laundering of profits, fraud and money laundering are more likely to occur.

Anti-money laundering systems have the potential to address environmental crime by detecting and tracing flows of money associated with such crimes, directing law enforcement efforts to the primary organizers and financiers. The goal is to 'follow the money trail' to high-level drivers and beneficiaries of environmental crimes, for the purpose of prosecuting them and recovering the proceeds of these crimes.

This differs from existing law enforcement efforts that focus on the physical movements of illegal fish and logs, which tend to capture more minor criminals involved in the operation and are also highly resource-intensive and subject to local corruption. By following the trail of money, anti-money laundering systems also have the advantage of allowing law enforcement agencies to seize and confiscate the proceeds of crimes. This not only ensures that criminals lose money or assets gained through the illegal activities but also contributes back to national revenue and can be specifically redirected back into law enforcement.

To combat the organized criminal efforts in timber and fisheries pillage and in money laundering, national forestry and fisheries and law enforcement agencies need good working relationships with their national financial intelligence units, usually located in central banks and national treasuries, to share information and to take a whole-of-government approach, as well as to work with relevant private sector stakeholders. There is a need to coordinate and, therefore, to integrate anti-money laundering and asset forfeiture mechanisms with law enforcement directed against fisheries and forest crimes and related corruption, generating integrated strategies across the whole of government.

Building such capacity to integrate financial intelligence will also enable governments to implement policies to ensure the legality of logging and fishing practices, which in turn strengthens traditional mainstream law enforcement capacity. Ultimately, improved law enforcement capacity should promote environmental sustainability and economic growth, and ensure that countries providing timber and fish receive adequate remuneration for their resources, rather than the value being funneled to corrupt individuals. Ultimately, enhancing the capacity of law enforcement and regulatory authorities to combat illegal logging and fishing using anti-money laundering systems might help prevent unsustainable practices in these sectors.

Transnational environmental law enforcement cooperation

Growing recognition of the significant adverse implications for development in the Asia-Pacific region of such environmental crime draws attention to the need for better law enforcement by regional governments.

A great deal of illegal exploitation and pollution occurs in countries with poor governance capacities, but much of the sale for profit and money laundering occurs in mature markets with well-developed governance capacities. The transnational dimension of these natural resources crimes creates opportunities for international cooperation in law enforcement to combat the crimes jointly. Law enforcement against white-collar crimes is relatively better established in countries with developed economies, where the statutes and jurisprudence, criminal procedure and institutional capabilities are at least modestly functional.

It follows that, given the limited law enforcement capacity of some regional source countries, international cooperation can usefully augment local opportunities for enforcement. Cooperation between mainstream traditional law enforcement agencies and white-collar crime regulatory agencies is imperative, not only within the domestic law enforcement arrangements of the source country but also across national borders. Foreign counterpart law enforcement agencies, such as police, customs and financial intelligence agencies, can be called upon to support a source country's law enforcement efforts. For example, Australia can provide useful financial intelligence and other law enforcement assistance to trace illegally harvested Indonesian products and their proceeds.

To optimize their effectiveness in providing support, foreign developed country counterpart agencies need to be aware of the risk profiles of logging sectors and of fisheries production factors throughout the region, in order to advise their financial intelligence units, and their financial sector stakeholders, of the risks associated with the natural resource industry in the source country. Improved appreciation of the potential for anti-money laundering cooperation may produce, therefore, information concerning suspect companies and products in the source countries, as well as specific requests by them for intelligence relating to the proceeds of forestry and fisheries crimes.

Scope, structure and synopsis of the book

In this volume, practitioners and academic specialists in the study of environmental crime and in the use of anti-money laundering systems share their understanding and insights of how to follow the proceeds of environmental crime. They consider natural resources governance, primarily the sustainable management of forests and fisheries, with a focus on transnational issues in the Asia-Pacific region and case studies especially of Australia and Indonesia.

Following this introduction, the book is structured into six parts that develop consecutive ideas about following the proceeds of environmental crime. Part II commences with a survey and analysis of the phenomenon of environmental crime in the Asia-Pacific region (Elliott) and a case study of Australia (Bricknell). Part III explains the tenets of anti-money laundering (Broome) and studies their application to environmental crime in Indonesia (Husein).

Parts IV and V then conduct case studies of illegal fishing and illegal logging respectively. Illegal fishing is considered through APEC (Asia-Pacific Economic Cooperation) regional efforts to improve fisheries governance (Johns), the cycle of Pacific Ocean tuna production (Barclay) and case studies of Indonesia and the Philippines (Palma). A case study of the application of anti-money laundering law enforcement techniques to illegal fishing in the Australian state of Victoria offers a fascinating model for possible application elsewhere (Parks). In relation to illegal logging, two chapters from the Centre for International Forestry Research paint a dramatic picture of timber crime in Indonesia (Dermawan, Obidzinski and Amira) and how to combat it by both 'following wood' and 'following the money' through an integrated law enforcement approach (Sinaga and Mardiah). A sobering and usefully critical response to the proposal to use anti-money laundering techniques considers the daunting legal challenges and complex technical obstacles that may obstruct this approach to combat illegal logging (Brack).

Part VI of the book concludes with ideas on how to enhance management of forests and fisheries resources by integrating criminal law enforcement with financial intelligence. This requires the construction of collaborative networks across management discipline boundaries at the national and regional levels (Pink) and the integration of intelligence functions into environmental law enforcement (Lehane). Ultimately, as considered in Part VII, international coordination across environmental management, financial intelligence and law enforcement functions is needed to address the inherently transnational nature of environmental crime (Rose).

Conclusion

In 2010, environmental and financial regulators, law enforcement and development assistance officials, policy analysts and academics from intergovernmental, governmental and private sector institutions – 130 people from across four continents and oceans – gathered together to discuss forests, fish and filthy lucre at a conference on 'Following the Proceeds of Environmental Crime'. The event was held at the University of Wollongong, Australia, in partnership with the Commonwealth of Australia Attorney-General's Department and supported by funds from the Australian Agency for International Development. The conference focused on the use of anti-money laundering systems to thwart organized crime syndicates engaged in illegal logging and illegal fishing in the Asia-Pacific and provided the impetus for the commissioning of thematic chapters for this book.

It is hoped that the book will contribute to greater awareness and a critical understanding of the opportunities to combat transnational environmental crime through international law enforcement cooperation, in particular, by using anti-money laundering techniques.

References

Alvazzi del Frate, A. and Norberry, J. (eds) (1993) *Environmental Crime, Sanctioning Strategies and Sustainable Development*, Rome: UNICRI Publication No. 50.

Australian Law Reform Commission (2002) *Principled Regulation: Federal Civil and Administrative Penalties in Australia*, Report No. 95.

Boister, N. (2003) 'Transnational Criminal Law?' *European Journal of International Law*, 14: 953–76.

Dupont, A. (2001) *East Asia Imperilled: Transnational Challenges to Security*, Cambridge: Cambridge University Press.

Edwards, S., Edwards, T. and Fields, C. (1996) *Environmental Crime and Criminality*, New York: Garland Inc.

Elliott, L. (2007) 'Transnational Environmental Crime in the Asia Pacific: an "un(der) securitized" security problem?' *The Pacific Review*, 20(4): 499–522.

Environment Investigation Agency (2008) *Environmental Crime: A Threat to Our Future*. Available online at www.eia-international.org/wp-content/uploads/reports171-1.pdf (accessed 21 January 2014).

European Commission (2004) *Study on measures other than criminal ones in cases where environmental Community law has not been respected in a few candidate countries*. Available online at http://ec.europa.eu/environment/legal/crime/pdf/cd_summary_report.pdf (accessed 10 August 2013).

Marine Resources Assessment Group (MRAG) (2005) *Final Report: Review of Impacts of Illegal, Unreported and Unregulated Fishing on Developing Countries*, London: MRAG. Available online at www.imcsnet.org/imcs/docs/iuu_fishing_synthesis_report_mrag. pdf (accessed 6 February 2014).

Meyer, F. (2006) 'Complementing Complementarity', *International Criminal Law Review*, 6: 549–83.

Michalowski, R. and Bitten, K. (2005) 'Transnational *Environmental* Crime', in P. Reichel (ed.) *Handbook of Transnational Crime and Justice*, Thousand Oaks, CA: Sage Publications.

Setiono, B. and Husein, Y. (2005) *Fighting Forest Crime and Promoting Prudent Banking for Sustainable Forest Management*, Bogor, Indonesia: Centre for International Forestry Research, Occasional Paper No. 44.

Sharman, J. (2011) *The Money Laundry: Regulating Criminal Finance in the Global Economy*, Ithaca, NY: Cornell University Press.

United Nations Interregional Crime and Justice Research Institute (UNICRI) (n.d.). Available online at www.unicri.it/topics/environmental/publications (accessed 10 August 2013).

United Nations Office on Drugs and Crime (UNODC) (n.d.) *Emerging Crimes*. Available online at www.unodc.org/unodc/organized-crime/emerging-crimes.html (accessed 10 August 2013).

White, R. (2008) *Crimes Against Nature: Environmental Criminology and Ecological Justice*, Devon: Willan Publishing.

White, R. (2009) *Environmental Crime: A Reader*, Devon: Willan Publishing.

White, R. (2011) *Transnational Environmental Crime: Towards an Eco-Global Criminology*, London: Routledge.

White, R. (ed.) (2010) *Global Environmental Harm: Criminological Perspectives*, Devon: Willan Publishing.

WWF-UK (2003) *Fighting forest crime and the illegal timber trade*. Available online at www.wwf.org.uk/filelibrary/pdf/fightingforestcrime.pdf (accessed 10 August 2013).

Part II

Environmental crime in the Asia-Pacific

2 Transnational environmental crime in the Asia-Pacific

Characteristics and key issues

Lorraine Elliott

Transnational environmental crime (TEC) is one of the fastest-growing areas of criminal activity, globally worth billions of dollars. It includes illegal logging and timber smuggling, wildlife trafficking, the black market in ozone-depleting substances (ODS) and other prohibited or regulated chemicals, the illegal trade in hazardous and toxic wastes, and what is known in the environmental governance lexicon as IUU (illegal, unreported and unregulated) fishing. TEC constitutes a seemingly intractable dimension of the non-compliance and enforcement problem that is central to global environmental governance. It is also an issue of increasing interest to the community of practice and scholars interested in transnational crime more generally. There is no doubt that those engaged in TEC include both resource-specific smuggling rings and organized crime groups for whom various individuals of fauna and flora, other environmental resources and pollutants are just one more commodity that can generate profit.

This chapter examines the growing 'transnationality' of environmental crime with a specific focus on the Asia-Pacific. It begins by identifying the key characteristics of this form of illegal activity. The second section provides a brief overview of some of the main impacts of TEC on environmental integrity, on governance, on communities and economies. The third section sketches the range of TEC activities in the Asia-Pacific. The fourth section examines and evaluates multi-scale governance responses. The conclusion offers some thoughts about a policy and research agenda to increase our knowledge about TEC globally and in the Asia-Pacific.

Mapping TEC: characteristics

The United Nations Convention against Transnational Organized Crime sets out the conditions for what makes a crime 'transnational'. Under Article 3 of the Convention, a crime is thus defined if it is committed in more than one state; is committed in one state but a substantial part of its preparation, planning, direction or control takes place in another state; or is committed in one state but has substantial effects in another state. Former INTERPOL Secretary General André Bossard characterizes it thus: a border must be crossed and the activity must be recognized as a criminal offence in at least two countries as a result of international or national law (Friman and Andreas 1999: 5). To put it even more simply still, a crime is transnational if the perpetrators, products and profits cross state borders. As with other forms of criminal endeavor, environmental crime has become increasingly transnationalized as those involved take advantage of economic liberalization and a globalizing of the world economy, increases in the frequency and volume of commodity shipments, fewer border controls and easier transfers of funds through global financial and banking systems that offer more opportunities to launder profits into 'legitimate' enterprise. Globalization, as Andreas (2002: 40) has noted, has 'create[d] a new opportunity structure for those involved in criminalized markets'.

Growing attention to transnational environmental crime as a problem of legality and criminality, rather than just environmental management and non-compliance, confirms that this is one of the fastest-growing areas of criminal endeavor. As with all other forms of transnational crime, the figures cited are estimates. Nevertheless, we can be certain that, taken together, the various sectors that fall under this category of transnational activity are globally worth billions of dollars. Estimates of the value of TEC to criminal groups around the world have ranged from US$31 billion a year (Lauterback 2005) to US$40 billion (Lovell 2002).

Compared with other forms of transnational crime – such as drugs or arms smuggling – TEC is an area of high returns and low risk. Transnational environmental crimes fall outside the serious crimes framework defined in the United Nations Convention against Transnational Organized Crime. National legislation rarely imposes the penalties of four or more years' imprisonment for activity such as timber smuggling or wildlife smuggling that are required for it to count as a 'serious crime' under the Convention. Nor, in many cases, do such activities meet domestic criteria on what constitutes a trigger crime for money laundering or other financial crimes such as tax and excise evasion. Fewer resources are given to the suppression, interdiction and prosecution of such crimes. Law enforcement and customs officials are not only less aware of and less interested in environmental crime, but they are often poorly trained to look for or recognize illegal environmental goods.

At least some of the activity that constitutes TEC at a global and regional level is opportunistic, or undertaken by individuals or by operators who work on a small scale. However, this is an area in which activity has become increasingly systematic, involving organized crime groups, sophisticated smuggling chains and complex trade routes with multiple forms of concealment. Even a quick review of the literature suggests that those involved in various sectors of TEC include Russian and Chinese crime groups, African-based smuggling rings, Japanese Yakuza and even South American drug cartels (see Cook, Roberts and Lowther 2002; Zimmerman 2003; Warchol 2004).

As a form of enterprise crime in pursuit of profit, the illegal transnational market in environmental goods and resources has multiple drivers at both the supply and demand ends of the chain of custody. Supply-side drivers include more than just the direct pursuit of profit. Engaging in illegal sourcing or trading of environmental resources, pollutants and wastes can be a means of avoiding excise, taxes and high disposal costs. Demand-side drivers apply particularly to wildlife smuggling. Animals, birds, insects, reptiles and plants, and parts thereof, are taken illegally in response to demands from private collectors and zoos for rare and unusual species, from research facilities for laboratory animals and from niche consumer markets for traditional Asian and African medicines and exotic foods such as reef fish and bushmeat. This illegal trade is also driven by a far more mundane demand for unusual pets such as Chinese three-striped turtles or the slow loris, and for fashion items such as ivory, tortoiseshell and shahtoosh shawls. Demand-side drivers are also at play in the trafficking of illegal or stolen timber, delivering cheaper timber products to processors and consumers, and in illegal fishing to deliver high-demand fish to consumer markets.

TEC serves also to generate 'venture capital' for other illicit activities such as drugs and arms. It can involve parallel trafficking – that is, using the same smuggling routes for different goods, combining illegal shipments or using ostensibly legal shipments such as wildlife to conceal other forms of illegal goods. Protected turtles, for example, have been found in the same shipments as marijuana (Cook *et al.* 2002). Live snakes – sometimes legally exported – have been found stuffed with condoms full of cocaine (Environment News Service 2002). Parrots and drugs have been smuggled together from Côte d'Ivoire to Israel (United Nations Commission 2002: 6). Illegal ODS imports into Italy were discovered during an investigation into arms trafficking, and at least some of those found to be smuggling ODS across the US–Mexico border had a history of working as drug mules (Newman 2001: 4). Illegal environmental goods are also sometimes used in barter trade. Protected birds have been smuggled from Australia and exchanged for heroin in Thailand (Cook *et al.* 2002: 15). Chinese crime groups are reported to be exporting the raw ingredients for methamphetamine to South African drug dealers in exchange for illegally harvested abalone which can fetch up to $US200 a pound in Asian retail markets (Schoofs 2007).

The most recent manifestation of this kind of 'venture capital' model of TEC has brought militia groups into illegal environmental activity. The Sudan-based Janjaweed militia is reported to be involved in elephant poaching in Chad. Rebel groups in the Democratic Republic of Congo are reported to have become actively involved in the illegal ivory trade, and the Kenyan Wildlife Service has identified armed groups from Somalia as the cause of an increase in elephant poaching within Kenya. Illegal logging and gun smuggling are reported to go hand in hand in places such as Liberia, generating the idea of 'conflict timber' to match the more familiar category of 'conflict diamonds' (FERN 2003). Recent reports from India's security, police and intelligence agencies suggest that Islamic militants linked to Al-Qaida are sponsoring poaching in reserves in north-eastern India as a way of generating funds (Levy and Scott-Clark 2007).

These are not occasional movements of goods. Large quantities of environmental contraband are daily moved across borders, sometimes using rather ordinary forms of concealment (in cars, luggage, express postbags and, as with drugs, hidden on the person) but also in bulk consignments by ship, barge, truck and plane. Environmental commodities are also moved in and out of the illicit economy. Trans-shipment through free trade zones or through third (or more) countries provide opportunities for 'laundering' of individuals of protected species or of prohibited pollutants or waste. Fraudulent or forged documentation can certify logs or processed timber as compliant with the Convention on International Trade in Endangered Species (CITES) (if they are specimens of CITES-controlled species) or as having come from legal or sustainable sources. Protected or endangered animal, bird and reptile species can be documented as bred in captivity or can be deliberately mislabeled as a related (but not protected) species or even different species altogether. Ozone-depleting substances are frequently mislabeled as something other than ODS or as having come from legitimate recycled sources. Hazardous and toxic wastes are also traded illegally using misleading certificates and documentation. Illegally taken fish stocks are intermingled with legally caught fish or are 'hidden' through the use of multiple log books and catch records.

TEC obviously requires a labor force at the source of supply – chainsaw operators and poachers, for example – but the illicit trade is rarely controlled by these source actors. As with other forms of transnational crime, the illicit networks involved in smuggling or trafficking illicit environmental goods, resources, pollutants and waste require complex personnel arrangements to sustain trading routes and concealment methods. Those arrangements involve intermediaries and brokers who can charter cargo vessels, arrange for fraudulent or fake documents, issue letters of credit and forge connections between buyers and sellers. They can involve multi-layered business arrangements and use of 'legitimate' companies. TEC networks also take advantage of (and are sometimes organized by) corrupt officials, politicians, members of the military and even law enforcement agencies. It is those complex arrangements that link environmental crime to crossover crimes such as corruption, fraud, document counterfeiting and money laundering – the 'filthy lucre' in the title of this book.

Why should we care: concerns and consequences

Environmental crime is not just a matter of concern because of the consequences for money laundering and the crimes of corruption and fraud that support it. TEC is a major factor in environmental degradation, habitat loss and continued pollution. It undermines the effectiveness of multilateral environmental agreements and the institutions and rule systems of global environmental governance. Wildlife trafficking is a major cause of species endangerment, often the second biggest threat to biodiversity after habitat loss (Zimmerman 2003: 1660; Banks and Newman 2004).

The trade in illegally logged timber – described by one observer as being of 'industrial scale' (Lawson 2004: 1) – is a significant component of what is an otherwise legal, although often unsustainable, global industry. It is a major driver of deforestation, habitat destruction and species endangerment. The ecological consequences include the loss of important environmental services such as soil quality, water retention and the stability of local climate systems. The illegal production and consumption of counterfeit chlorofluorocarbons (CFCs) and other ODS contributes to ozone depletion which, in turn, is implicated in an epidemiologically significant increase in skin cancers and cataracts, suppression of human and animal immune systems, increased vulnerability to infectious diseases and reduced productivity in plants and phytoplankton. The covert and illegal dumping of hazardous and toxic wastes results in poisonous pollution of water tables, river systems and local ecosystems, which affects animal, plant and human health, sometimes resulting in death or extreme disability and often in the world's poorest countries. Illegal fishing, part of the suite of activities described as illegal, unreported and unregulated (IUU) fishing, contributes to over-fishing of fish stocks, disruption of marine food chains and threats to marine biodiversity.

The consequences of environmental crime reach beyond impacts on ecosystems and habitat. As with other forms of transnational crime, TEC and associated crimes such as bribery, fraud and money laundering undermine good governance, corrode the institutions of the state and compromise core values such as democratic processes and the rule of law. It undermines the security of those people and communities who are most vulnerable to the consequences of illegally sponsored environmental degradation and to the violence that can accompany the demand for illegal resources. TEC also creates insecurity for those who constitute its labor force – fishing crew and chainsaw operators, for example – whose participation is often driven by need and survival rather than greed and profit, but who are often the most vulnerable to prosecution. Transnational environmental crime also has substantial economic consequences for developing countries and for their development prospects, and also for legitimate environmental markets. The World Bank (2006) estimates that the illegal trade in timber and timber products costs timber-producing countries about US$5 billion a year in lost government revenue.[1] This trade is also estimated to depress world timber prices (with consequences for the legal industry) by something between 7 and 16 per cent because the companies and agents involved pay no taxes or fees and are able to use cheap labor (The Economist 2006: 74). The High Seas Task Force (2006: 3) reports that IUU fishing 'imposes significant economic costs on some of the poorest countries in the world' through loss of resources available to stakeholders, lower export revenues and higher operating costs for legitimate fishers.

Asia-Pacific: a sketch map of TEC in the region

The patterns of activity described above are reproduced in the Asia-Pacific. Many of the chapters in this book provide more detail; the discussion here provides a brief overview only.

Logging

Illegal logging in the region involves a range of 'chain of custody' practices: extraction and harvesting crimes, processing crimes and transportation crimes.

Timber is smuggled from source countries to major regional hubs such as Singapore, South Korea and China (the largest consumer of stolen timber in the world). It is then processed or relabeled as a legally harvested product (timber laundering) and often re-exported outside the region to the United States and Europe, among other destinations. The extent of the trade would be impossible without a well-organized network of shipping companies and agents, brokers and middlemen in places such as Singapore, Malaysia, Hong Kong and China, who facilitate relabeling, processing and transportation crimes. 'Several major syndicates' are thought to be in operation (Newman and Lawson 2005: 17), involved in chartering cargo vessels, faking documents, issuing letters of credit and forging connections between buyers and sellers. While customs seizures of illegal timber have increased (especially since the hardwood species ramin was made subject to import and export controls under appendix III of CITES), the impact has not been extensive. The 155,000 cubic metres of smuggled timber seized by Indonesian officials in 2005, for example, makes only a minor dent in the trade compared with the 3.6 million cubic metres of round wood alleged to be moved illegally from Papua alone each year (The Economist 2006: 378(8470): 86). Corruption is also endemic in the illegal timber trade. This ranges from petty corruption of police and customs officials, who might destroy evidence or knowingly issue false transportation documents, through to allegations of financial involvement at the highest levels of political elites and military forces in countries such as Indonesia (see EIA/Telapak 2002; International Crisis Group 2001), Burma and Laos (The Economist 1999) and Cambodia (Global Witness 2007).

Fishing

Activities that constitute illegal fishing can take a variety of forms, including exceeding catch limits, illegal trans-shipment of fish at sea, fishing without appropriate licences or permission in exclusive economic zones (EEZs) and the use of prohibited fishing methods. Some estimates suggest that illegal fishing losses in the Asia-Pacific could be as high as 16 per cent of the overall annual catch (Meere 2009). A number of ports in the region are reported to be favored by fleets involved in illegal fishing, including Qingdao (China), Tanjung Priok (Indonesia), Tenjog Pelepas (Malaysia) and Singapore (High Seas Task Force 2006: 29). As well as a source of or haven for illegal fishing vessels and trans-shipment processes, countries in the region have also become a market for illegally sourced and 'laundered' fish. The High Seas Task Force (2006: 24) reports, for example, that Japanese investigations into imports of frozen tuna revealed 'widespread laundering of illegally caught catches from the Atlantic, Pacific and Indian Oceans'. This involved false data (including misleading information about the source and species of catch), mingling of unauthorized and legal catches, multiple logbooks and organized operations involving the owners and operators of fishing and freezer cargo vessels.

Wildlife

The Asia-Pacific is also a source of and trade route and market for other forms of transnational environmental crime and illegal environmental goods and pollutants. Southeast Asia alone, for example, is thought to be responsible for about a quarter of the world's illegal wildlife trade (Lin 2005: 201). Customs seizures reveal the range of wildlife smuggled into, through and out of the region: ivory, marine turtle eggs, pangolins and freshwater turtles, among others. While some of this is opportunity poaching, wildlife smuggling syndicates are now active in most areas of the trade. The trade is driven by the preferences of collectors and zoos, by the demand for exotic meats in niche markets such as Japan, South Korea and Thailand, and by a sustained market for traditional Asian medicines (TAM), even though, as Hayman and Brack (2002) point out, animal products constitute less than 10 per cent of the components of TAMs (and endangered species less than 3 per cent).

The expansion of the region's transport infrastructure has provided more opportunities for the movement of illegally sourced wildlife. High levels of illegal cross-border trade in wild species have been recorded in the tri-border area of Cambodia, Laos and Vietnam (Thomson 2002: 11). Singapore and Hong Kong have become major transit points. There is a growing illegal trade from China into the countries on its Himalayan borders – Nepal, India and Pakistan – involving threatened species such as the Tibetan antelope, the giant panda and the Saker falcon (Yi-Ming *et al.* 2000). Rhino horn and tiger parts are traded across the Sino-Burma border. Bear populations in East Asia have been the victim of the demand for bear gall bladder in the TAM pharmacopoeia. The consequences for wildlife numbers are grave. Tigers have been poached and killed to such an extent that fewer than 5,000 are estimated to remain in the wild (Banks and Newman 2004: 3). Tiger numbers in Vietnam are calculated at fewer than 150, and the population of Royal Bengal tigers in India has declined by half in the last decade, much of it as a result of poaching (Agence France Presse 2007). Along with illegal logging, wildlife smuggling now constitutes one of the major threats to the endangered Bornean orangutan and the critically endangered Sumatran orangutan.

Hazardous substances

The smuggling of pollutants is also a feature of TEC in the Asia-Pacific. China is a major source of CFCs, one of the key ozone-depleting substances, and Southeast Asia a major trade route. Illegal CFCs can be moved easily through Singapore, for example, to countries outside the region – to Nepal as a staging post for smuggling CFCs into India, or to South Africa (EIA/Telapak 2003: 2). In 2008, the United Nations Environment Programme reported that the illegal transboundary trade in ODS had increased 'dramatically' in the Asia-Pacific with serious discrepancies between import and export figures (UN Environment Programme 2008). Information on hazardous waste in the Asia-Pacific is much less comprehensive. Nevertheless, documentation of individual cases over the last decade or more suggests that there is regular illicit activity. Schmidt (2004: A101) suggests that European, Russian and Japanese crime groups have established an illegal market for hazardous waste in Asia, often in conjunction with money laundering and arms sales.

Responding to TEC: multi-scale governance

Formal responses to transnational environmental crime, in the region and globally, have, for the most part, been sector-specific although some NGOs have spread their investigative net over multiple sectors.[2] It is only recently (with one or two exceptions) that governments and international organizations have begun to look for synergies in their activities or to develop efforts to explore TEC as a multi-sectoral issue. The challenge for governments in establishing and implementing national frameworks, particularly but not entirely in developing countries, is, in part, a function of capacity. But it also raises questions about how to balance broad policy with more specific regulatory and operational strategies, and whether to embed those frameworks in environmental legislation, financial legislation or criminal legislation associated with money laundering and corruption. In effect, the challenge is how to deal with the product, the perpetrators and the profits simultaneously.

Treaties

International legal frameworks that provide tools to deal with transnational environmental crime range across multilateral environmental agreements (MEAs) and international crime agreements. The key MEAs are well known: the 1987 Montreal Protocol on Substances that Deplete the Ozone Layer, the 1972 CITES and the 1989 Basel Convention on the Control of Transboundary Movements of Hazardous Wastes and their Disposal ('Basel Convention'). None of these agreements are law enforcement or international crime agreements. Their purpose is to enhance conservation and environmental protection through establishing guidelines for the harvesting, production, use and trade of particular substances or species. It is something of an irony that the unintended consequences of the regulation or prohibition regimes established by these various agreements has been the creation of a black market and the incentives for criminal activity that goes with it. Of the three agreements identified above, only the Basel Convention refers specifically to illegal traffic, calling it 'criminal' (article 4(3)) and requiring parties to 'introduce appropriate . . . legislation to prevent and punish such traffic' (article 9). Article VIII of CITES also requires parties to penalize trade that violates the Convention but does not specifically describe such violations as criminal or illegal. The Montreal Protocol itself says nothing about illegal trade and it is generally accepted that the parties were unprepared for the possibility that the Protocol would generate such trade. Challenges associated with TEC have, however, been taken up by the secretariat, conferences of parties and various working groups of each of the MEAs above.

There is as yet no binding international treaty on deforestation, illegal logging or timber trafficking (except, in the latter case, for those timber species listed under CITES) although, as other chapters in this book explain, there is an increasing number of national legislative initiatives and international efforts to address these concerns. The latter rely, for the most part, on various declaratory statements of concern, voluntary partnerships and the use of market mechanisms. In November 2009, 91 member countries of the United Nations Food and Agricultural Organization approved a treaty to close ports to foreign fishing vessels involved in illegal fishing, but most of the governance framework for enforcement action against IUU fishing comes by way of guidelines and regional fisheries agreements.

International agreements on transnational crime provide potentially useful tools for responding to TEC. The preamble to the United Nations Convention against Transnational Organized Crime suggests that the Convention should constitute an effective tool against criminal activities such as illicit trafficking in endangered species of wild flora and fauna, but there is nothing in the body of the treaty about this. Governments and international organizations have also begun to turn to financial instruments, such as the United Nations Convention against Corruption and the Financial Action Task Force '40+9' recommendations, in attempts to stifle the profits associated with transnational environmental crime. In 2007, the UN Commission on Crime Prevention and Criminal Justice adopted a resolution on international cooperation on the illicit international trafficking in forest products (which included not just timber but wildlife and 'other forest biological resources'). Among other things, the resolution encouraged the United Nations Office on Drugs and Crime (UNODC) member states to use the conventions on organized crime and corruption in their efforts to address this particular challenge.

Institutions

Other international organizations that have become heavily involved in monitoring and establishing programs to deal with various aspects of international crime include the United Nations Environment Programme (UNEP), the World Customs Organization, the Food and Agricultural Organization, UNODC and INTERPOL. INTERPOL's Environmental Crime Committee dates back to 1992 and its Environmental Crime Programme now hosts three working groups – one on pollution crime, one on wildlife crime and a new one on global e-waste crime. Alongside this sit the efforts of regional organizations such as the European Union and global networks that involve various kinds of partnership arrangements between governments, NGOs, scientific bodies and the corporate sector. In this category one finds, for example, the Coalition Against Wildlife Trafficking (CAWT), the International Network for Environmental Compliance and Enforcement and the Global Forest and Trade Network established by the World Wide Fund for Nature (WWF).

These patterns are replicated in the Asia-Pacific region. The regional offices of UNEP and UNODC have both been addressing these issues, the former motivated by the environmental consequences of TEC and the latter with a concern about transnational crime. UNEP has been central to regional efforts on ODS and other prohibited chemicals, working in conjunction with the Regional Intelligence Liaison Office of the World Customs Organization on 'Project Sky-hole Patching' and, since 2007, the Multilateral Environmental Agreements Regional Enforcement Network (MEA-REN). The UNODC has taken steps to expand the mission of its Border Liaison Office Network in the Mekong to strengthen cross-border cooperation to tackle the illegal trade in timber, wildlife and hazardous waste. The Association of Southeast Asian Nations (ASEAN) has taken a lead in establishing the ASEAN Wildlife Enforcement Network with capacity-building support from NGOs such as the Freeland Foundation and TRAFFIC. Since 2005, the Asian Regional Partners Forum on Combating Environmental Crime (ARPEC) has brought government agencies, regional organizations and NGOs together to 'facilitate consultation, exchange of information, technical cooperation and coordination activities . . . to counter the alarming growth of environmental crime in the region' (UNODC n.d.).

Despite this growing coordinated effort that functions on multiple scales and at regional and global levels, and despite some successes in interdiction and prosecution of illegal environmental trade, TEC continues. Hoare (2007) identified a number of factors that undermine efforts to tackle the illegal environmental trade. This includes a lack of sufficient sanctions and legal tools, lack of capacity and resources, lack of coordination, lack of data, the increase in trade liberalization and globalization, and weak governance (Hoare 2007: 3). The High Seas Task Force, which brought together the governments of Australia, Canada, Chile, Namibia, New Zealand and the United Kingdom with the WWF, International Union for the Conservation of Nature and the Earth Institute at Columbia University, elaborated similar kinds of concerns as they apply to the problem of IUU fishing. In their 2006 report, the Task Force pointed to a number of concerns: failure by some states to participate in existing multilateral instruments; inadequate implementation of existing instruments at the regional level; lack of effective institutional arrangements; lack of coordination between regional bodies and inadequate harmonization of measures; inadequate flag state control over fishing vessels; and subsidies and other perverse signals that displace rather than eliminate unsustainable fishing (High Seas Task Force 2006: 44).

Conclusion

Responding to these gaps in governance and implementation, which include problems of capacity and material resources, is an important component of the battle against transnational environmental crime. At the same time, it is crucial to understand more about the nature of the illegal trade and the nature of the illicit networks that manage and sustain illicit chains of custody and profit laundering. Edwards and Gill (2002: 204) suggest that focusing research on 'the relationships of exchange between traders [and] markets' will make it possible to identify 'a continuum of licit–illicit markets and corresponding interventions directed at their regulation'. Understanding the way illicit networks function and the ways in which they facilitate trade will shed more light on the function of brokers (those who bring together disconnected sites or actors within a network) and critical nodes (those without whom the network is more vulnerable). Understanding the network structures and arrangements also involves attention to 'crossing points'. Those crossing points include not only the physical borders between states – and ways of getting around border, customs and law enforcement controls – but also the boundaries between the illicit and licit economies, a process that Williams (2001: 77) refers to as 'boundary spanning'. Through providing a more coherent and comprehensive understanding of the extent and nature of criminal networks involved in transnational environmental crime, this kind of research can help to provide the policy community with insights into more effective ways of responding to transnational environmental crime.

Notes

1 This may understate the loss. The Indonesian government has estimated its own annual revenue losses from illegal logging at approximately $US4.3 billion (Wadley, Shah and Lawson 2006: 1).
2 The Environmental Investigation Agency, based in London and Washington, DC, stands out in this regard. Greenpeace International has also explored wildlife smuggling, timber trafficking and the black market in ODS. TRAFFIC – the wildlife trade NGO that works closely with CITES – has also taken a lead role internationally in dealing with illegal and criminal activity in that particular sector.

References

Agence France Presse (2007) 'Wildlife smuggling in Asia still a roaring trade', 2 June. Available online at www.terradaily.com/reports/Wildlife_Talks_Focus_On_Survival_And_Human_Livelihood_As_Asian_Trade_Booms_999.html (accessed 10 August 2013).

Andreas, P. (2002) 'Transnational crime and economic globalization', in M. Berdal and M. Serrano (eds) *Transnational Organized Crime and International Security*, Boulder, CO: Lynne Rienner.

Banks, D. and Newman, J. (2004) *The Tiger Skin Trail*, London: Environmental Investigation Agency.

Cook, D., Roberts, M. and Lowther, J. (2002) *The International Wildlife Trade and Organized Crime: A Review of the Evidence and the Role of the UK*, Surrey: WWF-UK.

Edwards, A. and Gill, P. (2002) 'Crime as enterprise? The case of "transnational organized crime"', *Crime, Law and Social Change*, 37(3): 203–23.

EIA/Telapak (2002) *Above the Law: Corruption, Collusion, Nepotism and the Fate of Indonesia's Forests*, London and Jakarta: EIA/Telapak.

EIA/Telapak (2003) *Singapore's Illegal Timber Trade and the US–Singapore Free Trade Agreement*, London and Jakarta: EIA/Telapak.

Environment News Service (2002) 'Organized criminal gangs deal wildlife and drugs'. Available online at www.ens-newswire.com/ens/jun2002/2002-06-18-01.html (accessed 21 January 2014).

The Economist (1999) 'The fight against illegal loggers', *The Economist*, 351(8113): 34. Available online at www.economist.com/node/320457 (accessed 21 January 2014).

The Economist (2006) 'Down in the woods – the logging trade', *The Economist*, Special report, 23 March 2006. Available online at www.economist.com/node/5654971 (accessed 21 January 2014).

FERN (2003) 'Greenpeace intercepts a shipment of conflict timber in Italy', *EU Forest Watch*, 74 (May): 2. Available online at www.illegal-logging.info/content/greenpeace-intercepts-shipment-conflict-timber-italy (accessed 10 August 2013).

Friman, R.H. and Andreas, P. (1999) 'Introduction: international relations and the illicit global economy', in R.H. Friman and P. Andreas (eds) *The Illicit Economy and State Power*, Lanham, MD: Rowman & Littlefield.

Global Witness (2007) *Cambodia's Family Trees: Illegal Logging and the Stripping of Public Assets by Cambodia's Elite*, Washington, DC: Global Witness.

Hayman, G. and Brack, D. (2002) *International Environmental Crime: The Nature and Control of Environmental Black Markets*, London: Royal Institute of International Affairs.

High Seas Task Force (2006) *Closing the Net: Stopping Illegal Fishing on the High Seas: Final Report of the Ministerially-led Task Force on IUU Fishing on the High Seas*, London: IUU Fishing Coordination Unit.

Hoare, A. (2007) 'International environmental crime, sustainability and poverty', background paper prepared for the workshop, The Growth and Control of International Environmental Crime, London, 10 December 2007.

International Crisis Group (2001) 'Indonesia: natural resources and law enforcement', *International Crisis Group Asia Report*, 29.

Lauterback, A. (2005) Statement by the Chair, INTERPOL Environmental Crimes Committee to the 5th International Conference on Environmental Crime, Lyon, 2 and 3 June 2005.

Lawson, S. (2004) *The Ramin Racket: The role of CITES in Curbing Illegal Timber Trade*, London: Environmental Investigation Agency.

Levy, A. and Scott-Clark, C. (2007) 'Poaching for Bin Laden', *Guardian*, 5 May. Available online at www.guardian.co.uk/world/2007/may/05/terrorism.animalwelfare (accessed 10 August 2013).

Lin, J. (2005) 'Tackling Southeast Asia's illegal wildlife trade', *Singapore Yearbook of International Law*, 9: 191–208.

Lovell, J. (2002) 'Eco-crooks outwitting law agencies – experts', *Reuters News Service*, 28 May. Available online at http://forests.org/shared/reader/welcome.aspx?linkid=11490&keybold=wildlife%20black%20market (accessed 10 August 2013).

Meere, F. (2009) 'Assessment of impacts of illegal, unreported and unregulated (IUU) fishing in the Asia-Pacific'. Available online at http://publications.apec.org/publication-detail.php?pub_id=103 (accessed 10 August 2013).

Newman, J. (2001) 'The tricks of illegal trade: how criminals smuggle ODS', *OzonAction Newsletter Special Supplement*, 6: 14–15, 18–19.

Newman, J. and Lawson, S. (2005) *The Last Frontier: Illegal Logging in Papua and China's Massive Timber Theft*, London/Bogor: Telapak/EIA.

Schmidt, C.W. (2004) 'Environmental crimes: profiting at the Earth's expense', *Environmental Health Perspectives*, 112(2): A96–A10.

Schoofs, M. (2007) 'Traffic jam: as meth trade goes global, South Africa becomes a hub', *Wall Street Journal*, 21 May. Available online at http://online.wsj.com/news/articles/SB117969636007508872 (accessed 10 August 2013).

Thomson, J. (2002) 'Tiger protection gets a boost in Central Indochina', *TRAFFIC Dispatches*, 19 (March): 11.

United Nations Commission on Crime Prevention and Criminal Justice (2002) *Progress Made in the Implementation of Economic and Social Council Resolution 2001/12 on Illicit Trafficking in Protected Species of Wild Flora and Fauna: Report of the Secretary General*, UN ESCOR, 11th session, Provisional Agenda Item 5, UN Doc E/CN.15/2002/7 (26 February 2002).

United Nations Convention against Transnational Organized Crime, opened for signature 15 November 2000, 2225 UNTS 209 (entered into force 29 September 2003).

United Nations Environment Programme (2007) *Illegal Trade in Ozone Depleting Substances: Asia and Pacific Region*, 21 April. Available online at www.unep.fr/ozonaction/information/mmcfiles/6075-e-illegal-trade-asia.pdf (accessed 10 August 2013).

UN Office of Drugs and Crime (n.d.) 'Countering environmental crimes in South-East Asia'. Available online at www.unodc.org/eastasiaandpacific/en/2010/02/arpec/story.html (accessed 10 August 2013).

Wadley, J., Shah, P. and Lawson, S. (2006) *Behind the Veneer: How Indonesia's Last Rainforests are Being Felled for Flooring*, London/Bogor: EIA/Telapak.

Warchol, G.L. (2004) 'The transnational illegal wildlife trade', *Criminal Justice Studies*, 17(1): 57–73.

Williams, P. (2001) 'Transnational Criminal Networks', in J. Arquilla and D. Ronfeldt (eds) *Networks and Netwars: The Future of Terror, Crime and Militancy*, Santa Monica, CA: RAND.

World Bank (2006) 'Weak forest governance costs US$15 billion a year', news release, 16 September. Available online at http://web.worldbank.org/WBSITE/EXTERNAL/TOPICS/EXTARD/EXTFORESTS/0,contentMDK:21055716~menuPK:985797~pagePK:64020865~piPK:149114~theSitePK:985785,00.html (accessed 10 August 2013).

Yi-Ming, L., Zenxiang, G., Xinhai, L., Sung, W. and Niemela. J. (2000) 'Illegal wildlife trade in the Himalayan region of China', *Biodiversity and Conservation*, 9(7): 901–18.

Zimmerman, M.E. (2003) 'The black market for wildlife: Combating transnational organized crime in the illegal wildlife trade', *Vanderbilt Journal of Transnational Law*, 36(5): 1657–89.

3 What is environmental crime and how much is happening in Australia?

Samantha Bricknell

Environmental crime, defined simply, is the perpetration of harm (intentional or otherwise) against 'the environment' that violates current law. The term 'environmental harm' is often interchanged with 'environmental crime', and, for some, any environmental harm produced is considered an environmental crime. Towards the other end of the spectrum, environmental harm can only be described as a crime if it is subject to criminal prosecution and criminal sanction (Situ and Emmons 2000: 3). Adding to this complexity is the reality that a considerable proportion of environmental harm is '(quite) legal and takes place with the consent of society' (Korsell 2001: 133).

Environmental crimes, as stipulated in Australian law, comprise the activities of:

- pollution and contamination of air, land and water
- illegal discharge, transport or dumping of hazardous and other waste
- illegal trade in regulated substances
- illegal, unregulated and unreported (IUU) fishing
- illegal trade in fauna and flora, and harms against biodiversity
- illegal logging and timber trade
- illegal native vegetation clearance
- illegal take and use of water.

Other activities that have been included under the banner of environmental crime in Australia include littering, noise 'pollution' and the illegal trade in cultural heritage. In addition to these are what could be labelled adjunct environmental crimes, such as methods to defraud carbon offset schemes (e.g. double selling of credits, purchase of worthless credits) and emission trading schemes (Bergin and Allen 2008; Deloitte 2009; National Public Radio 2008; McCully 2008).

Grabosky (2003: 237) has described the primary drivers of environmental crime as 'ignorance' and 'greed'. Ignorance includes genuine lack of awareness about environmental responsibilities but may extend to uncertainty or misunderstanding about the often complex regulatory nature of these responsibilities. Greed refers to the benefits or gains (primarily financial) that may be obtained by committing environmentally harmful practices (e.g. trafficking in protected fauna and flora) as well as what can be saved by deliberately disregarding regulations as to how certain potentially harmful practices should be performed (e.g. depositing hazardous waste at undesignated sites and hence avoiding 'dumping' costs).

Australia's environment laws

The laws protecting Australia's environment are complex, if not labyrinthine. National controls against environmental harms are distributed primarily between the Commonwealth and Australia's eight states and territories; local government has some oversight for a select group of matters. Australia's environmental laws incorporate commitment to international principles as outlined in multilateral environmental agreements or similar instruments, and sovereign interests and standards.

Commonwealth environmental legislation primarily concerns the protection of biodiversity, management of fisheries in the Australian Fishing Zone, prevention of unauthorised disposal of waste into the ocean, prohibition of marine pollution by prescribed substances and regulation of the import and export of hazardous wastes, ozone-depleting substances and synthetic greenhouse gas replacements. Each state and territory has enacted statutes to cover some of these areas too, namely protection of biodiversity, fisheries management and prohibition of marine pollution, as well as laws on pollution and waste disposal (tied up in environment protection statutes), forestry practices, native vegetation clearance and water acquisition and use. These laws are supplemented by an extensive array of management plans, statutory instruments and government-sponsored incentive schemes.

Offences that are prescribed in Australian environmental laws extend across a broad spectrum of wrongdoing but can be generally classified as producing the harm or failing to comply with conditions attached to a regulated activity. The concept of harm is embedded in many environmental statutes and often tied to the severity of the offence and the associated maximum penalty (Bricknell 2010). Many activities that involve some interaction with, or impact on, the environment require formal consent, usually through the issue of a licence or permit. These consents come attached with strict provisions describing how an activity can be performed, and the majority of offences stipulated in Australian environmental law concern the breaching of these provisions. Most environmental offences are strict liability offences.

The nature and extent of environmental crime in Australia

Understanding the nature and extent of environmental crime in Australia remains a challenge. The detection of environmental offences relies on a combination of alert systems that include compliance monitoring, auditing, targeted operations, tip-offs and complaints, supplemented by episodes of chance observation or discovery (Bricknell 2010). Nonetheless, many environmental offences almost certainly go undetected, and recorded offences probably only represent a proportion of what is actually occurring.

A review of the literature on environmental crime in Australia (Bricknell 2010) noted the general absence of comparable *published* data on environmental offences. Much of the literature that quantifies or describes the types of offences being committed in Australia are corporate publications from regulatory authorities, which tend to publish statistics only on the more serious offences detected. Not all do, though, and where offence information is available, it is often described in very general terms. Another factor contributing to the currently incomplete picture of environmental crime in Australia is the paucity of active research in this area. There has been a modest but reasonably steady stream of research regarding Australian environmental regulation and judicial responses to environmental offences (see Bricknell 2010 for a list of these) but very little examination of the scope and nature of environmental offending.

Even if complete data were available, there needs to be some thought as to the best 'measure' to estimate extent. While an obvious candidate, quantitative measures can be misleading. A larger number of incidents for a specified category of environmental crime may indicate there is more criminal activity in this area. It may also indicate that the related offences are more readily detected than others, or simply reflect the larger number of offences that can be committed under one category of environmental crime compared with another. Fishing offences are a case of point.

In identifying hot spots of criminal activity, other indicators should be considered. Some examples include the seriousness of the harm produced, evidence for escalation in behaviour, apparent 'recalcitrance' among potential offenders, even facilitation of illegal behaviour. If we were to use these indices, hot spots for environmental crime in Australia could be identified as listed in Table 3.1.

The following sections briefly describe what can be discerned from the literature about the nature of environmental crimes committed in Australia. Given the focus of this compilation, they concentrate on illegal logging and illegal fishing; the situation for other environmental crime is summarised in Table 3.2.

Illegal logging

Forestry is a tightly regulated industry in Australia, with native forests and plantations managed by the Commonwealth, state or territory authorities, or private companies. With this comes a spread in tenure arrangements across

Table 3.1 Measures of environmental harm

Prevalence of illegal activity	Fishing offences
Seriousness of harm	Trade in highly threatened species
	Illegal water takes from stressed river systems
Escalation of behaviour	Illegal dumping of waste
Recalcitrance	Illegal native vegetation clearance
Facilitation	Illegal timber trafficking

Table 3.2 Nature and extent of environmental crimes in Australia

Pollution and illegal disposal of waste

- Based on data from regulatory reports, the most common polluting activity currently occurring is the illegal discharge and dumping of wastes, such as sewage, wastewaters from mining and animal production sites, and demolition and construction debris.
- Some acts are accidental or unintentional but a small majority (particularly dumping of waste) are done to cut corners and save money (e.g. fees related to safe disposal of waste at approved sites).
- There is possible infiltration of organised criminal activity in the waste disposal business. The structure of the business, the ease in which waste can be transported and the apparent formation of alliances between operators already working on the fringes of legality make it an ideal target.

Illegal trade in fauna and flora/harms to biodiversity

- The size of the trade, which involves the illegal export of native fauna and flora and illegal import of exotic species, is considered to be small when compared with overseas operations. However, the illegal trade may be on the increase.
- Between 2002–03 and 2006–07, over 26,500 wildlife and wildlife products were seized.
- Much of the detected trade involves wildlife, primarily birds/birds eggs, reptiles, turtles, spiders and insects.
- Both Australian and foreign nationals are involved in the trade, and in both directions of the trade. Fauna and flora are smuggled into and out of the country mostly by human couriers or through the post, but the use of fraudulent documentation (e.g. CITES permits) is another avenue taken.
- Most detection is of 'minor' infringements (e.g. tourists bringing back mementos from their holidays which contain animal products). Of the major cases, just under half were for the illegal export of native species (reptiles and birds) and a third for illegal import of exotics.
- The domestic market is not well understood but targets the same species. It is believed that in the domestic bird breeding industry, co-mixing of captured wild birds with captive-bred birds occurs, which might also be tied to inter-country smuggling.
- There is little information on harms perpetrated outside the trade cycle. Most offences committed refer to the harming of protected fauna, breach of licence conditions regarding the taking or treatment of native fauna or flora, or damage to important habitat.

Illegal native vegetation clearance

- Retaining high rates of compliance with native vegetation laws has proved to be a challenge. Audits of native vegetation laws in NSW and WA revealed substantial illegal clearing activity in various parts of the respective states – e.g. 40% of the 74,000 hectares cleared in 2005 was illegal.
- Acts of illegal clearance comprised clearance without prior consent or going beyond what the authorisation permits. Much of the illegal activity could be described as deliberate, committed by developers and rural landholders.
- Detection of illegal clearance has been hampered by inadequate resources and limited technology. Some states have invested in, or are looking to invest in, satellite surveillance and aerial photography to better map existing vegetation and monitor clearance patterns.
- Up until recently, very few cases of illegal native vegetation clearance (in NSW) were prosecuted or appropriate penalties handed down. A total of 29 prosecutions were pursued in NSW between 1998 and 2005, less than 5% of all detected breaches in that period.

(Continued)

Table 3.2   (Continued)

Water theft

- Water laws and water management plans have been revised to new restrictions on water access and use.
- The worsening water situation in Australia has led to the reduction of allocations, new licences not being issued for some regions or water systems, and rights to water no longer being tied to the land.
- Theft comes in multiple forms, including the taking of water for an unapproved purpose, from a source one is not entitled to, in excess of the amount allocated and/or tampering with metering equipment.
- There has been considerable speculation that water theft is 'rife', and anecdotal information suggests it is problematic in some parts of the country, but little to no information is published on rates of water theft.
- State and territory governments, notably NSW and SA, have acted on the purported increase in water theft (or risk of an increase) by reviewing penalty schemes and announcing considerable increases in pecuniary penalties for illegally taking water. In NSW, an offence of intentional, negligent or reckless taking of water was added to the Water Management Act 2000, increasing the maximum penalty from $132,000 to $1.1 million for individuals, with imprisonment up to two years, and a maximum penalty of $2.2 million for body corporate. In SA, the maximum penalty for an individual found illegally taking water was raised 20 fold to $700,000, and for a body corporate to $2.2 million.

Source: Bricknell 2010

different forest holdings and in the application of laws relating to conservation, native vegetation, national parks, environmental protection, water, planning and development, as well as those applicable to forestry activities *per se*.

In most Australian states, forests and plantations are managed by a mix of government regulators and commercial enterprises, the latter generally (but not necessarily solely) responsible for the management of commercial forestry operations. Alongside forest(ry) laws, jurisdictions have implemented forest management plans and timber production codes of conduct, or enacted complementary legislation, to ensure that sustainable forestry practices are followed (e.g. Sustainable Forests (Timber) Act 2004 (Vic)). Codes of practice serve as regulatory instruments and outline conventions regarding forest planning, management, harvesting and regeneration. Examples of these include Queensland's Code of Practice for Native Forest Timber Production on State Lands, Western Australia's Code of Practice for Timber Plantations, Tasmania's Forest Practices Code and Victoria's Code of Practice for Timber Production.

The Australian government has also entered into Regional Forestry Agreements (RFAs) (under the auspices of the Regional Forests Agreement Act 2002 (Cth)); at present there are 20 RFAs involving the states of New South Wales, Victoria, Western Australia and Tasmania. The RFAs outline 20-year plans to foster conservation and sustainable management of forests in these states.

Forestry activities are meant to be regularly audited for compliance with sustainable forest management and extraction practices, and with relevant laws prescribed in other environment protection and conservation statutes. In some jurisdictions, the results from these audits are made publicly available (see, for example, the Timber Production on Public Land audits that were published by the Victorian Environment Protection Authority). From the (albeit limited) data available, there is little to indicate that serious breaches are commonly or regularly committed, although they are not unknown. A recent case in New South Wales, for example, implicated Forests NSW in breaching laws from multiple environment protections statutes in three different state forests (Pugh 2009, 2010a, 2010b). The alleged breaches included the undertaking of activities that threatened protected species, and harvesting timber from old-growth rainforests. The NSW Department of Environment, Climate Change and Water commenced an investigation of NSW Forests regarding the alleged breaches (Cubby 2010); at the time of writing the outcome was still to be determined.

Nonetheless, it has been concluded that there is 'no evidence of systematic illegal logging taking place within Australia' (Schloenhardt 2008:79). Where Australia's complicity lies with illegal logging, and the broader effects of illegal logging, is through its consumption of illegally harvested timber imported from countries that do not have the same controls as Australia does, or the resources or political will to enforce these controls.

Australia's demand for timber and wood products is reported to be greater than what the local industry can supply (Schloenhardt 2008). There is little in the way of comprehensive information, however, on the volume of timber imported into Australia (other than that published by the International Tropical Timber Organization), the primary countries of origin or export, and the proportion of imports that have been deemed suspect. The most complete analysis so far was published in 2005 as part of an Australian government report on illegal logging; the Australian Government Department of Agriculture, Fisheries and Forestry (DAFF) has since commissioned a new report examining methods for estimating the volume and value of illegally harvested timber that is imported into Australia.

From this earlier study, it was estimated that 9 per cent (in value terms) of all timber and wood products imported to Australia between 1 July 2003 and 30 June 2004 was of suspect origin (Jaakko Pöyry Consulting 2005). Wooden furniture was particularly problematic – an estimated 22 per cent (in value terms) of this product was likely to have been constructed from illegally harvested timber – as was plywood (from hardwood sources: 19 per cent), veneer (16 per cent) and miscellaneous wood products (14 per cent). For other products, the quantity deemed suspect was less than 10 per cent.

The variation in the estimates for different categories of timber/wood product reflected the primary countries of origin for each product and the prevalence of illegal logging activity occurring in these countries. Indonesia, Malaysia and, to a lesser extent, Papua New Guinea were listed as important sources for products with an estimated higher illegal contribution; of similar significance is the importance of China as a key exporter of processed timber to Australia. Malaysia and especially Indonesia have become synonymous with illegal logging, predominantly as producers of illegal timber (EIA and Telapak 2004) although Malaysia has additionally played a central role in the smuggling of illegal timber out of

Indonesia (EIA and Telapak 2004, 2005). Based on wood-balance estimates, the current prevalence of illegal logging in Indonesia is 40 per cent of all forest production; in Malaysia, it is between 14 and 25 per cent of all forest production (Lawson and MacFaul 2010). While there have been substantial improvements in Indonesia – in 2000, it was estimated that almost 80 per cent of all forest production was illegal (Lawson and MacFaul 2010) – they are less evident in Malaysia. China's involvement in the illegal trade lies with its critical position in the timber market – as a key importer of timber for domestic use and as an exporter of processed timber to countries such as Australia – and it has been identified, in volume terms, as the largest importer of illegal wood (Lawson and MacFaul 2010). In 2008, 20 per cent of all timber imports to China were illegal, a 16 per cent drop since 2000–04 (Lawson and MacFaul 2010). Some of this decline can be attributed to a huge reduction in the import of illegal timber from Indonesia, but considerable discrepancies in log trade data between China and Malaysia (Greenpeace International and Greenpeace China 2006) and China and Burma (Global Witness 2009) indicate that illegal import is still thriving.

Australia's position as an 'unwitting' beneficiary of illegal timber is not unique, but compared with the European Union and the US, for example, Australia has been somewhat slower in implementing methods to halt the import of illegal timber into the country. The Australian government has established bilateral agreements with three producer countries – Papua New Guinea, Indonesia and Malaysia – which focus on capacity building in sustainable forest management and the development of measures to combat illegal logging, including the improvement of systems to verify the legal origin of timber and timber products and the establishment of a more robust chain of custody schemes (DAFF 2010). To assist Australian consumers, the Australian government has also been promoting the uptake of certification schemes. At present, three schemes are observed in Australia – the Australian Forestry Standard Limited, the Program for Endorsement of Forest Certification Schemes and the Forest Stewardship Council. The uptake of these schemes is not known.

As part of their 2007 election commitments, the incoming government stated that Australia would play a more decisive role in combating illegal logging through the banning of illegal timber and timber product imports. The Centre for International Economics was subsequently contracted by the Australian government to examine options to restrict the import of illegal timber into Australia. Among the report's conclusions were:

- Australia should follow a non-regulatory pathway, since regulation would be too costly to both industry and consumers;
- import regulation would be 'inefficient' (because the world timber trade represented only a small proportion – 15 per cent – of the timber trade, and Australia's share in that trade was similarly small) and the effect on illegal logging would be minimal; and
- a response from Australia would simply deflect trade elsewhere (Centre for International Economics 2010).

An earlier draft of the report spurned considerable criticism and comment regarding methodology and recommendations, both in Australia and from overseas (e.g. the European Commission; see Arup 2010; Crittenden 2010). The Australian government made the decision not to go with the report's recommendations and, during the 2010 federal election, the then Minister for Population/ Agriculture, Fisheries and Forestry, Tony Burke, announced that, if re-elected, the incumbent Labor government would pursue the implementation of legislation prescribing criminal and civil penalties for the import of illegal timber and timber products. Consequently, the Illegal Logging Prohibition Act 2012 (Cth) was enacted. Timber and timber product importers are required to follow due diligence to make sure that the timber they are sourcing is not illegally logged, and that they exercise due diligence in knowing the timber source country, the species and the verification or certification systems in place.

A small number of Australian peak industry bodies and companies have independently raised awareness about the issue and introduced measures to authenticate timber imported into the country. A group comprising representatives from the forest industry, wood product sector, furniture and hardware retailers, conservation and social welfare groups, and the Uniting Church in Australia, for example, have campaigned since 2007 to alert the Australian community to the problem of illegal logging and advertise their commitment to stopping the import of illegal timber/timber products (see, for example, ABC National Radio 2010; Greenpeace *et al.* 2010). Timber importers represented by the Australian Timber Importers Federation (ATIF) approved, in 2008, a code of ethics to support legal and sustainable forestry practices, which requires importers to verify that timber imports were harvested in accordance with the laws of the country of origin (ATIF 2008). In 2006, the Australian Plantation Products and Paper Industry Council (A3P) introduced guidelines for members which outlined due diligence measures that importers and processors should take to verify from their suppliers the legality of forest products (A3P 2006). Simmonds Lumber has taken the additional step of working in collaboration with a timber auditing company, Certisource, to implement a certification scheme based on DNA fingerprinting. The company was the first in the world to adopt the technology whereby records are compared between DNA samples taken from trees in legal concessions and samples drawn from logs processed in sawmills.

Illegal, unreported and unregulated fishing

While logging ventures in Australia are predominantly lawful, a not insubstantial amount of fishing is not, although most breaches discovered are relatively minor. The protection and management of Australia's fisheries is divided between the Commonwealth and the states and territories. The Commonwealth is responsible for the Australian Fishing Zone (AFZ) which incorporates just over 20 designated fisheries. States and territories manage all remaining marine fisheries as well as inland fisheries.

Illegal fishing in Australian fisheries involves both domestic and foreign fishers. Domestic fishers make up the majority of offenders but, for the most part, the scale of domestic fishing is considered to be relatively small and the majority of offending is likened to 'low level non-compliance' (Putt and Anderson 2007: 21). Nonetheless, it has been estimated that anywhere between 20 and 60 per cent of specific fish species (usually prized species) are illegally taken (Palmer 2004; Victorian Parliament Environment and Natural Resources Committee 2002). Both recreational and commercial fishers are complicit, flouting laws regarding bag and quota limits, taking of protected and/or undersized fish, and the use of illegal fishing equipment such as nets and traps, although administrative infringements (such as not completing or submitting log books) were by far the most common offence among domestic commercial fishers detained in the AFZ (Australian Fisheries Management Authority 2007, 2008, 2009; Fletcher and Santoro 2009, 2008, 2007; NSW Department of Primary Industries 2008, 2009b; Palmer 2004; Queensland Primary Industries and Fisheries 2009a–u; Victorian Parliament Environment and Natural Resources Committee 2002).

An ongoing problem in domestic illegal fishing is fishers masquerading as recreational fishers to hide commercial-size activity (Palmer 2004; Putt and Anderson 2007). These offenders are often well organised and usually target profitable species. Recent cases prosecuted in Victoria, South Australia and Western Australia involved 'recreational fishers' who were taking large quantities of protected species, such as abalone, rock lobster and Murray cod (New South Wales Department of Primary Industries 2009a, 2010a, 2010b, 2010c; Primary Industries and Resources South Australia 2010a, 2010b, 2010c; Victorian Department of Primary Industries 2010a–e; Western Australian Department of Fisheries 2009a, 2009b, 2010).

Fish species that are most vulnerable to domestic illegal fishing are abalone, shark (for their fins) and rock lobster; other targeted species include Murray cod, King George whiting, coral reef fish, barramundi, snapper, mud crab and prawns (Anderson and McCusker 2005; Palmer 2004; Putt and Anderson 2007; Tailby and Gant 2005; Victorian Parliament Environment and Natural Resources Committee 2002). Abalone and shark fin are primarily destined for the Asian market, whereas the other species are generally sold locally. Fisheries officers surveyed as part of Putt and Anderson's (2007) study of crime in the Australian fishing industry have detected the infiltration of organised criminal behaviour in the taking of profitable fish species. A quarter said that 'a lot' of the illegal activity occurring in their state could be described as organised, and 58 per cent said 'some' of it was organised; these observations varied between the states and territories, with between 40 and 50 per cent of fisheries officers responsible for monitoring Commonwealth, NSW, Victorian or South Australian fisheries stating that organised illegal fishing was common. Nonetheless, the majority of officers also believed that less than a fifth of the industry (including commercial and recreational fishers, fish receivers and processors) were actually involved in fishing-related crime (Putt and Anderson 2007).

Illegal fishing involving foreign fishers is dominated by Indonesian and Papua New Guinean nationals fishing in the northern waters of the AFZ, with much less (detected) illegal activity in Australia's southern waters. Primary targets for the former fishing ventures are shark fin, trepang and reef fish, and, in the latter, Patagonian toothfish and mackerel. Illegal fishing in Australia's northern waters intensified between 2000 and 2006; during this period the number of apprehended fishing boats increased from 78 to 368 (Australian Fisheries Management Authority 2000, 2009). To counter the influx of illegal fishing boats, the Australian government instigated a multi-agency and legislative response in which aerial and vessel surveillance was markedly increased, procedures related to the apprehension, detention and prosecution of fishers were streamlined, and, of particular significance, fishing vessels could be destroyed on a finding of guilt. Since this escalation in enforcement, there has been a distinct drop in the number of illegal foreign fishing vessels detected in the northern AFZ – 216 in 2006–07, 156 in 2007–08 and 27 in 2008–09 – and a displacement of illegal fishing ventures to the peripheries of the AFZ (Australian Fisheries Management Authority 2009).

Sanctioning environmental offenders

Historically, there has been a profusion of lesser penalties handed down for environmental offences, comprising remedial measures, regulatory action and administrative sanctions. For the most part, this is because the majority of environmental offences detected are described as 'minor', but it probably also reflects the facilitative approach preferred by regulators. Environmental authorities have been accused in the past of 'regulatory capture', and, in Australia, the leniency in penalties for environmental offences prompted a review of penalty schemes and a recommended shift back towards coercion (Martin 2003; Pain 1993). However, regulators who participated in an Australian Institute of Criminology roundtable on environmental crime have argued for balance in response. Not only does such an approach engender a beneficial relationship between regulated and regulator, which should encourage compliant behaviour from the regulated entity, but also the methodical pursuit of criminal penalties may not be the best outcome for punishing certain classes of environmental offender, nor the best method for deterring future transgressions.

When environmental offences are criminally prosecuted in Australia, fines are the predominant penalty handed down, although often at a fraction of the maximum that can be imposed (Abbott 2005; Bartel 2003, 2008; Cole 2008; Hain and Cocklin 2001; Hartley 2004; Martin 2003). Custodial sentences are available for more serious environmental offences but are rarely used. Bartel (2008) foresaw a possible increase in fines for illegal acts of native vegetation clearance, and sentences handed down in New South Wales in 2008 and 2009 have borne out this prediction.[1] There have also been not insignificant fines handed down for fishing offences. Some have questioned, however, the usefulness of fines to either punish or discourage environmental offending (Hain and Cocklin 2001; Cole 2008). Notwithstanding the adage that fines simply represent, for some, a 'cost of business', they cannot ameliorate the actual physical harm caused by environmental crimes nor produce a particularly great burden on the offender.

Alternative sentencing orders have been advocated as a particularly effective option in sentencing environmental offenders (Cole 2008; Hain and Cocklin 2001; Martin 2003; Preston 2007), especially those orders that require the offender to publicise the commission of the offence – preferably in peer-relevant media (Justice Preston 2009) – and produce or restore an environmental good. The latter generally come in the form of directions to rehabilitate the harmed environment or an environmental service order. Alternative sentencing orders are not universally prescribed in Australia's environmental legislation and not every court has the option to use them.

In addition to these are orders that target the illicit proceedings of crime – that is, confiscation or forfeiture orders. Forfeiture orders are prescribed in the Fisheries Management Act 1991 (Cth) and in fisheries statutes for each of Australia's six states and the Northern Territory. Items that may be ordered to be forfeited include the fish resources taken, fishing gear and related equipment, boat, vehicle or other forms of conveyance, and the proceeds derived from the sale for any of the previously listed items. There is variation between the jurisdictions regarding whether forfeitures are mandatory on conviction or a finding of guilt, as they are in Tasmania under ss 225–227 of the Living Marine Resources Act 1995 (Tas) and ss 109–110 of the Inland Fisheries Act 1995 (Tas), or are at the discretion of the court (the rest). For some offences, the court is obliged to order forfeiture of relevant assets, where there was the use of a foreign boat in the commission of a fishing offence in Western Australia (Fish Resources Management Act 1994 (WA) s 218(1)(a)) or in the Northern Territory (Fisheries Act (NT) s 46(1)(a)), or where the defendant had previous, multiple convictions for serious fishing offences (Fisheries Act 1995 (Vic) s 106(5)(a)).

Commonwealth

Provisions in the Proceeds of Crime Act 2002 (Cth) (POCA 2002) also allows for the restraint and recovery of assets associated with indictable fishing offences. The POCA 2002 includes provisions for both conviction-based and civil forfeiture of assets. Under s 19 of the POCA 2002, a court can impose a restraining order on property *suspected* of being the proceeds of indictable offences (such as s 105 of the Fisheries Management Act 1991 (Cth)) and under s 49(1) can make a forfeiture order for property covered by a restraining order and the proceeds of one or more indictable or foreign indictable offences.

Legislative amendment to the Fisheries Management Act 1991 (Cth) introduced the facility, under s 106A of the Act, for automatic forfeiture of foreign boats, and equipment and catch found on foreign boats, that were used in the commission of offences related to fishing and having a boat equipped for fishing in the AFZ. Unlike other forfeiture provisions in fisheries statutes, forfeiture in this instance is automatic on the suspicion, likelihood or allegation of an offence, not on conviction. Commentators including Blakely (2008) and White and Gibson (2010) have questioned the legitimacy of these provisions with respect to maritime law and outlined a number of cases in which boats were forfeited (and, in some cases, destroyed) when it was found the fishers were not breaking any Australian law or a court found no evidence of wrongdoing.

Powers to confiscate assets generated from or used in the commission of certain fisheries offences are prescribed in assets confiscation statutes enacted in NSW, Victoria, Queensland and South Australia. These are summarised below.

New South Wales

The Fisheries Management Amendment Bill 2009 elevated the offence of trafficking in fish (Fisheries Management Act 1994 (NSW) s 21) to an indictable offence, so that it fell within the definition of a 'serious offence' in the Confiscation of Proceeds of Crime Act 1989 (NSW). This amendment now allows for the ability to confiscate assets, under the Confiscation of Proceeds of Crime Act 1989 (NSW), from a person convicted for trafficking in an indictable species of fish (i.e. abalone or eastern rock lobster) or indictable quantity of said species.

Victoria

The Victorian parliament has also recently made changes to the state's assets confiscations scheme. Under Schedule 2 of the Confiscation Act 1997 (Vic), automatic and civil forfeiture orders may be used on conviction for offences against ss 111A, 111B or 111C of the Fisheries Act 1995 (Vic). These offences refer to the trafficking in, taking of (within a 24-hour period) or possession of a commercial quantity of a priority species (i.e. abalone, rock lobster, Murray cod or any species specified in the Regulations, Fisheries Act 1995 (Vic) s 4). The Confiscation Amendment Bill 2010 has amended the conditions under which assets can be recovered. In the previous iteration of the Act, asset recovery depended on a monetary threshold, calculated as export value, being surpassed; it is now determined on the commercial quantity of the catch recovered. Thus, assets can be recovered if the commercial quantity is no less than five times the commercial quantity prescribed for each priority species.

Queensland

Offences under the Fisheries Act 1994 (Qld) are prescribed in Schedule 2 of the Criminal Proceeds Confiscation Act 2002 (Qld) as an ancillary offence to an Item 1 offence that is punishable by imprisonment for five years or more.

South Australia

A 'serious offence', as prescribed in the Criminal Assets Confiscation Act 2005 (SA), under which assets can be forfeited, includes offences against ss 52, 53, 72 or 74 of the Fisheries Management Act 2007 (SA). These offences are respectively: engaging in commercial fishing without a licence or permit for the specified fishery; engaging in commercial fishing in an unregistered vessel; unauthorised sale, purchase or possession of an aquatic species; and unauthorised trafficking in a commercial quantity of a priority species. Priority species are abalone, rock lobster or a species of fish declared by the regulations.[2]

The Criminal Proceeds Confiscation Act 2002 (Qld) and the Criminal Assets Confiscation Act 2005 (SA) also list conservation and related offences from which assets can be forfeited. In the latter Act, these comprise offences against ss 47, 48, 48A, 51 and 60 of the Native Conservation Act 1992 (SA): taking and illegal possession of native plants, taking protected animals and illegal possession of animals.

Conclusion

The nature of environmental crime means that many illegal acts of environmental harm will go undetected. Compared with its near neighbours, the extent of environmental crime in Australia is, however, less of a problem. Many environmental offences detected in Australia are described as minor with respect to the harm produced, and Australia employs a multitude of laws and a multitude of agencies to protect different aspects of the environment. Nonetheless, the accrual effect of even minor infringements can and does produce significant and long-lasting detriments to the environment, and authorities can and do struggle with increasing compliance and enforcement demands (Bricknell 2010).

One of the challenges of combating environmental crime is instituting and applying a sanctioning system that reflects the seriousness of the harm produced, adequately punishes the offender and deters future transgression. Problems in the past with mounting successful prosecutions (for even serious cases of environmental harm), inadequate sentences and (probable) recidivism have led to the examination and application of alternative methods by which to penalise offenders or destabilise environmentally harmful activities.

Traditional penalties (mostly fines) are still the primary sentence imposed for criminally prosecuted incidents of environmental crime, but there is now greater use of additional or alternative sanctions, such as the orders described earlier in this chapter, in jurisdictions such as New South Wales and Victoria. Advocates of alternative sentencing orders suggest that these orders enable the creation of a sentence that matches the severity of the offence, provides a greater burden to the offender and produces a 'more acceptable social outcome' (Cole 2008: 96) – all attributes perceived as playing a crucial role in preventing future offending.

Forfeiture orders represent an alternative sanctioning method, one of which can act to incapacitate illegal activity. In recent years, forfeiture orders have been readily used for offences against the Fisheries Management Act 1991 (Cth) involving foreign fishing vessels found operating in the northern and southern waters of the AFZ, but rarely applied in cases of illegal fishing in state/territory waters. Part of this relates to the stronger forfeiture provisions under the Fisheries Management Act 1991 (Cth) and the perceived greater severity of fishing offences committed by foreign fishing ventures. Criticism has been levelled at the legality of Australia's forfeiture laws, chiefly provisions around automatic forfeiture and the potentially dire economic consequences that forfeiture (particularly of vessels) can exact on smaller operators (Fox, Therik and Sen 2002).

Stakeholders at an Australian Institute of Criminology roundtable on environmental crime collectively agreed that enforcement and sentencing options should address deterrence, incapacitation and rehabilitation (Bricknell 2010). Traditional penalties and additional orders act to serve these purposes, but there is the possibility that too much weight has been placed on some of these outcomes at the cost of others. One of the research recommendations that came out of the review of information on environmental crime in Australia was a need to better examine and assess enforcement and sentencing options to truly gauge the effectiveness of these. Given the large number of fishing offences committed each year, this category of environmental crime would benefit from such a study, particularly with respect to the role of alternative sentencing orders and forfeiture orders for cases of domestic illegal fishing.

Notes

1 See, for example, *Director General of Environment and Climate Change v Wilton* [2008] NSWLEC 297 (31 October 2008); *Director General of Environment and Climate Change v Rae* [2009] NSWLEC 137 (18 August 2009); *Director General of Environment and Climate Change v Hudson* [2009] NSWLEC 4 (11 February 2009).
2 These include crustaceans carrying external eggs (bug, blue swimmer crab, giant crab, slipper lobster, southern rock lobster, yabby, Murray River crayfish, south-east crayfish), western blue grouper, various scalefish, river blackfish, freshwater catfish, trout cod, silver perch and white shark.

References

Abbott, C. (2005) 'The regulatory enforcement of pollution control laws: the Australian experience', *Journal of Environmental Law*, 17(2): 161–74.

ABC Radio National, 'Timber politics', *Background Briefing*, 30 May 2010 (S. Crittenden). Available online at www.abc.net.au/rn/backgroundbriefing/stories/2010/2908767. htm (accessed 10 August 2013).

Anderson, K.M. and McCusker, R. (2005) 'Crime in the Australian fishing industry: key issues', *Trends and Issues in Crime and Criminal Justice*, 297.

Australian Fisheries Management Authority (2000) *Annual Report 1999–2000*, Canberra: Australian Fisheries Management Authority.

Australian Fisheries Management Authority (2007) *Annual Report 2006–07*, Canberra: Australian Fisheries Management Authority.

Australian Fisheries Management Authority (2008) *Annual Report 2007–08*, Canberra: Australian Fisheries Management Authority.

Australian Fisheries Management Authority (2009) *Annual Report 2008–09*, Canberra: Australian Fisheries Management Authority.

Australian Government Department of Agriculture, Fisheries and Forestry (2010) 'Australia's bilateral relationships on forestry'. Available online at www.daff.gov.au/forestry/international/regional (accessed 10 August 2013).

Australian Plantation Products and Paper Industry Council (2006) *A3P Member Guidelines: Stopping the supply of illegally logged forest products to Australia*, Barton: Australian Plantation

Products and Paper Industry Council. Available online at www.illegal-logging.info/sites/default/files/uploads/A3Pmemberguidelines.pdf (accessed 10 August 2013).

Australian Timber Importers Federation (2008) 'Code of Ethics'. Available online at www.atif.asn.au/index.php?option=com_content&task=view&id=23&Itemid=42 (accessed 21 January 2014).

Arup, T. (2010) 'EU spitting chips over timber plan', *Age*, 18 January. Available online at www.theage.com.au/national/eu-spitting-chips-over-timber-plan-20100117-medp.html (accessed 10 August 2013).

Bartel, R. (2003) 'Compliance and complicity: an assessment of the success of land clearing legislation in New South Wales', *Environmental and Planning Law Journal*, 20(2): 116–36.

Bartel, R. (2008) 'Sentencing for environmental offences: an Australian exploration', paper presented at the Sentencing Conference, 8 February 2008. Available online at http://njca.anu.edu.au/Professional%20Development/programs%20by%20year/2008/Sentencing%20Conference%202008/papers/Bartel.pdf (accessed 10 August 2013).

Bergin, A and Allen, R. (2008) 'The thin green line: climate change and Australian policing', *Australian Strategic Policy Institute Special Report*, 17. Available online at www.aspi.org.au/publications/special-report-issue-17-the-thin-green-line-climate-change-and-australian-policing (accessed 10 August 2013).

Blakely, L. (2008) 'The end of the *Viarsa* saga and the legality of Australia's forfeiture penalty for illegal fishing in its Exclusive Economic Zone', *Pacific Rim Law and Policy Journal*, 17(3): 677–705.

Bricknell, S. (2010) 'Environmental crime in Australia', *Australian Institute of Criminology Research and Public Policy Series*, 109. Available online at www.aic.gov.au/publications/current%20series/rpp/100-120/rpp109.html (accessed 10 August 2013).

Burke, T (2010) *Labor's plan to restrict illegally logged timber*, press conference, 10 August, Minister for Agriculture, Fisheries and Forestry, Minister for Sustainable Population. Available online at www.sciencemedia.com.au/downloads/2010-8-10-5.doc (accessed 10 August 2013).

Centre for International Economics (2010) *A Final Report to inform a Regulation Impact Statement for the proposed new policy on illegally logged timber: prepared for Department of Agriculture, Fisheries and Forestry*, Canberra: Centre for International Economics. Available online at www.daff.gov.au/__data/assets/pdf_file/0015/1510431/final-report-proposed-new-policy.pdf (accessed 10 August 2013).

Cole, D. (2008) 'Creative sentencing: using the sentencing provisions of the South Australian *Environment Protection Act* to greater community benefit', *Environmental and Planning Law Journal*, 25(1): 25–33.

Crittenden, S. (2010) 'Australia urged to ban illegal timber imports', *ABC News Online*, 28 May. Available online at www.abc.net.au/news/stories/2010/05/28/2912546.htm?section=justin (accessed 10 August 2013).

Cubby, S. (2010) 'Forests NSW investigated over logging breaches', *Sydney Morning Herald*, 18 August. Available online at www.smh.com.au/environment/forests-nsw-investigated-over-logging-breaches-20100817-128lo.html (accessed 10 August 2013).

Deloitte (2009) *Carbon credit fraud: the white collar crime of the future*, Sydney: Deloitte. Available online at www.deloitte.com/assets/Dcom-Australia/Local%20Assets/Documents/Services/Forensic/Carbon_credit_fraud.pdf (accessed 10 August 2013).

Environmental Investigation Agency (EIA) and Telapak (2004) *Profiting from Plunder: How Malaysia Smuggles Endangered Wood*, London/Bogor: EIA and Telapak. Online. Available online at www.illegal-logging.info/uploads/Profiting_from_Plunder.pdf (accessed 10 August 2013).

Environmental Investigation Agency (EIA) and Telapak (2005) *Stemming the Tide: Halting the Trade in Stolen Timber in Asia*, London/Bogor: EIA and Telapak. Available online at www.illegal-logging.info/uploads/reports114-1.pdf (accessed 10 August 2013).

Fletcher, W.J. and Santoro, K. (2007) (eds) *State of the fisheries report 2006–07*, Perth: Western Australian Department of Fisheries.

Fletcher, W.J. and Santoro, K. (2008) (eds) *State of the fisheries report 2007–08*, Perth: Western Australian Department of Fisheries.

Fletcher, W.J. and Santoro, K. (2009) (eds) *State of the fisheries report 2008–09*, Perth: Western Australian Department of Fisheries.

Fox, J.J., Therik, G.T. and Sen, S. (2002) *A Study of Socio-Economic Issues Facing Traditional Indonesian Fishers Who Access the MOU Box*, report prepared for Environment Australia. Available online at www.environment.gov.au/resource/study-socio-economic-issues-facing-traditional-indonesian-fishers-who-access-mou-box (accessed 10 August 2013).

Global Witness (2009) *A Disharmonious Trade: China and the Continued Destruction of Burma's Northern Frontier Forests*, Washington, DC: Global Witness Publishing. Available online at www.globalwitness.org/library/disharmonious-trade-china-and-continued-destruction-burmas-northern-frontier-forests (accessed 10 August 2013).

Grabosky, P. (2003) 'Eco-criminality: preventing and controlling crimes against the environment', *International Annals of Criminology*, 41(1–2): 225–42.

Greenpeace, IKEA, The Wilderness Society, Patio, Danks, Building Designers Association of Australia Ltd, Bunnings, Australian Conservation Foundation, The Woodage, Fantastic Furniture, Kimberly-Clark, Simmonds Lumber Pty Ltd, Uniting Church in Australia, Australian Plantation Products and Paper Industry Council, Timber Queensland, FIAA Australia, FSC, LifeStyle Furniture, WWF and Oxfam Australia (2010) 'Joint statement on eliminating illegal forest products in Australia', 9 December 2010, Ultimo: Greenpeace. Available online at http://assets.wwfau.panda.org/downloads/pr226_fs_environment_groups_welcome_laws_to_end_illegal_timber_imports_10dec10.pdf (accessed 10 August 2013).

Greenpeace International and Greenpeace China (2006) *Sharing the Blame: Global Consumption and China's Role in Ancient Forest Destruction*, Amsterdam/Hong Kong: Greenpeace International and Greenpeace China. Available online at www.illegal-logging.info/uploads/SHARING_THE_BLAME1.pdf (accessed 10 August 2013).

Hain, M. and Cocklin, C. (2001) 'The effectiveness of the courts in achieving the goals of environment protection legislation', *Environmental and Planning Law Journal*, 18(3): 319–38.

Hartley, A. (2004) 'Are criminal penalties the most effective sanction for offences under Part V of the Environmental Protection Act 1986 (WA)?' *Environmental and Planning Law Journal*, 21(4): 312–20.

Jaakko Pöyry Consulting (2005) *Overview of Illegal Logging*, report prepared for the Australian Government Department of Agriculture, Fisheries and Forestry, Melbourne: Jaakko Pöyry Consulting. Available online at www.daff.gov.au/__data/assets/pdf_file/0009/37593/illegal_logging_report_16sept05.pdf (accessed 10 August 2013).

Korsell, L.E. (2001) 'Big stick, little stick: strategies for controlling and combating environmental crime', *Journal of Scandinavian Studies in Criminology and Crime Prevention*, 2(2): 127–48.

Lawson, S. and MacFaul, L. (2010) *Illegal Logging and Related Trade: Indicators of the Global Response. Country Report Cards*, London: Chatham House. Available online at www.chathamhouse.org/sites/default/files/public/Research/Energy,%20Environment%20and%20Development/0710pr_illegallogging.pdf (accessed 10 August 2013).

Martin, R. (2003) 'Alternative sentencing in environment protection: making the punishment fit the crime', *Law Institute Journal*, 77(7): 32–6.

McCully, P. (2008) 'Discredited strategy', *Guardian Weekly*, 21 May 2008. Available online at www.guardian.co.uk/environment/2008/may/21/environment.carbontrading (accessed 10 August 2013).

National Public Radio, 'Carbon offsets: government warns of fraud risk', *All Things Considered*, 3 January 2008 (C. Joyce).

New South Wales Department of Primary Industries (2008) *Annual Report 2007–08*, Sydney: New South Wales Department of Primary Industries.

New South Wales Department of Primary Industries (2009a) 'Habitual abalone offender sent to jail', media release, 8 May.

New South Wales Department of Primary Industries (2009b) *Annual Report 2008–09*, Sydney: New South Wales Department of Primary Industries.

New South Wales Department of Primary Industries (2010a) 'Jail time for repeat abalone poacher', media release, 20 September. Available online at www.dpi.nsw.gov.au/__data/assets/pdf_file/0010/354565/100920-Jail-time-for-repeat-abalone-poacher.pdf (accessed 10 August 2013).

New South Wales Department of Primary Industries (2010b) 'Illegal fishing nipped in the bud', media release, 2 June. Available online at www.dpi.nsw.gov.au/archive/news-releases/fishing-and-aquaculture/2010/illegal-fishing-nipped-in-the-bud (accessed 10 August 2013).

New South Wales Department of Primary Industries (2010c) 'Fisheries officers continue to reel in abalone offenders', media release, 19 April.

Pain, N. (1993) 'Criminal law and environmental protection: overview of issues and themes', in N. Gunningham, J. Norberry and S. McKillop (eds) *Environmental Crime: Proceedings of a Conference Held 1–3 September 1993, Hobart*, Canberra: Australian Institute of Criminology.

Palmer, M. (2004) *Report on Illegal Fishing for Commercial Gain or Profit in New South Wales*, Sydney: New South Wales Department of Primary Industries.

Primary Industries and Resources South Australia (2010a) 'Major fines handed down for outback fishing offences', media release, 8 September.

Primary Industries and Resources South Australia (2010b) 'Jail sentence handed down for rock lobster offences', media release, 17 August.

Primary Industries and Resources South Australia (2010c) 'Abalone poachers nabbed at Stansbury', media release, 29 March.

Preston, Justice B.J. (2007) 'Principled sentencing for environmental offences – Part 2: sentencing considerations and options', *Criminal Law Journal*, 31: 142–64.

Pugh, D. (2009) *Preliminary audit of Yabbra State Forest compartments 162 and 163*, North East Forest Alliance. Available online at http://nefa.org.au/audit/Yabbra/Yabbra_audit.htm (accessed 10 August 2013).

Pugh, D. (2010a) *Preliminary audit of Girard State Forest compartments 44, 45, 46, 54, 55 and 56*, North East Forest Alliance. Available online at http://nefa.org.au/audit/Girard/Preliminary_Audit_of_Girard_State_Forest_1.pdf (accessed 10 August 2013).

Pugh, D. (2010b) *Preliminary audit of Doubleduke State Forest compartments 144, 145 and 146*, North East Forest Alliance. Available online at http://nefa.org.au/audit/Doubleduke/Prelim_Audit_Doubleduke_SF_1.pdf (accessed 10 August 2013).

Putt, J. and Anderson, K. (2007) 'A national study of crime in the Australian fishing industry', *Australian Institute of Criminology Research and Public Policy Series*, 76. Available online at www.aic.gov.au/documents/5/D/6/%7B5D6D36A1-3D6F-47BA-82AC-56DA79114CA6%7Drpp76.pdf (accessed 10 August 2013).

Queensland Primary Industries and Fisheries (2009a) *Annual status report 2009: Blue swimmer crab fishery*, Brisbane: Department of Employment, Economic Development and Innovation. Available online at www.daff.qld.gov.au/__data/assets/pdf_file/0009/59283/2011-MC-ASR-FINAL.pdf (accessed 10 August 2013).

Queensland Primary Industries and Fisheries (2009b) *Annual status report 2009: Coral fishery*, Brisbane: Department of Employment, Economic Development and Innovation.

Queensland Primary Industries and Fisheries (2009c) *Annual status report 2009: Coral reef fin fishery*, Brisbane: Department of Employment, Economic Development and Innovation.

Queensland Primary Industries and Fisheries (2009d) *Annual status report 2009: Coral reef fin fish fishery*, Brisbane: Department of Employment, Economic Development and Innovation. Available online at www.environment.gov.au/system/files/pages/959be80b-5bc8-4d52-baee-b84042801778/files/coral-reef-fin-fish-status-report-2011.pdf (accessed 10 August 2013).

Queensland Primary Industries and Fisheries (2009e) *Annual status report 2009: Deep water fin fishery*, Brisbane: Department of Employment, Economic Development and Innovation.

Queensland Primary Industries and Fisheries (2009f) *Annual status report 2009: East coast beche-de-mer fishery*, Brisbane: Department of Employment, Economic Development and Innovation. Available online at www.daff.qld.gov.au/__data/assets/pdf_file/0007/49597/AnnualStatusReport-ECBDM-2009-final.pdf (accessed 10 August 2013).

Queensland Primary Industries and Fisheries (2009g) *Annual status report 2009: East coast inshore fin fish fishery*, Brisbane: Department of Employment, Economic Development and Innovation.

Queensland Primary Industries and Fisheries (2009h) *Annual status report 2009: East coast Spanish mackerel fishery*, Brisbane: Department of Employment, Economic Development and Innovation.

Queensland Primary Industries and Fisheries (2009i) *Annual status report 2009: East coast trochus fishery*, Brisbane: Department of Employment, Economic Development and Innovation.

Queensland Primary Industries and Fisheries (2009j) *Annual status report 2009: Fin fish (Stout whiting) trawl fishery*, Brisbane: Department of Employment, Economic Development and Innovation.

Queensland Primary Industries and Fisheries (2009k) *Annual status report 2009: Gulf of Carpentaria developmental fin fish trawl fishery*, Brisbane: Department of Employment, Economic Development and Innovation. Available online at www.daff.qld.gov.au/__data/assets/pdf_file/0009/63837/GOCDFFTF-ASR-2009.pdf (accessed 10 August 2013).

Queensland Primary Industries and Fisheries (2009l) *Annual status report 2009: Gulf of Carpentaria inshore fin fish fishery*, Brisbane: Department of Employment, Economic Development and Innovation.

Queensland Primary Industries and Fisheries (2009m) *Annual status report 2009: Gulf of Carpentaria line fishery*, Brisbane: Department of Employment, Economic Development and Innovation. Available online at www.environment.gov.au/coasts/fisheries/qld/line/pubs/annual-status-report-2009.pdf (accessed 10 August 2013).

Queensland Primary Industries and Fisheries (2009n) *Annual status report 2009: Marine aquarium fin fishery*, Brisbane: Department of Employment, Economic Development and Innovation.

Queensland Primary Industries and Fisheries (2009o) *Annual status report 2009: Mud crab fishery*, Brisbane: Department of Employment, Economic Development and Innovation.

Queensland Primary Industries and Fisheries (2009p) *Annual status report 2009: Queensland eel fishery*, Brisbane: Department of Employment, Economic Development and Innovation.

Queensland Primary Industries and Fisheries (2009q) *Annual status report 2009: Otter trawl fishery*, Brisbane: Department of Employment, Economic Development and Innovation. Available online at www.daff.qld.gov.au/__data/assets/pdf_file/0005/66938/ASR_ECOTF2011.pdf (accessed 10 August 2013).

Queensland Primary Industries and Fisheries (2009r) *Annual status report 2009: River and inshore beam trawl fishery*, Brisbane: Department of Employment, Economic Development and Innovation.

Queensland Primary Industries and Fisheries (2009s) *Annual status report 2009: Rocky reef fin fish fishery*, Brisbane: Department of Employment, Economic Development and Innovation. Available online at www.daff.qld.gov.au/__data/assets/pdf_file/0016/66301/RRFFF-ASR-2009.pdf (accessed 10 August 2013).

Queensland Primary Industries and Fisheries (2009t) *Annual status report 2009: Spanner crab fishery*, Brisbane: Department of Employment, Economic Development and Innovation.

Queensland Primary Industries and Fisheries (2009u) *Annual status report 2009: Tropical rock lobster fishery*, Brisbane: Department of Employment, Economic Development and Innovation.

Schloenhardt, A. (2008) 'The illegal trade in timber and timber products in the Asia-Pacific region', *Australian Institute of Criminology Research and Public Policy Series*, 89. Available online at www.aic.gov.au/documents/B/D/4/%7BBD4B2E50-33B4-47F1-815E-901C0ACC7A43%7Drpp89.pdf (accessed 10 August 2013).

Situ, Y. and Emmons, D. (2000) *Environmental Crime: The Criminal Justice System's Role in Protecting the Environment*, Thousand Oaks, CA: Sage.

Tailby, R. and Gant, F. (2002) 'The illegal market in Australian abalone', *Australian Institute of Criminology Trends and Issues in Crime and Criminal Justice*, 225. Available online at www.aic.gov.au/documents/C/9/4/%7BC9422AC4-8412-42EE-8732-A54F4C98DAC4%7Dti225.pdf (accessed 10 August 2013).

Victorian Department of Primary Industries (2010a) *Annual Report 2009–10*, Melbourne: Victorian Department of Primary Industries.

Victorian Department of Primary Industries (2010b) 'Illegal fishing nets two men and a woman', media release, 30 August.

Victorian Department of Primary Industries (2010c) 'Abalone theft costs Noble Park mother and son $4,200', media release, 30 August.

Victorian Department of Primary Industries (2010d) 'Cape Schank abalone theft proved costly', media release, 22 July.

Victorian Department of Primary Industries (2010e) 'Four months jail for abalone theft', media release, 3 May.

Victorian Parliament Environment and Natural Resources Committee (2002) *Inquiry into fisheries management: second report*, Melbourne: Parliament of Victoria.

Western Australian Department of Fisheries (2009a) 'Big fines prove illegal rock lobster sale did not pay', media release, 18 November.

Western Australian Department of Fisheries (2009b) 'Another big fine over black market fish trade', media release, 13 July.

Western Australian Department of Fisheries (2010) 'Hefty fines handed out to illegal abalone fishers', media release, 2 February.

White, M. and Gibson, R. (2010) 'Fisheries and automatic forfeiture of vessels: draconian Commonwealth laws', *Australian Law Journal*, 84(5): 319–44.

Part III

Laundering the proceeds of environmental crime

4 Laundering the proceeds of crime

A global overview

John Broome

This chapter examines the nature of money laundering and the global responses to it over the last three decades. It looks at the way money is laundered and why, the international governmental and private sector responses, the new institutions and laws developed to respond to both money laundering and the ways in which the profits of environmental crimes might be laundered.

For immediate purposes it is enough to define money laundering as any activity designed to disguise the illegal origin of criminal proceeds. This is the general notion of money laundering as it is understood by most people. However, different countries have adopted different definitions of money laundering. In most cases the intention to disguise the criminal origin of the funds is a key element of the offence, but this is not always the case.

Criminals need to launder money

Not every crime gives rise to a need to launder its criminal profits. Indeed, most violent crime generates no criminal profit, and many property crimes do not involve the laundering of criminal proceeds. For example, a theft of items of property or relatively small amounts of cash obtained from a burglary might simply be used by the thief or spent on day-to-day expenses. The need to launder funds arises where criminal activity generates substantial profits, usually (but not always) in the form of cash. The criminal is confronted with a dual problem: spending large amounts of money can be conspicuous, and spending large amounts of criminal profits might attract the attention of both law enforcement agencies and other criminals. The criminal needs to disguise any obvious link to the crime that generated the profits and, at the same time, make those criminal profits secure from law enforcement investigators and other criminals alike. This is what gives rise to the need to launder the funds.

Money laundering is not a new phenomenon. The seventeenth-century highwayman needed to hide his bounty from those who enforced the law just as the cybercriminal of the twenty-first century seeks to avoid identification and prosecution. As Rider (2001) identified:

> Money laundering is nothing new. It is as old as the need to hide one's wealth from prying eyes and jealous hands. Of course, the modern money

launderer will adopt more sophisticated techniques than the gem carriers of India or the Knights Templar, but the essential *modus operandi* will be the same.

The means have changed but the essential process has not.

How big is the money laundering problem?

Across the globe, governments try to stem the rate of crime with mixed success. In many countries crime goes unchecked, particularly large-scale crime carried out by those close to or part of government. Government and private assets are systematically plundered and the funds moved to the financial capitals of the world – New York, London or Zurich – or the myriad of tax havens and offshore centres ready to accept funds and ask no questions. Corruption permeates governments across the globe. It also permeates many of the law enforcement agencies charged with the responsibility for identifying and investigating crime, the prosecutors who are supposed to bring the culprits to trial or the courts that apply the law.

No one knows the volume of criminal proceeds worldwide or the amount of that figure that is actually laundered. In 2011 a report by the United Nations Office on Drugs and Crim (UNODC) suggested that total global criminal proceeds are likely to be 3.6 per cent of global GDP, equivalent to about US$2.1 trillion in 2009 (UNODC 2011: 9).

The most quoted estimate of the amount of money laundering is that attributed to the International Monetary Fund (IMF). In 1998 the then Executive Director of the IMF released an estimate of 2–5 per cent of global GDP. While the basis for this estimate remains a mystery (the IMF has never revealed its methodology), more recent studies suggest this is a plausible estimate. According to the 2011 UNODC report:

> The best estimate for the amount available for laundering through the financial system, emerging from a meta-analysis of existing estimates, would be equivalent to 2.7 per cent of global GDP (2.1–4 per cent) or US$1.6 trillion in 2009. Still within the IMF 'consensus range', this figure is located towards its lower end.
>
> (UNOCD 2011: 7)

The process of money laundering

Money laundering is usually described as involving three sequential stages: placement, layering and integration (Reuter and Truman 2004: 25–43). Placement involves the placing of the physical funds or other funds derived from assets acquired criminally into traditional financial institutions (e.g. banks, securities brokers and insurance agents) or with non-traditional financial agents (e.g. bullion dealers, real estate agents, investment products and casinos). Layering refers to the subsequent movement of these funds through the financial system by using electronic transfers – domestic and international – monetary instruments, offshore centres, corporate structures and the use of financial markets such as those for derivatives, so as to obscure and subsequently remove links between the funds and the predicate offence. Integration is the step that involves the conversion of the layered funds into apparently legitimate earnings through normal commercial or financial activity. This last stage may involve the purchase of properties, businesses and other assets.

Of course, not all criminal proceeds are laundered, nor does all laundering involve all of the stages outlined above. Sometimes there is little attempt to hide ownership (US Senate Permanent Subcommittee on Investigations 2010: 269).[1] Simply placing cash into bank accounts using a number of transactions well below minimum reporting thresholds may suffice, as no one is really looking.

In many cases there is no need to launder at all because there is no fear that suspicion or even knowledge that the funds are the proceeds of crime will lead to any adverse consequence. It may be cheaper to bribe the police or the judges! There may be no real risk of detection even if the criminal behaviour is widely known as long as it is seen as 'normal' or at least 'acceptable'. This is the case in much of the corruption we see in Asia. Senior officials or national leaders may be immune from action and therefore simply transfer funds with impunity, at least until they lose office.

Legislative responses to combat money laundering

As recently as 30 years ago money laundering was not itself a criminal offence. Until the 1980s the focus of law makers and enforcement agencies was on the predicate offence itself rather than on the generated profits – the proceeds of crime. They focused on the underlying criminality, usually after the event. The growth in illicit drug trafficking that occurred in the 1980s led to both domestic and international responses developed around a focus on the way that proceeds of crime move through the economy, the so-called 'money trail'. New laws to identify and combat money laundering, referred to as anti-money laundering (AML) initiatives, were developed, each of which had common features:

- the creation of a separate money laundering offence defined laundering as involving the hiding of the profits of an earlier or predicate criminal activity;
- the laws provided the capacity to locate, freeze and confiscate criminally acquired assets;
- international cooperation through mutual legal assistance and extradition was recognised as an important element of the global response and new laws to facilitate this cooperation were introduced;
- financial intelligence, drawn from information about financial transactions, was recognised as a key element of responding to the drug trade; and
- the concept of the reporting of certain kinds of transactions to a central agency was developed.

Initially, these laws usually related to drug trafficking but they were gradually expanded to cover money generated by most, if not all, serious crimes. Money laundering was first criminalised in the United States (USA) by the Money Laundering Control Act of 1986,[2] and subsequently in the United Kingdom[3] (UK) and Australia.[4] In Australia, the Proceeds of Crime Act 1987 (Cth) (POCA 1987) applied to the proceeds of any indictable offence (POCA 1987 s 81).

At the same time, the United Nations (UN) was developing a global legal response to illicit drugs, namely the United Nations Convention against Illicit Traffic in Narcotic Drugs and Psychotropic Substances (the Vienna Drug Trafficking Convention). The Vienna Convention reflected the concepts that had been incorporated in the new legislation in the USA, UK and Australia. Subsequent UN conventions dealing with transnational organised crime and corruption, namely the United Nations Convention against Transnational Organized Crime and the United Nations Convention against Corruption, included more developed provisions dealing with money laundering also arising from transnational crime and corruption, as well as with international cooperation and the confiscation of proceeds of crime.

Locating, freezing and confiscating assets

The confiscation of criminally derived profits was a key strategy developed to deal with the drug trade. The thinking was straightforward. If criminal funds could be identified, they could be confiscated and they could also be used as a means to locate those involved in the organisation of major crime. This idea of 'following the money trail' was seen at the time as a major new initiative. While the concept was simple, its execution remains difficult.

Early legislation in Australia, namely the POCA 1987, included powers to locate, trace, freeze and confiscate criminally derived assets. It is important to note that there are often complex issues to be resolved, including the issue of third-party rights to the assets,[5] and the evidentiary basis on which confiscation proceedings can take place. Usually, a confiscation order will be made by a court following conviction of the defendant for the predicate offence. In a simple example, a person convicted of fraud may be subject to orders to confiscate the remaining funds if these have been located. Where the value of the located assets are less than the established value of the fraud, the prosecution may seek pecuniary penalty orders (up to the value of the offence) which would allow confiscation of additional assets if found or of subsequent assets obtained legitimately by the offender (Proceeds of Crime Act 2002 (Cth) pt 2–4 (POCA 2002)).

Most jurisdictions have conviction-based systems – that is, systems that require a criminal conviction for money laundering (or for a predicate offence) before the assets are forfeited. Some jurisdictions, however, such as Australia and the UK, have moved to also include a civil forfeiture regime that requires only that the prosecution establish to a civil standard that the assets in question were derived from criminal activity.[6] This approach is often used in cases involving proceeds of suspected drug trafficking. After an arrest of a person for trafficking (usually during an actual transaction) investigators may discover large amounts of assets which they believe are the results of previous undetected drug sales. Civil forfeiture allows the prosecution to establish, on the balance of probabilities, that these assets are the proceeds of crime (but not a particular crime). Of course, the respondent can always adduce evidence to show a legitimate source for the assets and thus rebut the prosecution case.

International assistance

It is essential that countries be able to seek and provide information and arrange for the obtaining of evidence from a foreign country in a form that would be admissible in legal proceedings in the requesting state.[7] Therefore, the provision of mutual legal assistance between states is not new. The European Convention on Mutual Assistance in Criminal Matters 1959 with its Additional Protocol has been in place since 1978, but increasingly the globalisation of trade and crime and the expansion of electronic communication has emphasised the need for countries to be able to cooperate in criminal investigations.

The extradition of suspected offenders to requesting states had been recognised in international law for many decades. Many current extradition arrangements reflect treaties developed in the nineteenth century. There were significant difficulties, however, in providing for both extradition and mutual legal assistance between civil law and common law jurisdictions.

As part of the development of the Vienna Convention, and in simultaneous bilateral negotiations, states developed processes to make both mutual assistance and extradition simpler. However, these remain issues often fraught with difficulty, particularly when political considerations are seen to be in play.[8] Other concerns relate to the need for dual criminality (the offence has to be an offence under the law in both requesting and requested country), possible prejudice to the sovereignty, security and national interest of the requested state, and concerns that the purpose of the request is to prosecute, punish or otherwise cause 'prejudice to a person on account of the person's race, sex, religion, nationality or political opinions' (Mutual Legal Assistance in Criminal Matters Act 1987 (Cth) s 8(1)(c)). More pragmatic concerns such as costs and resources also affect decisions on mutual assistance and extradition.

Financial intelligence responses to money laundering

Most criminal investigations involve the relevant agencies investigating a known crime (a murder, robbery, fraud, etc.) to identify and prosecute the suspected offender. In drug cases, police are usually unaware that an offence has occurred and therefore they often rely on the obtaining of information about possible criminal activities through informants, telephone intercepts and other covert activities. These transactions often involve movements of funds through financial institutions or the attempt to transfer value through buying and selling property.

One of the most important developments in law enforcement thinking in the 1980s was the recognition of the importance of financial intelligence in dealing with crimes that generated high levels of cash. Knowing that criminals would try to hide the criminal origins via various financial transactions, so that the proceeds could be spent with impunity, it was axiomatic that effective law enforcement needed access to information about these transactions.

The legislation in the USA, UK and Australia (which were the first jurisdictions to develop this approach) reflected the idea that the reporting of high-value cash transactions would generate valuable criminal intelligence. The reporting obligation was placed on those financial institutions that provided financial services in which large amounts of cash were involved.[9] Arbitrary reporting thresholds (AU$10,000 in Australia and US$10,000 in the US) were set, based on a view that only criminals would hold such large amounts in cash. Whatever the validity of that view in developed economies, it was quite irrelevant in cash-based economies where banking systems are less developed and accessible, and cash is often held in large amounts. In Asia, for example, the reality is that many transactions are conducted in cash and do not necessarily denote any criminal activity at all.

Identifying suspicious transactions

A second concept was the requirement that financial institutions report those transactions seen as unusual or suspicious in the light of the knowledge held by the institution of the financial circumstances of the customer. Although cash transaction reporting has not become a universal element of AML systems, the adoption of suspicious transaction reporting (STRs) has become a core element of such systems. This has evolved into what is now referred to as 'suspicious matter reporting' (e.g. the Anti-Money Laundering and Counter-Terrorism Financing Act 2006 (Cth) s 41), which goes further than individual transactions to cover surrounding circumstances. For example, a person may not actually undertake a transaction, but the fact that the person enquired about the possibility of obtaining a service may be enough to generate a report.

Financial intelligence units

It followed that if such reports were to be generated they needed to be received by an appropriate agency. The financial institutions wanted to be sure that the financial intelligence would be given to an agency that would understand its sensitivity and would use it appropriately. This was the basis of the development of financial intelligence units (FIUs).

The role of the FIU is to receive, analyse and disseminate financial intelligence obtained through the reporting processes which were mandated by the AML laws to law enforcement agencies whose role is to investigate the money laundering and its predicate criminal activity. It is one of the earliest innovations in following the money trail.[10] Most of these followed an administrative model, where the FIU is established within other agencies or as a separate body but outside traditional law enforcement agencies (LEAs).[11]

The early FIUs in the USA and Australia were created as separate from law enforcement agencies, although the UK took a different approach, initially using its National Criminal Intelligence Service (NCIS) as the recipient of its financial intelligence (this role is now carried out by the Serious Organised Crime Agency (SOCA)). Many countries, including most of the Asian economies, have located the FIU outside existing LEAs. In many cases, such as in China, the Philippines, Indonesia, Vietnam, Pakistan and Malaysia, the FIU has been created within the structure of the central bank. This approach was found useful as financial institutions in many countries were willing to pass customer information to central banks but were reluctant to see customer information passed directly to LEAs. This reluctance was driven by often justifiable concerns about corruption within the LEAs. Nevertheless, there has been a trend in recent years for the FIU to be moved within LEAs. For example, the FIU functions in Japan were moved from the Financial Supervisory Agency to the National Police Agency in 2007. Similar changes occurred in Hong Kong and Singapore.

Given that many money laundering transactions involve international transfers of funds, international cooperation is essential. An informal association, the Egmont Group of FIUs, was established in 1995 and now has 130 members. It provides the international framework for cooperation between FIUs. The Egmont Group has developed membership criteria and encourages members to develop memoranda of understanding (MOUs) to facilitate information exchanges (see Egmont Group (n.d.) for an outline of the membership criteria and process).

The exchange of information between FIUs is not automatic. FIUs want to be sure that the receiving FIU will deal with the information in accordance with agreed arrangements and for agreed purposes. Exchanges of financial intelligence between FIUs are usually conducted outside the formal requirements of mutual legal assistance treaties (MLATs) and can be carried out quickly if a MOU is in place and the capacity for electronic transfer of information has allowed for timely transfers between trusted partners.[12]

Coordinating a global response to money laundering

International cooperation to combat money laundering has always been difficult to achieve. Real and imaginary concerns about loss of sovereignty resource constraints, the potential for misuse of cooperative arrangements and legal and diplomatic processes which take interminable periods to produce even small results all combined to make effective international law enforcement more a dream than reality.

That said, the adoption of a suite of UN Conventions has seen the development of an international cooperative framework to deal with organised criminal activity, including corruption and money laundering.

There are many international initiatives directed at reducing the incidence of money laundering, including those undertaken by the United Nations through the work of the UNODC, which encourages legislative and regulatory approaches, supported by the provision of technical assistance through its own staff and consultants, by conducting research and analysis and by supporting the implementation of the Conventions (UNODC 2013). The work of the Basel Committee for Banking Supervision is mainly directed at providing a forum for central banks[13] on banking supervision issues. It has, however, issued guidelines on AML issues including the need to enhance Know Your Customer and customer due diligence (CDD) measures. The best practice recommendations of the Wolfsberg Group (made up of 11 major private banks) are intended to be financial services industry standards, for Know Your Customer, anti-money laundering and counter-terrorist financing policies (Wolfsberg Group 2012). Originally developed in 2000, these were revised in 2012.

The development banks and aid agencies have funded AML projects since the late 1980s. These projects usually involve the funding of experts to provide technical assistance including national and regional workshops, training, writing draft legislation and assisting countries to build new institutions, write procedural manuals and develop information technology systems to be used by the relevant agencies in the jurisdiction. Such projects have been funded by the Asian Development Bank (Asian Development Bank n.d.), World Bank (World Bank 2011), IMF (IMF 2013), the European Commission and by national aid agencies such as the Department for International Development (UK) and USAID, and through specialist national agencies on a bilateral basis.[14] Often a number of donors will coordinate responses in a particular country and the assistance is provided in response to needs analyses carried out by regional AML groups.[15]

Finally, three European Commission Directives (Council Directives 91/308/EEC of 10 June 1991, 2001/97/EC of 4 February 2001 and 2005/60/EC of 26 October 2005) are directed at improving AML and CFT (combating the financing of terrorism) activity with the European Union (EU).

However, the following section focuses on the main global coordination mechanism for AML, which is the Financial Action Task Force.

Financial Action Task Force (FATF)

The FATF was established by the G7 Leaders and the President of the EU in 1989 to draw up international best practice in identifying and combating money laundering. Initially, it consisted of the G7 countries, the European Commission and eight other countries. As the FATF tells it:

> The Task Force was given the responsibility of examining money laundering techniques and trends, reviewing the action which had already been taken at a national or international level, and setting out the measures that still needed to be taken to combat money laundering. In April 1990, less than one year after its creation, the FATF issued a report containing a set of *Forty Recommendations*, which were intended to provide a comprehensive plan of action needed to fight against money laundering.
>
> (FATF 2012a)

The membership of FATF increased over time as more economies were included.[16] It also undertook a programme of global expansion through FATF-style regional bodies which now cover all areas of the globe. The original 40 recommendations have been through four iterations, with the most recent adopted by the FATF Plenary in February 2012 following a substantial external consultation process.

Over time the FATF has come to be recognised as the global standard setter for AML activities and, after the terrorist attacks against the USA on 11 September 2001, also for CFT. More recently, it has become involved in attempts to combat the use of offshore centres for tax evasion and the application of UN sanctions linked to nuclear proliferation or terrorism concerns.[17] It also issues guidance material in relation to the implementation of the FATF standards and other documents such as UN Security Council Resolutions relating to the use of financial institutions.[18]

As a result of the global financial crisis, the FATF has been involved in the international discussions, notably through the Group of Twenty or G20,[19] to examine possible changes in global regulation of financial markets and participants.

These changes in focus and emphasis have seen the paradigms move from financial system protection to national security and terrorism, then to implementation of financial sanctions and now to financial and tax system integrity.

Implementing the FATF's 40 Recommendations

FATF has shown a remarkable ability to adapt to emerging concerns using the basic reporting, customer due diligence (CDD) and record keeping obligations which are at the heart of the 40 Recommendations. The initial 40 Recommendations set out legal, regulatory and law enforcement objectives. Countries were required to implement the Vienna Drug Trafficking Convention, remove laws providing for bank secrecy, criminalise money laundering and introduce laws to locate, freeze and confiscate proceeds of crime, provide for the reporting of suspicious transactions and establish entities to receive and analyse financial intelligence. The initial concept of financial institutions as published in the original FATF Recommendations of 1990 (designed to cover mainstream institutions such as banks, securities dealers, leasing companies, brokers and bureaux de change) quickly changed to include a wider list of non-bank financial institutions, with the 1996 iteration of the Recommendations containing a wider list of financial institutions in an annex. The concept of designated non-financial businesses and professions (DNFBPs), such as casinos, bullion dealers, gem dealers, real estate agents, lawyers, accountants and trust and company service providers, after being included in the 2003 iteration of the Recommendation, was added in 2003 (FATF 20 June 2003). The financial institutions and the DNFBPs are often referred to as reporting entities.

From the outset the Recommendations required financial institutions to identify customers (including verifying the documents provided for identification purposes) and to conduct customer due diligence. This meant ascertaining the likely nature of the business relationship so that transactions could be assessed against that expectation. Where circumstances changed, the financial institutions should ensure they had procedures to identify and react to those changes. In addition, anonymous accounts were outlawed. Records had to be maintained for at least five years. Financial institutions were to be protected from legal action where they met their reporting obligations and they were to be prohibited from tipping off customers who were the subject of reports. While the vulnerabilities to new technologies needed to be kept under scrutiny, institutions were encouraged to develop systems for safe and secure transfer of value. From 2003, DNFBPs were subject to the same requirements.

To facilitate international cooperation, countries were to enhance cooperation and the exchange of information and to enter into bilateral and multilateral agreements to facilitate international cooperation.

In the light of experience, the FATF moved from a rule-based approach to a risk-based approach. Essentially, countries were encouraged to develop AML systems that allowed both the financial institutions and the regulators to apply a risk-based approach (FATF 20 April 2012). Reporting entities could determine where they faced the highest money laundering risks and adapt their AML procedures to meet those risks. The regulators were to use a risk assessment as the basis for determining where they would devote their resources. This approach was supported by the reporting entities who thought it would reduce their workload and costs. In fact, it requires greater effort because it is premised on the existence of a thorough risk assessment across the entire business and continual reassessment of risk. Equally, many regulators seem content with a rule-based or 'tick the box' approach. The risk-based approach (RBA) is now specifically addressed in Recommendation 1 of the 2012 iteration of the Recommendations.

Many of the requirements of the 40 Recommendations are of doubtful relevance to developing economies where even basic banking services are unavailable to many in the country. For example, the requirement in Recommendation 10 that for every new customer a reporting entity should identify the customer and verify that customer's identity 'using reliable, independent source documents, data or information' is difficult to apply when there are no written records of birth, marriage or death and the customer is involved in subsistence agriculture. Many of the recommendations reflect practices only found in developed economies. Similarly, the need to identify beneficial owners of accounts is difficult where cultural norms often mean that one account may be used in a communal way by many members of a family. This was eventually recognised by FATF on 29 February 2008, but the 'one size fits all' approach is still largely applied. This causes many in the developing world to believe that, given high levels of non-compliance in FATF member jurisdictions, the standards are being used to require countries to legislate and implement requirements that are less than uniformly applied. Many developing economies question why costly procedures should be implemented for what they see, albeit incorrectly, as procedures only designed to meet the needs of developed economies but with little benefit to the developing economies. The FATF Recommendations are seen as a form of financial imperialism. They also object to the double standards that have been apparent in the non-compliance response processes.

FATF compliance system

The major focus of the FATF implementation programme has been to conduct mutual evaluations of members and non-members in relation to the level of compliance with the FATF standards. These mutual evaluations are conducted using a standard methodology and often involve organisations such as the IMF, World Bank and regional FATF-style bodies. Experts visit the country and conduct detailed investigations, including discussions with both public and private sector institutions, before preparing a report which is, after consideration by the FATF Plenary, made public. This 'name and shame' approach has provided a significant impetus for implementation of the FATF 40 Recommendations.

Supporting the FATF work is the development of a worldwide network of regional AML organisations. This began with the establishment of the Caribbean FATF in 1992 and the Asia-Pacific Group on Money Laundering in 1997. This was followed by a European group established by the Council of Europe in 1997 which covers Council of Europe members who are not members of the FATF (the Committee of Experts on the Evaluation of Anti-Money Laundering and the Financing of Terrorism (MONEYVAL)), and groups in Eastern and Southern Africa (the Eastern and Southern Africa Anti-Money Laundering Group (ESAAMLG)), West Africa (the Intergovernmental Action Group against Money Laundering in West Africa (GIABA)), South America (the Financial Action Task Force of South America GAFISUD)), Middle East and North Africa (Middle East and North Africa Financial Action Task Force (MENAFATF)) and Eurasia (the Eurasian Group on Combating Money Laundering and Terrorist Financing (EAG)).

FATF has placed emphasis on identifying money laundering and terrorist financing typologies (methodologies) and has conducted workshops and published reports identifying new trends. They have also focused on areas seen as high risk, such as trade-based money laundering, laundering proceeds of corruption, human trafficking, new payment methods, use of trust and company service providers, the securities sector, the football sector and casinos (FATF 2012b), and published guidance material on how to reduce these risks.

Undoubtedly, the FATF 40 Recommendations (which have now effectively become requirements) have been the basis for legislation in most countries to deal with money laundering and terrorism financing. That is not to say that the standards are universally implemented. They are not. Even the FATF's own mutual evaluations disclose widespread failure by FATF members to implement the standards.

This has not stopped the FATF from implementing a number of programmes designed to identify and encourage sanctions against non-complying countries (other than members). In 2000, FATF set out 25 criteria it would use to determine which jurisdictions were to be considered Non-Cooperative Countries and

Territories (NCCTs) and later that year listed 15 jurisdictions and recommended members impose financial constraints on them. This process continued for a number of years but had effectively petered out by 2005. As FATF itself says:

> A total of 47 countries or territories were examined in two rounds of reviews (in 2000 and 2001). A total of 23 were listed as NCCTs –15 in 2000 and 8 in 2001. The FATF has not reviewed any new jurisdictions since 2001 in the framework of the NCCT initiative. As of October 2006, there are no Non-Cooperative Countries and Territories in the context of the NCCT initiative.
>
> (FATF 23 August 2012)

That did not mean that all of the countries listed had fully implemented the FATF Recommendations. One could seriously debate the delisting of some jurisdictions on the basis of the FATF's own criteria. Some decisions were clearly political, such as the removal of Russia despite its non-compliance, so that it could become a member of FATF. FATF decided, correctly, that Russia should be 'inside the tent' and as first step removed it from the NCCT list in 2002.

Instead, in 2007, FATF established its International Cooperation Review Group (ICRG). It analyses high-risk jurisdictions and recommends specific action to address the money laundering/financing terrorism risks emanating from them. It was, therefore, a continuation of the 'naming and shaming' approach applied under the NCCT policy. It issues public statements and seeks to influence changes of policy and law in the named jurisdictions. But it goes further.

> For two of these jurisdictions, Iran and DPRK, the FATF took the additional step of calling upon its members and urging all jurisdictions to apply counter-measures to protect their financial sectors from money laundering and terrorist financing risks emanating from them. Based on continued lack of progress by both jurisdictions, the FATF reiterated its call for countermeasures at each subsequent Plenary meeting.
>
> (FATF 24 October 2012)

The process is, in part, a mechanism to place pressure on those jurisdictions seen to be the most recalcitrant in applying the FATF 'rules'. This process is also used as part of other global attempts to exert pressure on countries such as Iran and the Democratic People's Republic of Korea to try to impose pressure on these counties to stop their nuclear proliferation programmes.

While the NCCT and ICRG processes have been aimed at non-compliance by non-FATF members, there has been no specific action to deal with significant non-compliance by members or the major financial institutions operating in FATF member jurisdictions. Major regulatory failures[20] within FATF members may be reflected in mutual evaluation reports, but there is no FATF mechanism to deal with regulatory failures outside the mutual evaluation process.

This international effort has also resulted in substantial tightening of regulatory regimes, increased compliance costs, greater pressure on financial institutions to identify suspicious transactions and the inclusion of many businesses and professions outside traditional financial institutions within the regulatory and reporting regimes imposed to combat money laundering and the financing of terrorism.

The changing reasons for a global approach

FATF has become a body with varied and, one can argue, incompatible functions: policy formulator, rule maker, investigator of rule breakers, prosecutor of 'offenders' and judge and imposer of sanctions.

While the original focus on money laundering in the 1980s was a means to an end – that is, identifying, investigating and prosecuting criminals – it was also believed that, if enough criminal proceeds could be identified and recovered, the financial motive for crime might be removed or at least significantly lessened. This latter objective has proved impossible to obtain. The volume of proceeds recovered worldwide, even in those countries enjoying reasonable levels of success, is a fraction of the estimated value of criminal behaviour.[21] There are many reasons for this failure and these include resource constraints, the failure of law enforcement agencies to focus on proceeds recovery in addition to investigation of the predicate offence, the success of money laundering techniques and the use of tax havens and offshore centres which may prevent the tracing of transactions and corruption.

The focus soon turned to other objectives: protecting the integrity of the financial system. (That now may seem an oxymoron given the events of the 2009 global financial crisis and ongoing problems with major financial institutions that constantly fail to meet legislated and regulatory standards.) There was also a concern, which remains today, that large amounts of criminal proceeds moving through small or poorly governed economies might result in their becoming failed states or states where the financial system was compromised.

By 1989, when the finance ministers of the G7[22] (as it then was) had the issue of money laundering placed on the G7 Leaders' Meeting agenda, the new paradigm was protection of the financial system. The result was that, to a large extent, the international models and most of the AML processes now in place are more concerned with protecting financial markets, supporting sanctions regimes and combating terrorist financing than with the original objectives of law enforcement. That is not to say these new objectives are unimportant but that the resources and the focus of much AML activity over the last decade has shifted considerably.

Indeed, the implementation of AML processes and adherence to rules have become ends in themselves, rather than a means to a law enforcement end. An illustration of this thinking is seen in the following comment by Min Zhu, Deputy Managing Director of the IMF:

> Money laundering and the financing of terrorism are financial crimes with economic effects. They can threaten the stability of a country's financial sector or its external stability more generally. Effective anti-money

laundering and combating the financing of terrorism regimes are essential to protect the integrity of markets and of the global financial framework as they help mitigate the factors that facilitate financial abuse. Action to prevent and combat money laundering and the financing of terrorism thus responds not only to a moral imperative, but also to an economic need.

(IMF 31 March 2013)

Much of the emphasis placed by the IMF on AML has been on the protection of the financial system. Other objectives, however, have also been concerned about the effects of money laundering on economic development (Bartlett 2002). In any event, almost from the time of the creation of the FATF in 1989, the paradigm through which money laundering was examined has shifted from law enforcement to the protection of the financial system.

Countering the financing of terrorism

Activities of the UN Security Council (UNSC), regional organisations and national governments to deal with the threat of terrorism have focused in part on combating the financing of terrorism. This has been resource-intensive with relatively poor results. It has not, for example, seen a significant reduction in the incidence of terrorist attacks. International terrorism statistics can be unreliable due to different definitions of terrorism and the way incidents are counted.[23] That said, broad conclusions can be drawn from the longitudinal data that is available. The National Consortium for the Study of Terrorism and Responses to Terrorism (START) at the University of Maryland publishes a Global Terrorism Database which shows 31,148 incidents from 1991 to 2000 and 26,782 incidents from 2001 to 2010 (START 2011). The most notable feature of the statistics is that the number of incidents was decreasing up to 2001 and has been increasing since 2001. In the ten years prior to the attacks on 9/11, the three years with the highest incidence of attacks were 1991 (4,663), 1992 (5,081) and 1993 (4,954). From 1994 to 2000 the average number of incidents was 2,350. From 2001 the figures show the reverse trend. The three years with the highest number of incidents are 2008 (4,769), 2009 (4,619) and 2010 (4,640), while the average for the previous seven years is 1,822.

One consequence of the political pressure to deal with terrorist threats is that law enforcement agencies and reporting entities tend to place less emphasis on detecting money laundering. Although money laundering and terrorism financing both involve the movement of funds through the financial system, they are in fact completely opposite phenomena. Money laundering involves the movement of criminal proceeds through the financial system in order to hide its criminal origins, whereas most terrorism financing involves legitimate funds being moved to fund a subsequent criminal act.[24]

The immediate linking of the CFT initiatives to the AML system involved a 'marriage of convenience'. In the immediate aftermath of 9/11, the FATF convened, at the request of the USA, a special meeting to consider special recommendations to combat terrorism financing. By the time this meeting was held in late October, the UNSC was already looking at responses and the USA Patriot Act was already law. An underlying thread was that the way to locate terrorists was to 'follow the money trail', the core idea behind the early AML responses. The existence of a global framework that allowed suspicious transactions to be reported, customer due diligence to be applied and for record keeping to be required was seen as a perfect fit for the emerging CFT agenda. The result was that the CFT agenda was joined to the AML processes. The problem was that it asked financial institutions to look at where funds might be going rather than where they might be from. It also meant looking for small amounts rather than large amounts. Logically, this was always going to be very difficult and so it has proved.

Links between money laundering and corruption

One of the main sources of criminal proceeds is corruption. This occurs at many levels. It may involve kickbacks for the awarding of government contracts, the use of government assets for private gain, the use of related parties to siphon off government revenues, receipt of licences and contracts to which the recipient is not entitled or which occurs without open competition, or simply large-scale theft of public monies. However obtained, these proceeds need to be moved offshore to be stored or returned as laundered funds to be used and invested in 'legitimate' businesses.

There are well-documented cases of grand corruption by former national leaders such as Presidents Pinochet (Chile), Abacha (Nigeria) (Maton and Daniel 2012: 418–28), Suharto (Indonesia) and Marcos (Philippines). Huge sums are also obtained by other senior officials, such as military officers and family members,[25] in corrupt regimes. The numerous post-mortems of corrupt activities by various dictators, potentates and presidents often contain evidence of widespread contemporaneous knowledge within financial markets and even regulators of the movement of these funds, but little action to seize the funds or bring the perpetrators to justice.

Lest this be thought unfairly critical, the following description of the action taken by the Financial Services Authority in the UK in relation to attempts to recover funds moved to the UK by Abacha are illustrative:

> Virtually no action was taken by the United Kingdom authorities following Nigeria's request for mutual legal assistance that was lodged in June 2000. The Financial Services Authority, which was involved in the early part of the enquiry in the United Kingdom, only reprimanded the banks involved in laundering US$1.2 billion through the City of London; it took no steps to initiate a domestic criminal investigation into money laundering, nor would it disclose the names of the banks involved.
>
> (Maton and Daniel 2012: 426)

Of course, even where there are attempts to locate, freeze and recover assets laundered offshore, these are often plagued by long delays. Adverse decisions lead to interminable appeals by the corrupt and proceedings are terminated. Often decades pass before the proceedings are concluded, a fact not lost on those who undertake corruption on a grand scale. The Zardari/Bhutto cases (Tariq 2008: 178) in Pakistan and elsewhere show how this can be done. Often Western governments, which purport to be committed to dealing with corruption, let other strategic interests influence their inaction in such cases.[26] While Zardari and his wife were both imprisoned in Pakistan for alleged corruption at various times, there are still large amounts of funds said to be held in Switzerland by Zardari as well as assets in the USA and the UK.

Recognising that politicians, high-placed officials and their families – referred to as politically exposed persons (PEPs) – posed higher money laundering risks, FATF recommended in 2003 that such persons should be subject to higher levels of scrutiny, including a need for acceptance of such customers being subject to senior management approval (FAFT 20 June 2003: Recommendation 6). Of course, in many cases senior management was well aware of the fact that such people were customers and they are often given very special treatment, including assistance in moving funds obtained through corruption to safe havens. Even where the accounts were conducted under false names, the banks were well aware of the identities of the customers.

The scrutiny of accounts and other transactions involving PEPs is important because of the high incidence of corruption amongst PEPs in many countries.

In the most recent iteration of the FATF 40 Recommendations, the relevant provision relating to PEPs is as follows:

> Financial institutions should be required, in relation to foreign politically exposed persons (PEPs) (whether as customer or beneficial owner), in addition to performing normal customer due diligence measures, to:
>
> (a) have appropriate risk-management systems to determine whether the customer or the beneficial owner is a politically exposed person;
> (b) obtain senior management approval for establishing (or continuing, for existing customers) such business relationships;
> (c) take reasonable measures to establish the source of wealth and source of funds; and
> (d) conduct enhanced ongoing monitoring of the business relationship.
>
> Financial institutions should be required to take reasonable measures to determine whether a customer or beneficial owner is a domestic PEP or a person who is or has been entrusted with a prominent function by an international organisation. In cases of a higher risk business relationship with such persons, financial institutions should be required to apply the measures referred to in paragraphs (b), (c) and (d).
>
> The requirements for all types of PEP should also apply to family members or close associates of such PEPs.
>
> (FAFT February 2012: Recommendation 12)

Since 2012 the FATF has specifically recommended that both foreign and domestic PEPs[27] should be subject to enhanced diligence. Previously, the formal recommendation only applied to foreign PEPs (FATF 20 June 2003), although the interpretive note suggested domestic PEPs should also be scrutinised. As the FATF has become more involved with anti-corruption initiatives, application of Recommendation 12 has been given greater prominence, including the provision of guidance to financial institutions (FATF 20 July 2012).

Corruption and environmental crime proceeds

One area of corruption of particular relevance to environmental offences is the granting by corrupt officials of apparently legitimate licences or permits which may provide a cover for illegal logging or fishing. In such cases, the official who issues the licence may receive substantial payments which are laundered out of the jurisdiction. The permits provide cover for the illegal loggers to justify the receipt of payment for the product by offshore entities to which the logs are sent.

This can work in a number of ways. For example, if the purchaser of the logs is a manufacturer based in Canada or Australia, the remitting bank might (but almost certainly would not) ask for documentary evidence that the funds being transmitted to, say, Indonesia are for a legitimate purpose. The wood producer can then produce documents, including the logging permit in the name of the company, as well as invoices and other correspondence making the transaction appear entirely legitimate. The remitting bank offshore would never be expected to contact the issuing agency in Indonesia and, back at the receiving bank, the company can repeat the process of document production in the unlikely event that the inwards transfer is questioned. The funds may well be sent to an account in a third country instead, further reducing the risk of scrutiny. Of course, even if the permit was entirely false, the process can still work effectively.

This kind of scheme to legitimise illegal proceeds is simply a variation on the various trade-based money laundering schemes which can be used.

Conclusion

Most crimes that generate large profits lead to the need to launder the proceeds of those crimes. Environmental crimes are no different. Large profits may be generated by the sale of illegally obtained products, from the failure to declare the true profits obtained from legally obtained products (taxation fraud) and from the failure to implement required and costly environmental protections. These profits may arise in the country of origin, in those countries to which illegally obtained products are exported or where the companies involved may operate or place their funds.

In cases where the profits are derived from exporting illegally obtained products to developed economies, the flow of cash back to the illegal operators should attract attention from banks which are required to have in place effective AML processes. But, of course, many do not. They are often not only involved in seeking to ignore those requirements but also engaged in actively circumventing them.[28]

This means that the very institutions which should be identifying money laundering activities are deeply and knowingly involved in the practice. It is little wonder that the worldwide effort to identify and combat money laundering has been largely ineffective. The result is that the methodologies that might assist in identifying and prosecuting environmental criminals and in recovering their criminal proceeds are not delivering the expected results. Until this situation is addressed there is little hope of effective action to combat environmental crime.

Notes

1 At 269, the 2010 report of the US Senate Permanent Subcommittee on Investigations details attempts by the then Governor of the Angolan Central Bank to transfer $50,000,000 to a private account in his own name. In this case, given that there was no attempt to hide the origin of the money (the central bank), the initial transfer may not have been money laundering but subsequent transactions within the USA certainly were.
2 18 USC §§ 1001, 1956–7.
3 Drug Trafficking Offences Act 1986 (UK).
4 Proceeds of Crime Act 1987 (Cth), Mutual Assistance in Criminal Matters Act 1987 (Cth) and the Financial Transaction Reports Act 1988 (Cth).
5 For example, where there are assets held jointly by a defendant and another person not involved in the offence. See Proceeds of Crime Act 2002 (Cth) pt 2–2 div 5 (POCA 2002).
6 See the POCA 2002 and the Proceeds of Crime Act 2002 (UK) pt 5. The POCA 2002 now not only deals with criminal and civil forfeiture but also allows recovery of unexplained wealth and other assets obtained as a result of previous criminal activity such as through literary proceeds orders. Civil forfeiture was included in POCA 2002 following an extensive examination of the issue by the Australian Law Reform Commission (ALRC). In its 1999 Report, *Confiscation That Counts: A Review of the Proceeds of Crime Act 1987* (ALRC Report 87), the ALRC based its recommendation on the principle that a person should not be able to enrich themselves as a result of illegal activity. Chapter 4 of the Report discusses the issue of criminal and civil forfeiture at length.
7 The language adopted in these treaties is to refer to the state making the request for assistance as the 'requesting state' and the country providing the assistance as the 'requested state'.
8 For example, multilateral and bilateral treaties usually contain a political offence exception allowing a requested state to refuse cooperation where the offence involved is seen as 'political'. Of course, this often begs the question of what is 'political'.
9 In Australia, 'cash dealers' is defined by s 3 of the Cash Transactions Reports Act 1988 (Cth) to include banks, building societies, credit unions, securities brokers and insurance companies, but also includes bullion dealers, casinos and bookmakers.
10 Although the concept of reporting certain transactions to a central repository was initiated in the USA by the Currency and Foreign Transactions Reporting Act of 1970 (now known as the Bank Secrecy Act), it was not until 1990 that the US FIU, FinCEN was established within the US Treasury.
11 The Australian FIU, AUSTRAC, was established by the Financial Transaction Reports Act 1988 (Cth) as the first standalone FIU. There are four types of FIUs: administrative, law enforcement, judicial or prosecutorial and hybrid (IMF 2004: 9–17).

12 It may be necessary for the information and relevant documents to be subsequently obtained under an MLAT or other formal agreement for it to be admissible in legal proceedings.

13 The Bank for International Settlements (BIS) is essentially the organisation of central banks established in 1930. The Basel Committee is a sub-group within the BIS (BIS n.d.).

14 For example, AUSTRAC (Australia's FIU) has provided extensive regional AML assistance (AUSTRAC 8 March 2013). Many other national FIUs also provide such assistance.

15 The Asia/Pacific Group on Money Laundering (APG) coordinates regional AML CFT activity (APG n.d.).

16 Membership of the FATF is limited to developed economies or those thought by FATF to be sufficiently important to be included. In August 2012, it had 36 members. In addition to the members of the OECD, it includes Russia, China, Argentina, Brazil, India, South Africa, the European Commission and the Gulf Cooperation Council. Eight regional FATF-style bodies are associate members and 26 international organisations are observers, including the UN, the IMF, World Bank, the regional development banks, IOSCO, IASIS, WCO, the Basel Committee on Banking Supervision, the Al-Qaida and Taliban Sanctions Committee (1267 Committee) and the Gulf Cooperation Council.

17 Measures include, for example, UNSC Res 1989 (2011) on the Al-Qaida Sanctions List, UNSC Res 1988 (2011) on the Taliban Sanctions List, UNSC Res 1737 (2006) on the Iran Financial Sanctions List and UNSC Res 1718 (2006) on the DPRK Financial Sanctions List.

18 See, for example, UN SC Resolution 1803 (2008) (concerning financial links with Iran) which welcomes 'the guidance issued by the Financial Actions Task Force (FATF) to assist States in implementing their financial obligations under resolution 1737 (2006)'.

19 The G20 is the premier international forum for cooperation on the most important aspects of the international economic and financial agenda. It includes 19 country members and the European Union, which together represent around 90 per cent of global GDP, 80 per cent of global trade and two-thirds of the world's population. The objectives of the G20 are to assist policy coordination to achieve global financial stability, reduce risk, enhance regulation and develop new financial architecture (G20 n.d.).

20 The fines imposed in July and August 2012 by US regulators on Standard Chartered Bank and HSBC for breaches of the sanctions regimes against economic ties with Iranian banks are arguably examples of regulatory failure as these major examples of non-compliance were not identified by US regulators for years. Given the importance of the sanctions regimes to meet strategic foreign policy objectives, closer scrutiny of the legislated rules could have been expected.

21 In 2011, the UNODC estimated that in 2009 global criminal proceeds were in excess of $2 trillion.

22 The G6 was established in 1975 as a result of a meeting of the leaders of France, Germany, Italy, Japan, UK and the USA, convened by French President, Valéry Giscard d'Estaing. It became the G7 when Canada joined in 1976, and G8 when Russia (which had been an observer) joined in 1997. It is not an international organisation but an informal meeting of leaders without a permanent secretariat. The presidency rotates annually. It provides a forum for leaders and also provides a framework for meetings of Foreign and Finance Ministers. See www.g8.utoronto.ca (accessed 30 August 2012).

23 The US National Counterterrorism Center (NCTC) was established by Presidential Order in 2004 and its role codified by the Intelligence Reform and Terrorism Prevention Act of 2004, 50 USC § 401. It produces the Worldwide Incidents Tracking System

(WITS) based on a definition of terrorism as 'premeditated, politically motivated violence perpetrated against noncombatant targets by subnational groups or clandestine agents' specified by 22 USC § 2656f(d)[2]. On the other hand, the National Consortium for the Study of Terrorism and Responses to Terrorism (START) at the University of Maryland uses a 75-point coding system of incidents and produce its Global Terrorism Database (GTB). The WITS results produce significantly higher numbers than the START figures. For example, the WITS number of incidents for 2010 is more than 11,000 while the START figure is 4,640.

24 The IRA, for example, were known to undertake robberies to fund their activities, but most recent terrorism appears to be funded through legitimate donations to various causes or by state players. Although the act of financing terrorism is itself an offence, it is not using proceeds of crime.

25 On his father's death, Tommy Suharto controlled more than $1 billion in assets and it is believed that the family acquired more than $30 billion during Suharto's presidency (Maton and Daniel 2012: 435).

26 President Zardari of Pakistan has been the subject of ongoing proceedings in Switzerland since 1998 (and elsewhere) in relation to a variety of well-documented claims of corruption. These included receipt of $15 million in bribes from two Swiss companies for which both Zardari and his wife (Benazir Bhutto) were convicted in Switzerland, *in absentia*, and sentenced to serve six months in gaol and return $11.9 million to the Pakistan Government, but these orders were suspended on appeal. The former Prime Minister of Pakistan, Yousuf Raza Gilani, was removed from office on 19 June 2012 for being in contempt of the Supreme Court which had ordered Gilani to reopen the mutual assistance request made of the Swiss authorities in 1998 but terminated by the Gilani Government in 2008 after it came to power. The case remains dormant as it has not been reopened by Mr Gilani's successor.

27 PEPs are defined in the 2012 iteration of the Recommendations as follows:
Foreign PEPs are individuals who are or have been entrusted with prominent public functions by a foreign country – for example, heads of state or of government, senior politicians, senior government, judicial or military officials, senior executives of state-owned corporations, important political party officials.
Domestic PEPs are individuals who are or have been entrusted domestically with prominent public functions – for example, heads of state or of government, senior politicians, senior government, judicial or military officials, senior executives of state-owned corporations, important political party officials.

28 The New York Department of Financial Services settled charges of money laundering and sanctions breaches by Standard Chartered Bank for $340 million on 14 August 2012. In the same month, HSBC announced it had made provision of $700 million to meet expected penalties to be imposed by US regulators as a result of finds by a US Senate Committee. In June 2012 ING Groep NV settled similar charges for $619 million in penalties and forfeitures. Previous settlements for similar matters by US regulators involved Lloyd's Banking Group Plc, ABN Amro Bank NV, Barclays Plc and Credit Suisse Group AG. No criminal action has been taken to date against any individual in any of these entities.

References

APG (n.d.) *Technical Assistance and Training*. Available online at www.apgml.org/ta-and-t/page.aspx?p=df174e0e-3e75-4810-902f-caf56d2e0ea5 (accessed 4 February 2014).

Asian Development Bank (n.d.) *Anti-Money Laundering/Combating Terrorist Financing (AML/CFT)*. Available online at www.adb.org/themes/governance/aml (accessed 30 August 2012).

AUSTRAC (8 March 2013) *Technical Assistance and Training*. Available online at www.austrac. gov.au/technical_assistance_and_training.html (accessed 1 July 2013).

Bartlett, B. (2002) 'The Negative Effects of Money Laundering on Economic Development', *Platypus*, 77.

BIS (n.d.) *Basel Committee on Banking Supervision*. Available online at www.bis.org/bcbs (accessed 30 August 2012).

Egmont Group (n.d.) *About the Egmont Group*. Available online at www.egmontgroup.org (accessed 31 August 2012).

FATF (20 June 2003) *The Forty Recommendations*, Paris: FATF. Available online at www.fatf-gafi.org/topics/fatfrecommendations/documents/internationalstandardsoncombatin gmoneylaunderingandthefinancingofterrorismproliferation-thefatfrecommendations. html (accessed 30 August 2012).

FATF (29 February 2008) *Guidance on Capacity Building for Mutual Evaluations and Implementation of the FATF Standards within Low Capacity Countries*, Paris: FATF. Available online at www.fatf-gafi.org/media/fatf/documents/reports/Capacity%20building%20LCC. pdf (accessed 4 February 2014).

FATF (20 April 2012) *FATF Guidance on the Risk-Based Approach to Combating Money Laundering and Terrorist Financing – High Level Principles and Procedures*. Available online at www.fatf-gafi.org/topics/fatfrecommendations/documents/fatfguidanceontherisk-basedapproach tocombatingmoneylaunderingandterroristfinancing-highlevelprinciplesandprocedures. html (accessed 30 August 2012).

FATF (2 July 2012) *Corruption: Specific Risk Factors in the Laundering of Proceeds of Corruption – Assistance to Reporting Institutions*. Available online at www.fatf-gafi.org/topics/corruption/ documents/specificriskfactorsinthelaunderingofproceedsofcorruption-assistancetore portinginstitutions.html (accessed 30 August 2012).

FATF (23 August 2012) *High-Risk and Non-Cooperative Jurisdictions: About the Non-Cooperative Countries and Territories (NCCT) Initiative*. Available online at www.fatf-gafi.org/topics/ high-riskandnon-cooperativejurisdictions/more/aboutthenon-cooperativecountriesan dterritoriesncctinitiative.html (accessed 26 August 2012).

FATF (24 October 2012) *High-Risk and Non-Cooperative Jurisdictions: More about the International Co-operation Review Group (ICRG)*. Available online at www.fatf-gafi.org/topics/high-riskandnon-cooperativejurisdictions/more/moreabouttheinternationalco-operationre viewgroupicrg.html (accessed 25 June 2013).

FATF (2012a) *About Us: History of the FATF*. Available online at www.fatf-gafi.org/pages/ aboutus/historyofthefatf (accessed 26 August 2012).

FATF (2012b) *Documents*. Available online at www.fatf-gafi.org/documents/documents. jsp?lang=en (accessed 30 August 2012).

G20 (n.d.) *Russia G20*. Available online at www.g20.org/about_g20/g20_members (accessed 4 February 2014).

IMF (2004) *Financial Intelligence Units: An Overview*, Washington, DC: IMF.

IMF (2013) *The IMF and the Fight Against Money Laundering and the Financing of Terrorism*. Available online at www.imf.org/external/np/exr/facts/aml.htm (accessed 27 June 2013).

Maton, J. and Daniel, T. (2012) 'The Kleptocrat's Portfolio Decisions', in P. Reuter (ed.) *Draining Development? Controlling Flows of Illicit Funds from Developing Countries*, Washington, DC: World Bank.

Reuter, P. and Truman, E.M. (2004) *Chasing Dirty Money: The Fight Against Money Laundering*, Washington, DC: Institute for International Economics.

Rider, B.A.K. (2001) 'Washing Wealth – The Criminal Perspective', paper presented at New Zealand Law Society Conference, Christchurch, October 2001.

START (2011) *Global Terrorism Database*. Available online at www.start.umd.edu/gtd (accessed 3 September 2012).

START (2012) *START*. Available online at www.start.umd.edu/start (accessed 22 January 2014).

Tariq, A. (2008) *The Duel: Pakistan on the Flight Path of American Power*, New York, NY: Scribner.

United Nations Convention against Corruption, opened for signature 9 December 2003, 2349 UNTS 41 (entered into force 14 December 2005).

United Nations Convention against Illicit Traffic in Narcotic Drugs and Psychotropic Substances, opened for signature 20 December 1988, 1582 UNTS 95 (entered into force 11 November 1990).

United Nations Convention against Transnational Organized Crime, opened for signature 15 November 2000, 2225 UNTS 209 (entered into force 29 September 2003).

UNODC (2011) *Estimating Illicit Financial Flows Resulting from Drug Trafficking and Other Transnational Organized Crimes*, Vienna: UNODC.

UNODC (2013) *About UNODC*. Available online at www.unodc.org/unodc/en/about-unodc/index.html?ref=menutop (accessed 30 August 2012).

US Senate Permanent Subcommittee on Investigations (2010) *Keeping Foreign Corruption out of the United States: Four Case Histories*, Washington, DC: US Senate.

Wolfsberg Group (2012) *Global Banks: Global Standards*. Available online at www.wolfsberg-principles.com/index.html (accessed 30 August 2012).

World Bank (2011) *Technical Assistance*. Available online at http://web.worldbank.org/WBSITE/EXTERNAL/TOPICS/EXTFINANCIALSECTOR/EXTAML/0,contentMDK:21996447~pagePK:210058~piPK:210062~theSitePK:396512~isCURL:Y,00.html (accessed 30 August 2012).

5 Combating environmental crime with anti-money laundering initiatives

Indonesian experiences

Yunus Husein

Indonesia has the world's third largest expanse of forest, exceeded only by Brazil and the Democratic Republic of Congo. Indonesia's forests are commercially valuable because they are densely populated with hardwood timber trees, making them much more profitable to log than forests elsewhere in the tropics where merchantable trees are rarer and are typically of lower value. Although Indonesia has one of the world's largest areas of remaining forest, it also has one of the world's highest deforestation rates, and in recent years almost half of all Indonesian timber has been logged illegally.

Indonesia's sovereign marine area amounts to 75.3 per cent of the total area of Indonesian land territory. Indonesian waters are also crossed by many commercial ships from around the world. Flanked by two continents and two seas, it has a very strategic position in geopolitical and geo-economic terms. Around 90 per cent of world aquaculture occurs in the Asia-Pacific region and Indonesia has the highest fish consumption in the region.

Environmental crimes in Indonesia are readily seen in the forms of illegal logging and illegal fishing. In Indonesia, illegal logging is not classed as an environmental crime as such. Rather, illegal logging and environmental crime are separate offences. Each is a distinct predicate offence for the further crime of money laundering. Article 2 of Law No. 25 of 2003 states that the proceeds of crime shall be assets derived from the offences of: corruption, bribery, smuggling of goods, smuggling of workers, smuggling of immigrants, banking offences, capital market offences, insurance offences, narcotics offences, psychotropic substance offences, trade in people, illegal trading in arms, kidnapping, terrorism, theft, embezzlement, fraud, counterfeiting of currencies, gambling, prostitution, taxation offences, forestry offences, environmental offences, maritime offences, or other offences for which the penalty that may be imposed is a sentence of at least four years' imprisonment. Despite their distinctness, forestry and environmental offences are closely related and, in this chapter, illegal logging is treated as a type of environmental crime. In contrast, illegal fishing is not listed as a separate predicate offence for the crime of money laundering and would have to be considered to be included in the class of environmental crimes.

Illegal fishing in Indonesia

Illegal fishing refers to activities conducted by national or foreign vessels in waters under the jurisdiction of a state, without the permission of that state, or in contravention of its laws and regulations. Other illegal activities include those conducted by vessels flying the flag of states that are members of relevant regional fisheries management organisations but operate in contravention of the con- servation and management measures adopted by them and by which the flag states are bound. Similarly, breaches of relevant provisions of the applicable international laws or violation of national laws or international obligations, including those undertaken by states cooperating with a relevant regional fisheries management organisation, contribute to the crime of illegal fishing.

Indonesia has long been a magnet for foreign illegal fishing activity due to poor law enforcement. Illegal fishing in Indonesia is performed by fishing boats that operate without fishing permits. This is a major issue because it causes large state revenue losses as illegal fishers do not report their catch or pay the taxes they owe to the government.

Illegal fishing activities also impact on traditional and local fishers' abilities to continue to earn their living. The Indonesian government needs to improve its surveillance fleet's technology to ensure effective monitoring to combat illegal fishing. Most regional marine authorities only have speedboats available to monitor coastal waters and are unable to explore deeper waters. Indonesia needs at least 120 patrol vessels to combat illegal fishing. Most illegal fishing that happens in the Indonesian region occurs in the eastern part of Indonesia – for example, in Bali and East Java. Table 5.1 shows the number of illegal fishing violations proven against foreign vessels from 2005 to 2009.

Illegal logging in Indonesia

Illegal logging is the harvest, transportation, purchase or sale of timber in viola- tion of the law. The harvesting procedure itself may be illegal, including using corrupt means to gain access to forests, extraction without permission or from a protected area, the cutting of protected species, or the extraction of timber in excess of agreed limits. Illegal logging seriously impacts the environment and human life, contributing to deforestation and global warming, loss of biodiversity

Table 5.1 Illegal fishing violations proven against foreign vessels

Year	Illegal fishing violations
2005	165
2006	139
2007	155
2008	104
2009	93

Source: Ministry of Marine Affairs and Fisheries

and undermining of the rule of law. Illegal logging also has serious economic and social implications for the poor and disadvantaged. Furthermore, the illegal trade of forest resources undermines international security and is frequently associated with corruption, money laundering, organised crime, human rights abuses and, in some cases, violent conflict.

According to a 2005 analysis conducted by the WWF and World Bank, illegal logging is happening in all the world's tropical forests because of increasing demand for cheap wood from China, Europe, Japan and the USA. Indonesia supplies about 50 per cent of the total global timber trade. Market demand for illegal timbers plays a significant role in Indonesian deforestation. Illegal logging and forest exploitation results in the loss of timber estimated to be worth US$5 billion, and loss of Indonesian state income is estimated to be US$1.4 billion per year.

According to Forest Ministry data in 2006, the area of forests that are damaged and are not functioning reached 59.6 million out of 120.35 million hectares of total Indonesian forest area. Based on current rates, analysis from Forest Watch Indonesia and Global Forest Watch indicates that in 50 years Indonesian forests will decrease in area by about another 40 per cent.

The crime of illegal logging in Indonesia is found in two pieces of legislation: Law No. 41/1999 concerning Forestry (as amended) and Law No. 5/1990 concerning Natural Resources Conservation and the Ecosystem. Indonesian forest law enforcement efforts have been largely ineffective. Sometimes, the law enforcement officers themselves are a part of the illegal logging scenario and therefore the criminals behind the illegal logging have immunity from the law. Table 5.2 shows illegal logging violations from 2005 to 2007.

Environmental crimes as predicate crimes

In the case of illegal logging in Indonesia, the perpetrators are not working alone but with other parties who benefit from the proceeds of crime. The first step is the illegal cutting down of trees. Loggers will send the wood to either domestic or international customers using one of two methods: road or river transportation. This mechanism of illegal logging is shown in Figure 5.1.

From Figure 5.1 it can be seen that illegal logging involves a large number of parties, both domestically and internationally. These parties include timber buyers, non-timber buyers, community leaders, government regulators and law enforcement officials. It reflects how truly organised environmental crime is as part of transnational organised crime.

Table 5.2 Illegal logging violations

Year	Illegal logging violations
2005	9,700
2006	916
2007	300

Source: Minister of Forestry (Waspada 1 August 2009)

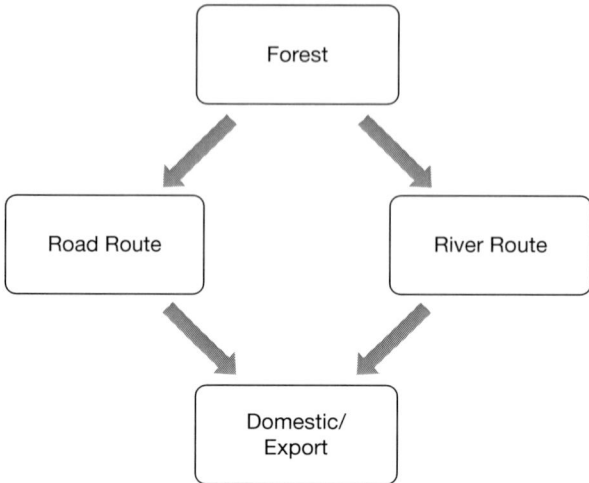

Figure 5.1 Road and river routes used for illegal logging exports

Illegal logging is commonly facilitated through local agents and accomplices (both Indonesian and non-Indonesian citizens) who operate as financial backers and have connections with corrupt government officers. Illegal documents are used in attempts to bribe government officers and illegal timbers are smuggled across borders in the process of timber laundering. These laundered illegal timbers are usually delivered to a go-between country (e.g. Malaysia) before being delivered to the destination country. Accomplices operating in Indonesia (e.g. in Sumatra, Kalimantan and Papua) cooperate with local communities who live inside and around forest areas. They offer money and promise to build relatively cheap infrastructure (e.g. streets, schools, mosques, churches) but gain great profit.

Anti-money laundering approach to combat environmental crime

There are several difficulties faced by the Indonesian government in its attempts to put the masterminds of environmental crime, especially illegal logging and illegal fishing, into gaol. When the police do have the courage to investigate a case of illegal logging, they bring a case only against truck drivers, local loggers or the captains of river boats transporting illegal logs that were actually caught by the forestry law enforcement officers. It is the same in the case of illegal fishing. Mostly, illegal fishing law enforcement convicts fishermen or boat captains. They are usually sentenced to less than one year in prison or other minimum penalties.

In addition, assets derived from these criminal acts are generally not spent or used directly by the perpetrators as such assets can be easily traced by law enforcement agencies. Instead, perpetrators usually try to bring tainted assets into the financial system, especially into the banking system, where they expect that law enforcement agencies will be unable to trace the origins of such assets.

Accessing their illegally obtained assets is essential to financial backers and that is why they conduct money laundering activities to hide the origins and make them difficult or impossible to trace by law enforcement agencies.

With the enactment of Law No. 25/2003 regarding money laundering crimes, Indonesia gained an opportunity to promote prudent banking and sustainable development while curtailing environmental crimes. It seems that if the flow of assets through the international banking system could be cut off, the activities of environmental criminals would decline.

There are two methods that can be used to trace money laundering from environmental crimes: the proactive method and the reactive method.

Proactive method

The proactive method of tracking money laundering crimes is driven by suspicious transaction reports (STRs). It obliges banks and other financial service providers to 'know their customers'. According to the 'customer due diligence' (CDD) principles guided by the 40 recommendations of the Financial Assistance Task Force (FATF), established by the Organisation for Economic Cooperation and Development (OECD), domestic financial institutions should put in place systems for knowing their customers. Prudent banks and financial institutions are required to have adequate policies, practices and procedures in place, including strict CDD rules, to make sure that no criminals or suspected criminals add money from illegal businesses and criminal activities into the banking system.

Responding to the 40 FATF recommendations, the Indonesian Central Bank and Indonesian Capital Market and Financial Institutions Supervisory Agency issued regulations regarding CDD in July 2009. The Indonesian Central Bank issued regulation number 11/28/PBI/2009 and the Indonesian Capital Market and Financial Institutions Supervisory Agency issued regulation V.D.10 on December 2009.

Using CDD, the first step is the tracking by financial providers of suspicious financial transactions and making suspicious transaction reports. Banks and other financial institutions are required to report customers engaged in suspicious transactions and customers making major cash transactions of more than Rp500 million (about US$50,000) to the Indonesian National Transactions Reporting and Analysis Commission (INTRAC). Figure 5.2 illustrates the proactive approach.

In the case of illegal logging, the Ministry of Forestry can help banks and other financial providers to identify suspicious transactions. It can also help banks to develop a reasonable suspicion regarding bank customers suspected of illegal logging and corruption in the forestry sector – especially those that operate in Kalimantan, Sumatra and Papua – by providing information on parameters for the normal transaction patterns of forestry-related customers. To this end, it

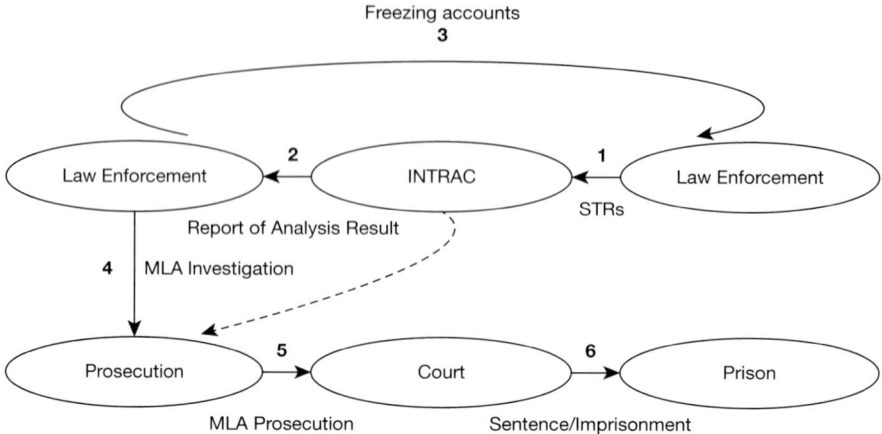

Figure 5.2 Proactive approach to anti-money laundering

signed a Memorandum of Understanding with the Indonesian Transaction Reporting and Analysis Centre (INTRAC) at the end of March 2005.

Banks should report to INTRAC any customers that are reasonably suspected of having connections with illegal logging crimes. A bank should have its reasonable suspicion backed up by information from many sources, including but not limited to law enforcement agencies (e.g. police investigators and state prosecutors), government institutions (e.g. Ministry of Forestry), civil society (e.g. forestry NGOs), news media, as well as Bank Indonesia, INTRAC and its own records. Figure 5.3 sets out these information flows.

The second step is analysis, by INTRAC, of STRs and cash transaction reports (CTRs). INTRAC can integrate into the analysis information from several

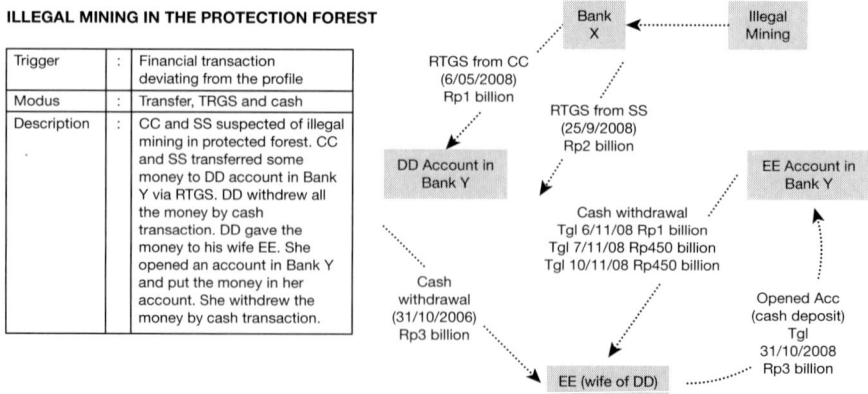

Figure 5.3 Proactive method case study

databases, including information from other financial intelligence units (FIUs), news, cross-border cash carrying reports, law enforcement agency intelligence, regulator information, and so on.

The third step is law enforcement action. The anti-money laundering legislation provides law enforcement officers with new powers. First, they have access to financial information, including flows and analyses of suspected transactions. With the assistance of INTRAC, an investigator can locate the proceeds of crimes, identify all the parties involved in the crime and start collecting evidence. The police investigator only then needs a letter signed by the Chief of the Indonesian National Police or a Regional Chief of Police to collect evidence from a bank. There are no requirements to get approval from the Governor of the Central Bank or the Minister of Finance to look into the accounts of suspects of money laundering crimes. The law enforcement officers also have the power to request that a bank freeze the bank accounts of suspects. They do not need to wait for a court order.

As part of the law enforcement process, new tools provided by the anti-money laundering legislation include a protection programme for reporting parties and witnesses, especially in court. This can involve personal security protections that extend to the protection of the families of the reporting parties and witnesses, as well as their assets. It can be used to conceal the identity of reporting parties and witnesses, or allow witnesses to provide information without having to meet face to face with the defendants at each level of court proceedings. Reporting parties can be any person who submits a report to INTRAC regarding STR and CTR, or any person who voluntarily provides investigators with reports on money laundering cases. A witness is a person who can provide information for the purpose of investigation, prosecution or court proceedings regarding a money laundering case that he or she experiences for him- or herself.

Another new innovation in the prosecution stage of law enforcement is the reversal of the burden of proof. In court proceedings, defendants will have the burden of proving that their assets were not derived from crimes. The anti-money laundering legislation shattered standard court norms by reducing the evidentiary burden borne by prosecutors and investigators to prove the criminal origins of the money under investigation. Unlike court cases involving predicate crimes such as illegal logging itself, in money laundering cases the prosecutors can force the defendants to explain the sources of their assets.

It should be noted that the reversal of burden of proof only applies in the courtroom. Investigators and prosecutors may not use this measure during the investigation and collection of evidence, so as to discourage them from abusing their power or soliciting bribes.

In addition to rules on legal evidence under the Criminal Procedure Law (KUHAP), the anti-money laundering legislation considers as legal evidence information written, sent, received or saved in electronic form (i.e. maps, designs, photographs, letters, signs, numbers, symbols or 'perforations which have meaning').

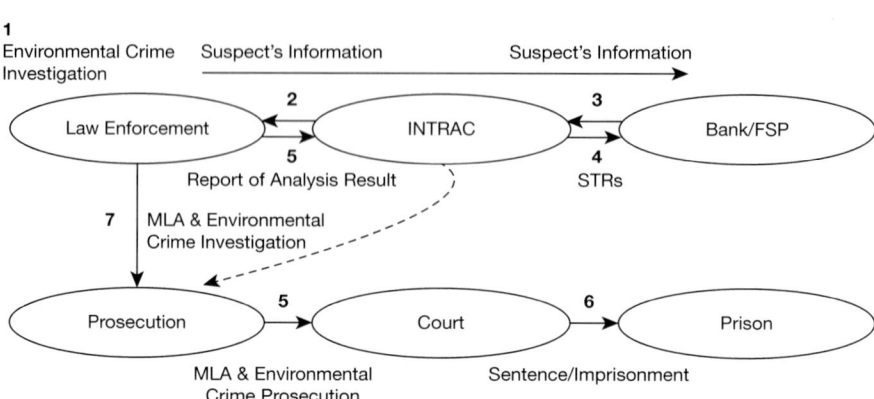

Figure 5.4 Reactive approach to anti-money laundering

Reactive method

The differences between the proactive approach and reactive approach are only in the first step. Whereas, under the proactive approach, INTRAC analysis is driven by financial provider delivery of STR reports, under the reactive approach, INTRAC first receives reports of environmental crimes, illegal logging or illegal fishing in the form of criminal intelligence from law enforcement authorities or financial intelligence from other national FIUs. INTRAC then queries the financial providers and requests that they submit more information, such as STRs or CTRs, to INTRAC. Figure 5.4 illustrates the reactive approach.

The proactive and reactive approaches have differing time, skill and information requisites, as shown in Table 5.3.

Cooperation and coordination

Proceeds of crimes can be transferred to other parties in other jurisdictions. Information from other foreign FIUs regarding illegal logging and illegal fishing

Table 5.3 Distinctions between proactive and reactive methods

Description	Proactive method	Reactive method
Analytical skill of financial provider	High	Medium
Suspicion levels	Certain	Uncertain
Detection period	Long	Short
FIU challenge	Every financial provider must have forensic auditors	Depend on law enforcement officers query

Table 5.4 Domestic and international cooperation

Domestic cooperation	International cooperation
Signed 24 MoUs with Indonesian government institutions (included Ministry of Forestry)	Signed 34 MoU with other national FIUs
Signed 11 MoUs with Indonesian universities	Active in multilateral fora (APG, FATF, Egmont Group, ASEAN SOMTC, etc.)
	Signed 1 MoU with the Indonesia-based Center for International Forestry Research

Key: APG – Asia-Pacific Group on Anti-Money Laundering; FATF – Financial Assistance Task Force; Egmont Group – an informal international gathering of national financial intelligence units; ASEAN – Association of Southeast Asian Nations; SOMTC – ASEAN Senior Officials Meeting on Transnational Crime.

is therefore often very useful in tracing the flow of the money. INTRAC has realised that combating transnational crimes such as illegal logging and illegal fishing needs international cooperation and coordination, and has established international cooperative arrangements to assist in international tracking of proceeds of crime. Domestic and international cooperation arrangements with INTRAC are shown in Table 5.4.

Conclusion

Illegal logging and illegal fishing are prominent forms of environmental crime in Indonesia. Concerning illegal logging, the Indonesian government has taken law enforcement steps. However, those efforts have not solved the problem in the field and have been unable to target the masterminds of illegal logging. Lack of coordination and differing perceptions between the law enforcement agencies, as well as the weaknesses of law enforcement agencies, are factors in this failure.

A new approach, not relying only on prosecutions under the forestry law, could use other legal instruments to catch the criminal masterminds. Law No. 25 of Year 2003 concerning money laundering includes forestry and environmental crimes among its predicate offences. The predicate forestry offences are set out in Law No. 41/1999 on forestry and, for illegal fishing, environmental crime predicate offences could apply generally. The money laundering law can be used in investigations and prosecutions where a person is suspected of conducting money laundering crimes predicated on illegal logging or illegal fishing. So far, however, even if the financial backers' cases have been investigated and finally prosecuted, they are either sentenced to less than six months' imprisonment or acquitted due to lack of evidence that they were involved in illegal logging or illegal fishing.

Financial intelligence is necessary to trace the flow of the money and it requires cooperation with domestic and international agencies. The Indonesian Transactions Reporting and Analysis Centre engages in the collection of intelligence and in inter-agency cooperative arrangements to support prosecution for laundering money derived from environmental crimes of illegal fishing and illegal logging.

Sources

Banks, B., Davies, C., Gosling, J., Newman, J., Rice, M., Wadley, J. and Walravens, F. (2008) *Environmental Crime: A Threat to Our Future*, London: Environmental Investigation Agency (EIA). Available online at www.unodc.org/documents/NGO/EIA_Ecocrime_report_0908_final_draft_low.pdf (accessed 10 August 2013).

Clifford, M. (1998) *Environmental Crime: Enforcement, Policy and Social Responsibility*, Gaithersburg: Aspen: 26.

Environmental Investigation Agency (EIA) and Telapak (2005) *The Last Frontier: Illegal Logging in Papua and China's Massive Timber Theft*, Jakarta: EIA/Telapak.

Human Rights Watch (2009) '*Wild Money': The Human Rights Consequences of Illegal Logging and Corruption in Indonesia's Forestry Sector*, USA: Human Rights Watch. Online. Available online at www.hrw.org/sites/default/files/reports/indonesia1209webwcover.pdf (accessed 10 August 2013).

Indonesian Financial Transaction Report and Analysis Center (2008) *Submission of Information on the Crime of Money Laundering in Forestry and Natural Resources Conservation*.

Law No. 25 of 2003 on Money Laundering (Republic of Indonesia).

Ministry of Forestry, Republic of Indonesia (n.d.) Available at www.dephut.go.id (accessed 22 January 2014).

Ministry of Marine Affairs and Fisheries, Republic of Indonesia (n.d.) Available at www.kkp.go.id/en/ (accessed 22 January 2014).

Setiono, B. (2005) *KYC Principles for Forestry Related Customers, Governance Brief*, Bogor: Centre for International Forestry Research.

Setiono, B. and Husein, Y. (2005) 'Fighting forest crimes and promoting prudent banking for sustainable forest management: The anti-money laundering approach', *CIFOR Occasional Paper*, 44.

Situ, Y. and Emmons, D. (2000) *Environmental Crime: The Criminal Justice System's Role in Protecting the Environment*, Thousand Oaks, CA: Sage.

Sugianto, I. and Lembaga Pengembangan Hukum Lingkungan Indonesia (2006) *Manual Invesitigasi Illegal Logging: Dengan Pendekatan UU Kehutanan, UU Tindak Pidana Pencucian Uang, UU Pemberantasan Tindak Pidana Korupsi*, Jakarta: Indonesian Center for Environmental Law (ICEL).

Part IV

Illegal fishing

Combating crime and following the proceeds

6 Regional plan of action to promote responsible fishing practices in the Southeast Asia region

Cooperative mechanisms

Murray Johns

The Regional Plan of Action (RPOA) to Promote Responsible Fishing Practices Including Combating Illegal, Unreported and Unregulated Fishing in the South East Region was endorsed in May 2007 by Ministers responsible for fisheries from its member countries. The 11 member countries are Australia, Brunei Darussalam, Cambodia, Indonesia, Malaysia, Papua New Guinea, the Philippines, Singapore, Thailand, Timor-Leste and Vietnam. The RPOA operates under the direction of a Coordination Committee – a high-level strategic group comprising senior officials who meet annually to review RPOA implementation and formulate a forward work programme. Four regional fisheries organisations provide technical advice and assistance. They comprise: FAO/Asia-Pacific Fishery Commission; Southeast Asian Fisheries Development Centre; InfoFish; and Worldfish Center.

Fishing activity is vitally important to the food security and economic well-being of the Southeast Asia region. However, overexploitation and increasing illegal fishing activity have hastened the depletion of many fish stocks. For this reason, ministers of the 11 RPOA member countries agreed that fishery resources need to be managed sustainably and more responsible fishing practices should be promoted across the region. The purpose of this chapter is: (1) to outline the structure, purpose and focus of the RPOA, with particular attention to fisheries monitoring, control and surveillance (MCS); (2) to examine why and how illegal fishing continues in Southeast Asia; and (3) to draw some conclusions on how stronger inter-agency links might be forged between fisheries agencies and financial investigation units.

RPOA objective and framework

The objective of the RPOA is to strengthen the overall level of fisheries management in the region in order to sustain fisheries resources and the marine environment. Principal actions cover the conservation of fisheries resources, managing fishing capacity and combating illegal, unreported and unregulated

(IUU) fishing in the areas of the South China Sea, Sulu-Sulawesi Seas and the Arafura and Timor Seas.

The RPOA is a voluntary instrument and takes its core principles from already-established international fisheries instruments for promoting responsible fishing practices, including the United Nations Convention on the Law of the Sea 1982 (UNCLOS), in particular articles 61–4, 116–19 and 123; United Nations Fish Stocks Agreement' 1995 (UNFSA); the United Nations Food and Agriculture Organization (FAO) Compliance Agreement 1993; and the FAO Code of Conduct for Responsible Fisheries 1995. The RPOA also draws on the FAO International Plan of Actions (IPOAs), including the IPOA to Prevent, Deter and Eliminate Illegal, Unreported and Unregulated Fishing.

The RPOA is consistent with existing treaties, agreements and arrangements and all other plans and programmes relevant to the sustainable management of the region's living marine resources, including a regional plan of action developed in 2009 under the Coral Triangle Initiative (CTI). Whereas the work of the CTI regional plan of action is focused more on the sustainability of coastal marine ecosystems and coral reefs, that of the fisheries RPOA is focused on the sustainability of fish stocks and their supporting ecosystems which, importantly, includes combating IUU fishing. As such, both the fisheries RPOA and the CTI are complementary, with strong links assured through their overlapping country memberships. Indonesia provides the Secretariat for the RPOA.

RPOA focus

The RPOA identifies a number of measures to promote responsible fishing practices and to combat illegal fishing. These measures include: understanding the current resource and management situation in the region; implementation of international and regional instruments; working with regional and multilateral organisations; implementing coastal state measures; enforcing flag state responsibilities; developing port state measures; considering regional market measures; developing regional capacity building (human and institutional); strengthening monitoring, control and surveillance (MCS) systems; and controlling transhipment at sea.

Since its inception in 2007 there have been seven RPOA implementation meetings and/or workshops. In addition, in 2008 the RPOA carried out a survey of member countries helping to define the region's key issues, needs and concerns, all with the aim to better focus efforts to develop fisheries management arrangements.

From the broader perspective, the workshops and survey identified the all-important need for greater human and institutional capacity building in fisheries governance across the full spectrum of fisheries management arrangements. This includes the need to strengthen MCS systems – both at regional and sub-regional levels. Functional MCS systems are a key factor in the fight against IUU fishing.

Monitoring, control and surveillance systems

Monitoring, control and surveillance (MCS) systems are the 'eyes and ears' of a fishery, from the catching sector through to fish landings and marketing. Drawing on a UN Food and Agriculture Organization (FAO) expert consultation in 1981, in very broad terms, MCS can be defined as:

- *monitoring* – the ongoing measurement of fishing effort characteristics and resource yields;
- *control* – the regulatory conditions under which the exploitation of the resource may be conducted; and
- *surveillance* – the degree and types of observations required to maintain compliance with the regulatory controls imposed on fishing activities.

MCS systems better enable fisheries and enforcement agencies (at national, sub-regional, regional and international levels) to quickly share information on vessel details (vessel location, name, species on board, ownership and fishing history), ports used (home port, unloading port and/or transhipment at sea) and other relevant information and intelligence. However, functional MCS systems rely heavily on advanced technology, such as satellite-based vessel monitoring systems, and sophisticated catch documentation schemes which enable trace-ability (chain of custody) of both vessel and catch from the point-of-catch to the point-of-landing.

Mechanisms to enhance regional cooperation, such as MCS systems as described above, are critical for the long-term sustainable protection of the living marine resource and the marine environment. Although some of the root causes of the depletion of fisheries resources can be addressed at the national level, many can only be successfully addressed through regional action. This is particularly the case in the areas with interdependent marine ecosystems, adjoining maritime boundaries and shared or migrating fish stocks.

So important are MCS networks that the RPOA has established four networks – one regional and three sub-regional: Regional MCS Network; Southern and Eastern Area of the South China Sea and the Sulu-Sulawesi Seas Sub-regional MCS Network; Arafura and Timor Seas Sub-regional MCS Network; and Gulf of Thailand Sub-regional MCS Network.

The RPOA further promotes participation by member countries in the work of the International MCS Network. Created in 2001, the International MCS Network aims to improve the efficiency and effectiveness of fisheries-related MCS activities through enhanced cooperation, coordination, information collection and exchange among national organisations and institutions responsible for fisheries-related MCS. The current RPOA participants who are members of the International MCS Network are Australia, Papua New Guinea, the Philippines and Vietnam.

The nature of overfishing/illegal fishing in the region

Notwithstanding RPOA initiatives to date, overfishing and illegal fishing continue in the region. This is driven by a combination of: strong regional and global demand for fish protein; the 'need' of fishers to improve their financial position in the face of diminishing fish stocks; a failure by countries to adequately implement their flag state responsibilities, resulting in unregulated fishing activity by national fleets; illegal fishing operations in national waters and the waters of neighbouring countries; the increasing use of carrier/support vessels; and official corruption – fisheries and others.

A casual review of the region's media indicates that illegal fishing continues to be practised by vessels flagged to RPOA member countries, and this is happening both in their own waters and in the waters of other RPOA member countries. According to the media articles, methods used by foreign poachers to avoid detection typically include: unauthorised entry and opportunistic forays into a neighbour's waters; document falsification (e.g. fishing licences and catch records); flag falsification; using fishing gear not in accordance with the regulations; falsifying vessel names; and bribery of officials.

Adding to the reasons why illegal fishing continues in the region is the lack of, or difficulty in, coordination between fisheries agencies and other national agencies that share regulatory control over fishing vessel movements. For example, a priority request from the fisheries agency for a port inspection to be carried out on a foreign fishing vessel unloading its catch may not be a priority for the port authority and so the vessel is not subjected to inspection. Although on the face of it this is an issue to be resolved at the national level, it is also an issue for the region as the intelligence and original request may have come from elsewhere within the region, or even from outside the region.

Opportunities to further enhance regional cooperation

Within the ambit of the RPOA, and more specifically the MCS Network, there is scope to still further enhance the pursuit of fisheries resource sustainability and regional food security. As the 'eyes and ears' of a fishery, MCS systems are repositories of information and intelligence on fishing operations and fish catches including, to the extent that it is possible, information on illegal operations.

In the fight against illegal fishing, however, there is the added dimension of tracking the financial transactions involved in the movement of the illegally caught product along the supply chain. Although tracking financial returns from illegal fishing is, largely, outside the operational scope of fisheries MCS systems, there is a bank of operational data and intelligence that can assist other agencies, such as financial investigation units (FIUs) and forensic accountants, in their tracking of the ill-gotten gains of illegal fishers.

Information held by MCS systems and networks (national, sub-regional, regional and international) can be used to give context to, and support for, investigations undertaken by FIUs and, where appropriate, be used by FIUs as evidence in prosecutions. Information on suspected illegal vessels – such as details about their fishing locations and fishing methods, possible name changes, flag(s) used, falsification of catch records, fish species on board, a history of infractions/ sanctions, vessel ownership and gear types on board – can help draw a pattern around illegal operations that can, potentially, corroborate evidence collected by the FIUs.

In addition to the vessel information just described, data on vessel movements and ports used by suspected illegal fishing vessels – such as the home port, ports used to unload or tranship catches and the use of mother ships at sea to tranship their catches – can, potentially, be very useful to FIUs. Once transhipped, it is very difficult to track the chain of custody due to mixing of species, on-board fish processing, false labelling of containers and document falsification generally. Nevertheless, any information on such aspects of illegal operations should be shared between the MCS systems and the FIUs.

Conclusion

Opportunities for RPOA member countries to advance the tracking of ill-gotten gains from illegal fishing should be pursued and built over time. It would be worthy of consideration by the RPOA Coordination Committee to develop, in partnership with FIUs, training and capacity-building programmes to foster more inter-agency cooperation between fisheries MCS units and financial intelligence units, anti-money laundering agencies and anti-fraud and corruption units. In addition, the potential for greater compatibility and support between legislative frameworks for fisheries enforcement and financial tracking should be explored. The more that fisheries agencies and financial tracking agencies can work together, the more they will cause disruption to, and a reduction in, illegal fishing.

Reference

RPOA, (n.d.) Available online at www.rpoa.sec.kkp.go.id (accessed 12 December 2013).

7 Following the proceeds of illegal fishing in the Asia-Pacific

Supply chain intervention points

Kate Barclay

Introduction

It is vitally important that illegal fishing practices not be allowed to undermine the effective management of tuna resources in the region, for the sake of marine eco-systems, world seafood supplies and the economic development of Pacific Island countries. Tunas are predatory fish, so declines in stocks have a destabilizing effect on oceanic food chains. As yet, the Western and Central Pacific Ocean (WCPO) tuna stocks are relatively less damaged by human activities, including fishing, than tuna stocks in other parts of the world, but scientists have been highlighting stock declines in some species and calling for restrictions on fishing mortality for several years (Sibert *et al.* 2006). The WCPF Convention Area tuna fishery is the largest in the world, supplying around sixty per cent of the world's tuna, and in 2012 the 'delivered' (ex fishing vessel) value of the catch was US$6,590 million (Williams and Terawasi 2013). Some of the richest fishing grounds in the region are in the exclusive economic zones (EEZs) of Pacific Island countries, many of which are in a precarious economic situation. One report estimates that between 21 and 46 per cent of catches for this region are illegal (Agnew *et al.* 2008).

The tuna fisheries of the region may be divided by species, fishing method and end market. The main species fished commercially in the tropical zone are skipjack, yellowfin, bigeye and albacore. In cooler waters further north and south, bluefin are also caught. The main types of fishing are purse seine, longline and pole-and-line.[1] End markets are those for fresh and frozen fish (including sashimi as well as tuna steaks), canned tuna and smoked *katsuobushi* (used as flavouring in Japanese cuisine). Issues of illegality most often come up to do with tunas sold in sashimi markets, which may fetch tens of thousands of dollars per fish at auction. The most valuable sashimi tunas caught in the region are the southern bluefin tuna and bigeye. Bluefin is mostly caught in temperate waters, while bigeye is mostly caught in tropical waters and is therefore significant in Pacific Island and Southeast Asian fisheries. This chapter focuses on longline fishing of bigeye for sashimi markets, with some discussion of southern bluefin tuna and cannery tuna where relevant. Routes to market are mapped as supply chains, with major players highlighted. Then key points for intervention to address illegal fishing practices are canvassed.

Illegal, unreported and unregulated (IUU) fishing

Illegal fishing is usually discussed under the umbrella term 'IUU', which means fishing not compliant with national and/or international rules for fisheries conservation and management. Tuna species are highly migratory, crossing through the waters of many countries and the high seas in the course of their lives, so as a resource they must be managed internationally. This is done through regional fisheries management organizations (RFMOs), such as the Western and Central Pacific Fisheries Commission (WCPFC). Member governments agree on measures, and are obligated to implement these in their national jurisdictions. Bluefin tuna stocks declined drastically due to overfishing from the 1960s to the 1980s and quotas have been implemented in relevant RFMOs to try to limit fishing to sustainable levels. Bigeye populations around the world are considered to be in the 'overfishing' phase (not yet overfished but on the way there), so the RFMOs have highlighted bigeye as a species in need of protection, but not all RFMOs have agreed on measures to limit bigeye catches.

Transnational crime is often described as existing in 'parallel' with legitimate international business networks (van Schendel and Abraham 2005; Nordstrom 2008). This is very much the case with IUU tuna fisheries in the Asia-Pacific region. There is not a clearly demarcated group of hidden-from-view illegal fishing vessels with distinct routes to 'black' markets run by criminals. Sometimes IUU fish is caught by vessels that are not appropriately licensed and registered for fishing in the WCPO, but often IUU fish is caught by vessels that are largely compliant. Non-compliant catch is then laundered into the legitimate catch at various points along the supply chain and sold in the main sashimi markets, potentially passing through any of the businesses involved.

Issues with underreporting southern bluefin tuna catches demonstrate how IUU practices can occur within legitimate operations. Member governments of the Commission for the Conservation of Southern Bluefin Tuna (CCSBT) RFMO have, since the early 1990s, agreed to limit their catches of southern bluefin tuna to specified national quotas. However, in 2005, a survey of the amount of southern bluefin tuna caught by a Japanese fleet (determined by an analysis of the amount of bluefin tuna available in the market and in cold storage) revealed that the fleet had been catching as much as double the agreed quota, possibly for more than a decade. Australia was the second biggest producer of southern bluefin tuna. There have also been accusations that the systems used for calculating the catch and monitoring mortality in the tuna ranching enterprises based at Port Lincoln allow the Australian fleet to underreport their catch.[2] In both cases the whole industry and government systems for monitoring catches are implicated.

Bigeye sashimi supply chains

Sashimi is a style of raw fish cuisine originating in Japan. Japan is still the main market for sashimi fish (80 per cent or more of the sashimi market is in Japan), although there are markets in other countries that have developed a taste for sushi and sashimi, including the USA, Taiwan and Korea. In the WCPO there are two main types of vessels catching bigeye for sashimi markets. Large, high-tech long-line vessels with ultra-low temperature (ULT) freezing capacity can store their catch for long periods. Tuna flesh turns brown and unappetizing for sashimi unless it is treated very carefully. Normal freezing temperatures are not suitable, but if tunas are frozen at $-60°C$ they can be stored for months or years at sashimi-grade quality. These large vessels are called 'distant water' ships and roam the globe without needing to offload or return to their home port for a year or more. They may have catches from the Atlantic and Indian Oceans as well as the Pacific Ocean in their hold. Then there are smaller, low-tech longline vessels with no ULT freezing capacity which operate from shore bases and return sashimi catches to shore quickly in order to airfreight it to market 'chilled' on ice (see Figure 7.1 below).

The Japanese longline fleet was the first to target bigeye for sashimi in the Pacific Ocean in the 1970s. They had been focusing on albacore for cannery markets but, due to changing costs of production, availability of ULT freezing technology and changing market conditions, moved to the higher-value sashimi sector, with large, high-tech vessels. Taiwanese and Korean longline fleets soon followed them, both with and without ULT capacity. From the late 1980s and into the 1990s, fleets of small longliners (without ULT) based in Pacific Island countries emerged, some owned by local citizens, others by Taiwanese and Chinese investors (Barclay n.d.; Williams and Terawasi 2010).

Both the WCPFC and the Pacific Islands Forum Fisheries Agency (FFA) maintain databases of vessels licensed to operate in the region, including information on registered owner companies.[3] These databases show a vast number of fishing companies operating in the region, with no major consolidation visible in terms of registered vessel ownership. However, it should be noted that there are a variety of more or less legitimate reasons that the 'beneficial' ownership (who gets the benefit of the activities of the vessel) of a vessel may be obscure. One reason is that vessels usually operate under a chartering arrangement rather than simply being owned by the people managing the fishing. There are many different kinds of chartering arrangements, from 'bare boat' to something more like a fishing contract (where everything from crewing to fishing is managed by the entity supplying the charter). Another is that vessels may be based in a country other than that of their owner, for various reasons. Tariff exemption arrangements for processed fish often have 'rules of origin' that include the nationality of the fleet (Campling *et al.* 2007). Several Pacific Island countries have 'domestication' policies that encourage foreign fishing companies to base their vessels locally, as does a regional multilateral fisheries access arrangement called the Federated States of Micronesia Arrangement, which came into effect in 1995 (Barclay and Cartwright 2007). Finally, companies may choose to register ownership of their vessels in a country in which the owner does not reside in order to reduce costs and/or avoid regulations, a practice called flag of convenience (FOC). Panama, Belize and Vanuatu have been associated with FOC tuna fishing in the region.

There is no indication that the lack of transparency about vessel ownership, however, hides an underlying consolidation of vessel ownership among a few major players. Vessel ownership does seem to be widely dispersed among many companies in many countries. Furthermore, fishing companies are 'price takers' within supply chains consolidated in the fishing nodes. A node is a part of the fishing enterprise that is distinct in terms of the processes involved. Imagine a horizontal axis representing a process such as harvesting, packing or trading. Prices, and other production factors such as quality standards, are generally set well down the supply chain – imagine a vertical axis – by traders and retail buyers. While illegal fishing is conducted in the production node of the supply chain, downstream nodes of the chain may be implicated because they create conditions that encourage illegal fishing by putting downward pressure on prices, demanding large volumes and failing to ensure that their products have been sourced legally.

The trading node of sashimi supply chains is highly concentrated. This node involves getting the fish from the fishing vessel to the auction, or to a retail buyer in strands of supply chains that bypass Japan's wholesale auctions (see Figure 7.1). The seafood company Mitsubishi is estimated to control around 70 per cent of the global trade in sashimi-grade tuna. Other large seafood trading companies involved in this node include Maruha and Nippon Suisan. There are also very small companies involved in trading sashimi tunas, but many of these are in effect subsidiaries of the large trading houses, set up by former employees who deal exclusively with the one trading house.

Some fishing vessels supply both sashimi and cannery markets. A detailed discussion of cannery supply chains is beyond the scope of this chapter, but one point worth noting in cannery supply chains is that the 'trading' node of the supply chain – moving fish from fishing vessels to carrier vessels and/or landing fish in ports – is also highly consolidated. Companies keep their trading relationships confidential so there is no public data about exactly how much fish is traded through which company, but industry people estimate that in excess of 75 per cent of the world's tuna catch bound for canneries is funnelled through three companies: FCF Fishery Company, Itochu Corporation and Tri Marine. Tri Marine does not trade in sashimi tuna, but FCF and Itochu both trade in sashimi as well as fish for canneries. For example, FCF has an exclusive contract to supply the Pafco processing plant managed by Bumble Bee in Fiji. FCF has arrangements with many tuna fishing companies as part of this deal, including Taiwanese and Fiji-based companies that supply both cannery and sashimi markets, so when dealing with vessels that offload to the Pafco factory FCF is also likely to be buying sashimi from some of the same vessels (see Figure 7.1).

It is not easy to trace where particular batches of fish go as they move from fishing vessel through the importation (or landing for the Japanese fleet) and wholesale processes. Governments require traceability in seafood supply chains where food safety is of concern. Since sashimi is eaten raw, it might be assumed traceability would be required; however, there is no official traceability system for ensuring food safety for sashimi in the Japanese market. Food safety, along with quality more generally, is guaranteed by relationships of trust between the people buying and selling the fish. Some unofficial traceability exists in strands of supply

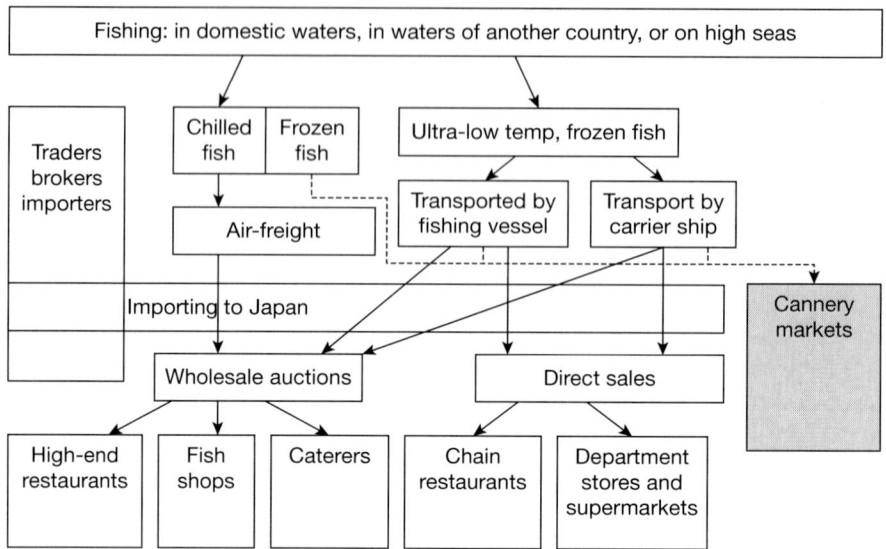

Figure 7.1 Sashimi supply chains

chains ending up in the big auctions, such as the famous Tsukiji in Tokyo, because the buyers in these auctions want to know (for quality reasons) which fishing master caught the fish and where it was caught. This capacity to trace where the fish came from in the auction strand of the supply chain, however, lasts only until the 'outer ring' of Tsukiji (where wholesalers buy at auction). Restaurateurs trust their wholesalers to supply quality fish and generally do not require information about where the fish came from (Bestor 2004; Issenberg 2007).

Sashimi sold in high-end department stores and supermarkets is labelled with its origin as the region in which it was caught as well as whether it was 'wild-caught' or farmed. An increasingly significant portion of the Japanese food retail market, including sashimi, also has traceability for its products as part of a move to provide consumers with information about how their food is produced, to enhance perceptions of food quality, safety and sustainability, but this practice is yet to be substantially implemented for sashimi tunas. The direct route to market for tuna that bypasses the 'middle-men' layers of the auction system facilitates traceability as it is less complex than the auction route in the supply chain. However, direct sales of sashimi are mostly to large chains of supermarkets, department stores and restaurants, and these buyers want predictable volume and quality, and so tend to favour farmed product. Wild-caught bigeye from the Pacific is most likely to end up in the auction strand.

IUU in bigeye sashimi supply chains

In 2004 Japan accused Taiwan of laundering IUU bigeye tuna from the Atlantic Ocean, disguising it as catch from the Indian Ocean and, to a lesser extent, the

Pacific Ocean. Tuna fishing in the Atlantic is managed under the auspices of the International Commission for the Conservation of Atlantic Tunas (ICCAT) RFMO. Heavy fishing over many years had diminished bigeye stocks in the Atlantic so the ICCAT had stipulated catch limits for this species. Some Taiwanese vessels fishing in the Atlantic, however, worked around the catch limit by record-ing some of their Atlantic bigeye as having been caught in other oceans (RFMOs for the Indian and Pacific Oceans have yet have to set catch limits for this species). Japan's evidence included analyses of changes in Taiwanese bigeye production, noting improbable shifts in the regions in which fish were recorded as having been caught and the types of vessels recorded as having caught them. Also, the Japan Coastguard arrested two freezer cargo vessels (vessels that take ULT frozen fish from fishing vessels to market in Japan) and found evidence of tuna laundering. The cargo vessels had duplicate log books falsifying information about where fish was caught, which vessels had caught fish and when/where the fish was transhipped to carrier vessels. The crews of these vessels told prosecutors that these fish laundering practices were widespread throughout the Pacific, Indian and Atlantic Oceans. Taiwan countered some of the Japanese claims about shifts in production – arguing that some of the changes in production records were due to legitimate changes in business model, misunderstandings of vessel capacities and mistakes in data – while also acknowledging that there was a significant level of criminal activity needing to be addressed.[4]

Japan's accusations of Taiwanese bigeye laundering in 2004 took place after Japan and other members of ICCAT had for several years been putting increasing pressure on Taiwan to more strongly enforce flag state controls on its tuna fleet. Despite some efforts by the Taiwanese government to reduce fishing capacity through vessel buy-back schemes in the 1990s, the Taiwanese fleet had a reputation for flouting efforts to restrict their catch by laundering practices such as those outlined above, and also for simply evading Taiwanese regulation by using flags of convenience. The Taiwanese Fisheries Agency was prevented from extending greater control over the fleet because of the electoral importance of the tuna fishing industry around the port city of Kaohsiung (Chen 2009a). ICCAT was unimpressed by Taiwan's efforts to rein in its fleet and in 2005 took the unprecedented step of implementing strong sanctions against Taiwan. Taiwan's 2006 quota of bigeye for the Atlantic was cut from 16,500 to 4,600 tons, a cut worth about US$100 million to the industry, and the numbers of Taiwanese vessels permitted to fish in the Atlantic was reduced from around 100 in 2005 to just 15 for 2006 (Fisheries and Oceans Canada 2005). These cuts sent the Taiwanese longline industry into financial chaos and caused a turnabout in attitudes to government regulation of their activities. The industry now needed the Fisheries Agency to regulate them effectively enough that they would regain good standing as a fishing fleet. Fisheries Agency measures to reduce the capacity of the fleet (such as requiring companies to scrap an old vessel for every new vessel they build) and to reduce the use of flags of convenience have been much more convincing since 2005 (Chen 2009a).[5]

It is important to note that although the Taiwanese fleet was at the centre of this IUU fishing scandal, culpability was certainly not limited to people of any one nationality. Indeed, it was somewhat ironic for Japan to be pointing the finger at Taiwan in the bigeye laundering scandal, as Japan was the main market for the IUU fish. Although Taiwanese domestic politics had prevented better fisheries management, no doubt the desire for cheap sources of bigeye on the part of some interest groups influenced Japanese policies. We tend to speak of national fleets as distinct entities, but the commercial reality of these supply chains is transnational. For example, *Suruga 1* was one of the ULT freezer carrier vessels arrested by Japan in 2004. *Suruga 1* was flagged in Panama but described as being operated by a Japanese company at the time of inspection. Of the 13 Taiwanese longliners that had supplied fish found on the *Suruga 1*, six were found to have laundered fish. One of the laundering practices was to record fish that was caught by a vessel that should not have been catching that fish as having been caught by another vessel that was licensed to catch those fish. Some of the vessel names used were from vessels registered in the People's Republic of China. (Currently *Suruga 1* is on the list of vessels licensed in the Solomon Islands; it is still flagged in Panama but is 'held' by the (South) Korean company Mako.[6] Mako is not a fishing company *per se*, but is an agent for Korean vessels that tranship their catch in the Solomon Islands.)

Networks between Japan, Taiwan, Korea and China in regional tuna fishing were established during the twentieth century and underpin regional tuna industries. Fisheries were a key part of Japan's empire building from the late 1800s. Japanese fishing companies were moving into Korean waters as early as the 1880s and were one of the main commercial pillars of colonialism in Taiwan from 1895, later spreading into Southeast Asia and parts of the Chinese mainland occupied by Japan (Koh and Barclay 2007; Chen 2009b). Korean and Taiwanese fishing industries developed in the context of the Japanese Empire, with strong links to Japanese fisheries and markets. These business ties continued even after decolonization, especially from the 1970s as Japan's economy took off and domestic fisheries production costs increased so that many Japanese fishing and seafood trading companies looked overseas for cheaper sources of production. Japanese companies utilized pre-War connections in Taiwan, Korea and, later, as China's market reforms took hold, in the Shandong and Liaoning Peninsulas. Then, as Taiwan and Korea's own economies strengthened, their seafood companies also utilized transnational connections to reduce their production costs, particularly in mainland China, utilizing ethnic connections between communities on either side of their shared borders.[7]

Intervention points

There are various points along the bigeye sashimi supply chain at which interventions to deter IUU activities may be targeted: (1) the harvesting/fishing node; (2) the transhipping/trading node; and (3) the point of importation or landing in the country in which the fish is retailed. Most types of interventions are in the form of government regulation. Government regulations are developed in the RFMOs and then implemented by members: coastal states, fishing (flag) states, port states and end-market states. Private measures to ensure seafood is sourced from legal fishing operations are also becoming influential, due to the increasing importance of corporate social responsibility in the public relations of food retailers (Roheim 2008). Non-governmental organizations (NGOs, both industry and environmental) are important players because of the pressure they bring to bear on governments and companies to strengthen fisheries conservation measures. Some of the key NGO players in tuna fisheries in the region include: Greenpeace; the Marine Stewardship Council (MSC); WWF; International Seafood Sustainability Foundation (ISSF); Organization for the Promotion of Responsible Tuna Industries (OPRT); and the Japan Fisheries Association.

Fisheries regulation has conventionally targeted fishing activities, and there are well-established systems for intervening at this node of the supply chain. Some of the systems of monitoring, control and surveillance (MCS) for fisheries include: (1) coastguard operations; (2) placement of government observers on fishing vessels to give independent information to cross-check with company logbooks; (3) use of satellite tracking vessel monitoring system (VMS) equipment on vessels for tracking their movements; and (4) linking licensing of vessels to their standing on public lists of vessels complying (or not) with regulations ('black' lists). Unfortunately, these measures have not been sufficiently effective. One reason is the sheer difficulty of mounting effective MCS in the extremely large national waters of many countries in the region, with limited government resources. Government will is another problem. In some cases, the will to effectively enforce fisheries regulations is weakened by corruption, or by competing demands on government – the short-term economic health of the fishing industry may trump enforcement, or scarce government resources may be diverted to other priorities, understandable in the developing country context. The fact that there are thousands of companies involved in fishing for sashimi tunas and that the fishing node of the chain is not very powerful relative to other nodes also means that targeting fishing companies for interventions may not be as effective as targeting companies further downstream in the supply chain.

The next node in the supply chain is when fish are moved from the fishing vessel – landed at a fish market, landed for airfreight to market or transhipped to a carrier vessel to take it to market. When catches are landed or transhipped in port there are government monitoring systems in place – by Fisheries officers and officers from other departments, such as Customs. By contrast, transhipping at sea facilitates the laundering of IUU catches (Greenpeace 2009). Longliners do most of their fishing in the region in high seas areas. They are not required to report via VMS while on the high seas, and furthermore may tranship on the high seas, where as yet there is no effective monitoring. A vessel fishing on the high seas with its VMS turned off may stray into a nearby EEZ for which it is not licensed and fish those national waters, and then go back to the high seas and tranship the catch. The portion of the catch from the EEZ would be IUU because of the licensing issue, but also IUU because it will be misreported as coming from somewhere other than where it was actually caught (distorting the statistics on which resource management decisions are based). Purse seiners in the WCPO have for many years been required to tranship in port to reduce the opportunities for IUU, and the WCPFC has been negotiating measures to bring more longline transhipments into ports and increase the monitoring of high seas transhipments.

When considering the scope for more intervention in the transhipping node of sashimi supply chains, it is useful to bear in mind that this stage of the journey from ocean to plate is largely managed by a relatively small number of companies. The tuna traders' business is facilitating the supply of fish from longline vessels to sashimi wholesale markets or canning processors, so presumably the companies Mitsubishi, FCF and Itochu can influence practices in the transhipping node of supply chains.

In recent years, 'trade-related measures' have been added to conventional fisheries regulation in an attempt to strengthen conservation measures overall. One kind of trade-related measure is that the importing state can refuse to accept fish not accompanied by appropriate documentation certifying that it was caught in compliance with relevant regulations. This type of intervention occurs at the point in the supply chain of landing the catch in the end-market country. Insofar as they are related to 'trade', these measures only apply to imports, and it is important also to encompass domestic catches with interventions at this point in the chain. For example, with Japan's overcatching of southern bluefin tuna mentioned earlier, the catch from Japan's domestic fleet had been exempt from a level of monitoring imposed on imported fish in a 'trade documentation scheme' implemented by Japanese customs authorities. When the overcatching was revealed in 2005, Japan agreed that its domestic catches should also be subject to greater scrutiny, although stopped short of including them in the same documentation scheme as the imports.

Measures to monitor catches at the point of landing in the end-market country relies on the accuracy of the documentation certifying that the catch was caught according to relevant regulations. That is, the documentation must enable officials to accurately trace the path the fish has taken back to the fishing vessel and pinpoint when and where it was caught. The scheme used for the South Georgia toothfish fishery under the RFMO the Commission for the Conservation of Antarctic Marine Living Resources is one model. It is certified by the Marine Stewardship Council and uses a system with barcodes on boxes of fish (Roheim 2008). As mentioned earlier, there is no thorough scheme in place for traceability in sashimi tunas. There is, however, traceability for canned tuna, and this system might be adapted for sashimi tunas.

For canned tuna, both importing governments and retail buyers require the importing agent to be able to quickly and accurately work out exactly where in the supply chain any food safety problem occurred, and identify all other fish in that batch for the purposes of a recall. It is in the commercial interests of everyone in the supply chain for these traceability systems to be very accurate so that all the fish needing to be recalled can be, while the recall is limited to the affected fish only. All the information needed to trace canned tuna is contained in the code printed on the flat side of the can. This traceability system as it currently exists is for food safety rather than conservation purposes, and most of the information used for the traceability is commercially sensitive and therefore sits with the companies managing supply, rather than with governments, so it may be that this system is not amenable to cooption for conservation purposes. Nevertheless, traceability for accurate catch documentation schemes is necessary for effective intervention at the importation/landing node of sashimi tuna supply chains, and lessons may be learned from existing traceability in cannery tuna supply chains.

Conclusion

Various kinds of organizations have a role to play in addressing the laundering of IUU catches in transnational tuna supply chains. RFMOs are the main international bodies for discussing and agreeing on measures that then must be implemented by members, including coastal states, fishing states, port states and market states. Private measures related to concerns with corporate social responsibility are also influencing practices, with retailers increasingly requiring suppliers to ensure the product has been legally sourced. Industry organizations and environmental organizations have an impact through lobbying of RFMOs, governments and companies to improve fisheries conservation.

Interventions to deter IUU fishing may be implemented at several points along the supply chain. Interventions in the fisheries node of the supply chain have been tried and tested over many years. More recently, measures have been developed for implementation further downstream, in the transhipping, landing and importation nodes of the chain. The effectiveness of fisheries regulations implemented downstream from the fishing node depends on traceability – the ability to accurately trace the fish back to the point at which it was caught.

Some of the challenges facing attempts to stem IUU sashimi tuna practices include the capacities (and political will) of governments and the complexity of intervening at several points in supply chains that operate across multiple jurisdictions and the high seas. Factors in favour of more effective enforcement include the increasing importance of corporate social responsibility, potentially making IUU fish harder to sell, and the high level of consolidation at both the trading node and the end-market country node of the supply chain.

Notes

1 For explanation about these types of fishing, see the FAO fish capture technology website: www.fao.org/fishery/topic/3384/en.
2 For official accounts of southern bluefin tuna underreporting issues, see the CCSBT meeting reports at: www.ccsbt.org/site/reports_past_meetings.php.
3 The WCPFC fishing vessel database is available at: www.wcpfc.int/record-fishing-vessel-database. The FFA vessel list is available at: www.ffa.int/licence_lists.
4 Japan submitted versions of an 'Information Paper' on this topic to ICCAT and the Preparatory Conference for the WCPFC, and Taiwan submitted versions of an

'Explanatory Note' in response. See Papers Submitted by Delegations for the Preparatory Conference on the WCPFC website: www.wcpfc.int/preparatory-conference/conference-documents/papers-submitted-delegations. One of the issues Japan raised was that old Taiwanese vessels built prior to 1980 were recorded as having caught sashimi, whereas Japan asserted that vessels this old would not have the ULT capacity to supply sashimi-grade fish (they would only be able to supply cannery-grade fish). Taiwan countered that its fleet had had ULT capacity since the 1970s and in any case it was possible to retro-fit ULT freezing equipment in older vessels.

5 Weichen Wang, third-generation owner/manager of Taiwanese tuna longlining company (Wu Pioneers Seafoods), personal communication, 18 November 2009.
6 The list of vessels licensed to operate in Pacific Island countries is available on the website of the Pacific Islands Forum Fisheries Agency: www.ffa.int.
7 The political standoff between China and Taiwan means Taiwanese companies are not supposed to work with Chinese companies, but mingled Taiwanese and Chinese investment is not uncommon in regional tuna industries (McCoy and Gillett 2005).

References

Agnew, D., Pearce, J., Peatman, T., Pitcher, T. and Ganapathiraju, P. (2008) *The Global Extent of Illegal Fishing*, Marine Resources Assessment Group and Fisheries Eco-systems Restoration Research, Fisheries Centre, University of British Columbia. Available online at www.mrag.co.uk/Documents/ExtentGlobalIllegalFishing.pdf (accessed 24 November 2013).

Barclay, K. (2014) 'History of Industrial Tuna Fishing in the Pacific Islands', in M. Tull and J. Christensen (eds) *Historical Perspectives of Fisheries Exploitation in the Indo-Pacific*, Germany: Springer, MARE Publication Series Vol 12.

Barclay, K. and Cartwright, I. (2007) *Capturing Wealth from Tuna: Case Studies from the Pacific*, Canberra: Asia Pacific Press.

Bestor, T. (2004), *Tsukiji: The Fish Market at the Center of the World*, Berkeley, CA: University of California Press.

Campling, L., Havice, E., Ram-Bidesi, V. and Grynberg, R. (2007) *Pacific Islands Countries, The Global Tuna Industry and the International Trade Regime – A Guidebook*, Honiara: Pacific Islands Forum Fisheries Agency.

Chen, H.T. (2009a) 'Japan–Taiwan Relations in the 21st Century: From the Perspective of Tuna Disputes in the Atlantic Ocean', unpublished paper, China Research Centre, University of Technology, Sydney.

Chen, H.T. (2009b) *Taiwanese Distant-Water Fisheries in Southeast Asia 1936–1977*, Newfoundland: International Maritime Economic History Association.

Fisheries and Oceans Canada (2005) 'Unprecedented Sanctions Invoked by ICCAT for Overfishing Bigeye Tuna', news release. Available online at www.marketwired.com/press-release/DFO-Unprecedented-Sanctions-Invoked-ICCAT-Overfishing-Bigeye-Tuna-Organization-also-568738.htm (accessed 12 November 2013).

Greenpeace (2009) *End the High Seas Heist: Briefing to the Fifth Regular Session of the Western and Central Pacific Fisheries Commission Scientific Committee*, Kolonia: Greenpeace. Available online at www.wcpfc.int/node/2189 (accessed 2 December 2013).

Issenberg, S. (2007) *The Sushi Economy: Globalization and the Making of a Modern Delicacy*, New York: Gotham Books.

Koh, S. and Barclay, K. (2007) 'Traveling through autonomy and subjugation: Jeju Island under Japan and Korea', *Asia Pacific Journal: Japan Focus*. Available online at www.japanfocus.org/-Kate-Barclay/2433 (accessed 2 December 2013).

McCoy, M.A. and Gillett, R.D. (2005) *Tuna Longlining by China in the Pacific Islands: A Description and Considerations for Increasing Benefits to FFA Member Countries*, Honiara: Pacific Islands Forum Fisheries Agency.

Nordstrom, C. (2008) 'Global fractures', *Social Analysis*, 52(2): 71–86.

Roheim, C. (2008) *Seafood Supply Chain Management: Methods to Prevent Illegally-Caught Product Entry into the Marketplace*, International Union for Conservation of Nature. Available online at http://cmsdata.iucn.org/downloads/supply_chain_management_roheim. pdf (accessed 11 December 2013).

Sibert, J., Hampton, J., Kleiber, P. and Maunder, M. (2006) 'Biomass, size, and trophic status of top predators in the Pacific Ocean', *Science*, 314(15 December): 1773–6.

van Schendel, W. and Abraham, I. (2005) *Illicit Flows and Criminal Things: States, Borders, and the Other Side of Globalization*, Bloomington, IN: Indiana University Press.

Williams, P. and Terawasi P. (2010) *Overview of Tuna Fisheries in the Western and Central Pacific Ocean, Including Economic Conditions – 2012*, Western and Central Pacific Fisheries Commission, Ponhpei, Federated States of Micronesia, http://www.wcpfc.int/ meetings/9th-regular-session-scientific-committee, accessed 12 May 2014.

8 Integrating monitoring, control and surveillance and anti-money laundering tools to address illegal fishing in the Philippines and Indonesia

Mary Ann Palma-Robles

Introduction

For decades, states have raised concerns about the need to address resource- and environment-related offences within the framework of transnational criminal law,[1] such as the illegal trade in wildlife, illegal trade in ozone-depleting substances, dumping and illegal transport of hazardous waste, and illegal logging and trade in timber (Environmental Investigation Agency 2008; Brack and Hayman 2002). However, to date, the classification of illegal fishing activities as an environmental crime has not been uniformly and clearly established in international or domestic law.

Recently, however, propositions to promote the adoption of an international legal framework to combat opportunistic participation by transnational criminal groups in certain illegal fishing activities have been taken up in the international agenda. In March 2010, the United Nations General Assembly (UNGA) adopted Resolution 64/72 on sustainable fisheries where it noted concerns about possible connections between international organised crime and illegal fishing in certain regions of the world, and encouraged states to study the causes and methods of, as well as contributing factors to, illegal fishing, bearing in mind the distinct legal regimes and remedies under international law applicable to illegal fishing and international organised crime (UNGA Resolution 63/112: 59).

In response to the call of the UNGA, the UN Office of Drugs and Crime (UNODC), an international body responsible primarily for assisting states in addressing transnational crime, released a report on organised crime in the fishing industry in April 2011. The report highlighted certain issues related to organised crime in fisheries, including: abuse of fishers trafficked for the purpose of forced labour on board fishing vessels; frequency of child trafficking in the fishing industry; human trafficking in persons on board fishing vessels; vulnerability of fish licensing systems and foreign access rights to corruption; and use of fishing vessels for the purpose of trafficking of illicit drugs, illegal trafficking of weapons; and acts of terrorism (UNODC 2011). This UNODC study has not only revived the global campaign to address illegal fishing as an environmental crime, but also encouraged states to find a collective approach that will bridge the gap between the legal regimes on sustainable fisheries and combating transnational organised crime.

Pending agreement towards an international framework that will address transnational crime in fisheries, one can examine how current domestic legal frameworks may be utilised and strengthened to assist states in addressing the issue. This chapter focuses on how fisheries' enforcement mechanisms such as monitoring, control and surveillance (MCS)[2] may be utilised to supplement anti-money laundering tools to address illegal fishing. The fisheries enforcement framework of two countries, Indonesia and the Philippines, are analysed here in this respect. Examples of MCS tools in the two countries include logbook systems, port and market inspections and audit, fishing patrols, vessel monitoring systems, port and market denial, and catch certification systems.

This chapter is presented in four sections. The first section summarises some of the illegal fishing activities confronting the Philippines and Indonesia, and the importance of addressing the transnational criminal aspects of this illegal activity. The second and third examine key aspects of fisheries implementation using MCS tools and of fisheries-relevant anti-money laundering laws, respectively, in the Philippines and Indonesia. The fourth section provides options to bridge the gap between legislation on fisheries and anti-money laundering to establish a clear connection between illegal fishing and other illicit activities. It also gives examples of how fisheries MCS and anti-money laundering tools may be integrated to curtail the problem.

Illegal fishing and transnational crime in the Philippines and Indonesia

Illegal fishing in the Philippines and Indonesia is a longstanding problem confronting both commercial and small-scale fisheries. The two countries not only share common boundaries but also experience ongoing illegal fishing within areas under their national jurisdiction. The most common illegal fishing activities in the two countries are: illegal fishing by foreign fishing vessels, mainly vessels flying the flags of distant-water fishing nations; use of illegal fishing gears and destructive fishing methods such as blast fishing, cyanide poisoning, and fine-meshed nets; use of fake licences and registration papers; and other violations such as failure to comply with reporting requirements. Illegal fishing activities occur in rich fishing grounds both in coastal and offshore areas with ineffective fisheries enforcement measures in place.

Indonesia estimates that the country loses US$4 billion annually due to illegal fishing activities, while the Philippines loses about US$1 billion annually. These economic loss estimates are mainly based on apprehension records and only account for the value of caught fish and do not reflect further environmental and social losses incurred from associated destruction of fish habitats and the marine environment. As an example, the value of damage to coral reef by destructive fishing could be as much as US$2 billion over a period of 20 years (Department of Environment and Natural Resources *et al.* 2001: 2). Illegal fishing by foreign fishing vessels is also associated with the illegal trade in corals, which, based on shipment to the United States alone, is estimated to be valued at about US$1 million per annum (de Jesus 1999: 29). Illegal foreign fishers may also be involved in the illegal trade of endangered and protected species such as marine turtles (see Ticke 2002: 14). Depending on the extent and value of these activities and where they take place, such activities may qualify as 'smuggling of fish' or 'laundering of catch', as characterised by some regional fisheries management organisations.

A coral reef that has been destroyed by such fishing methods can only produce 4 tonnes of fish per square kilometre every year, compared with the 20 tonnes that a healthy coral reef can produce (White, Vogt and Arin 2000: 600). It also takes about 38 years for a dynamited reef to recover 50 per cent of its hard coral cover (White *et al.* 2000: 600). Similarly, cyanide kills corals and reef invertebrates along with many non-target fish. It has been estimated that over 1 million kilograms of sodium cyanide has been used on the Philippine reefs since the 1960s (Barber and Pratt 1998: 11).

While these incidents and estimates highlight various fisheries violations in the Philippines and Indonesia, there are no official records of involvement of transnational criminal groups in these activities. However, a number of areas in fisheries may be considered to be most susceptible to other unlawful activities associated with transnational crime. These activities include the use of fishing vessels to transport migrants and drugs, smuggle goods and arms, and trade in high-value species such as live reef food fish entering the markets of Hong Kong, Taiwan, China, and Singapore.

Indonesia and the Philippines have a long history of maritime criminal activities such as smuggling of goods, illegal transport of people, trafficking in drugs and arms, and piracy at sea. Although these illicit activities are not directly related to fisheries, they all have elements of 'transit by sea and ports' which may involve the use of fishing vessels. As an example, there has been anecdotal evidence of fishing vessels, either sourced from or transiting through Indonesia, that are used as conduits for the illegal transport of migrants to northern Australia. This is one example of the type of activities within the nexus of fisheries and transnational crime that need further investigation on the part of the Indonesian and Philippine governments.

One specific fishery that exhibits most of the characteristics of a business involving unlawful activities is live reef fish trade originating from Indonesia and the Philippines. First, live reef fish trade is a highly lucrative industry (Sadovy *et al.* 2003: 29), involving high-value low-volume species, which is a characteristic of the illegal trade in abalone in Australia and other parts of the world. Second, the live reef fish trade is largely unregulated and unreported (Scales, Balmford and Manica 2007: 989). For decades there has not been accurate trade information or proper reporting of reef fish trade in exporting countries such as Indonesia and the Philippines. Other illegal fishing activities also occur within the live reef fish trade, such as the use of cyanides and trade in fish fry and juvenile reef fish (Ishak and Hooi 2008: 65). Numerous stakeholders are involved in live reef fish trade in the Philippines and Indonesia, from the catching, rearing, transport, to the trade and sale of reef fish, sometimes involving business ventures that are not adequately monitored or regulated. Most of the financial benefits go to unknown middlemen and business owners rather than to local fishers or communities involved in the fishery.

Licensing is one of the key aspects of fisheries most vulnerable to fraud and corruption. Fraud in licensing fishing vessels or gear may involve falsification of licences, logsheets, and catch documents, and tampering with vessel monitoring systems (VMS) equipment. Corruption may include bribery of fisheries officers to obtain the necessary licences, of enforcement officers to avoid detection, and of fisheries observers to prevent the reporting of inaccurate information. Thus, some of the illegal fishing activities in Indonesia and the Philippines demonstrate elements of transnational crime in fisheries that need further investigation and adoption of measures that would detect and deter potential problems.

Fisheries law and enforcement tools in the Philippines and Indonesia

The conservation, management, and use of fisheries resources in the Philippines and Indonesia are governed by a number of laws, including fisheries-, marine conservation-, environmental-, shipping-, and trade-related laws. Provincial, city, district, or municipal laws also apply since some fisheries functions are decentralised to local governments. The domestic framework for addressing illegal fishing in the two countries remains in the realm of fisheries management, however, and does not necessarily include instruments that relate to (maritime) security in the broadest sense, where issues such as transnational organised crime are discussed. However, as discussed below, the Indonesian fisheries framework is progressing, through recent amendments to its fisheries legislation, towards addressing transnational crime in fisheries.

Features of national fisheries legislation

In the Philippines, the main piece of fisheries legislation is the Republic Act (RA) No. 8550, An Act Providing for the Development, Management and Conservation of the Fisheries and Aquatic Resources, Integrating all Laws Pertinent thereto, and for other Purposes (RA No. 8550), also known as the Philippine Fisheries Code of 1998. The basic objectives of the Philippine Fisheries Code of 1998 are the conservation and protection of fisheries and aquatic resources, alleviation of poverty, utilisation of offshore and deep-sea resources, improvement of aquaculture, and the upgrade of post-harvest technology (RA No. 8550 s 2(g)). The Philippine Fisheries Code of 1998 implements general fisheries management principles such as the setting of total allowable catch based on maximum sustainable yield, temporal and spatial limitations such as the establishment of closed seasons, closed areas, fish refuges, and sanctuaries, and licensing fees as resource rent. The Philippine Fisheries Code of 1998 also implements basic policies on the protection of subsistence fisheries in the use of communal fishing areas (RA No. 8550 s 2(d)) and the promotion of the constitutional right to limit fishery access in Philippine waters to the exclusive use and enjoyment of Filipinos (RA No. 8550 s 2(b)). This implies that no foreign vessels are allowed to fish in Philippine waters.

The Philippine Fisheries Code of 1998 does not contain any provision on grave offences in fisheries that may be likened to transnational crime. Sections 86 to 106 provide fisheries prohibitions which include: authorised fishing or fishing without a licence; fishing by foreign vessels; fishing using explosives or poisonous substances; use of fine mesh nets; use of prohibited gears in municipal waters; use of methods and gears that are destructive to coral reefs and marine habitats; conversion of mangroves to fishing areas; fishing in overfished areas and during closed seasons; fishing in fishery reserves; taking of rare, threatened, or endangered species; capture and exportation of breeders and spawners; illegal trade of fish or fishery species; violation of catch ceilings; and aquatic pollution. Other violations under the Philippine Fisheries Code of 1998 include: failure to comply with minimum safety standards; failure to report aquaculture-related activities; illegal gathering and marketing of shellfish; illegal construction and operation of fish cages and corrals; and obstruction of navigational areas. Although no reference is made in legislation to how these fisheries violations can be made predicate offences to money laundering, it can be noted that some of these provisions describe characteristics of transnational crime in fisheries, such as illegal use of fishing gears and methods, illegal trade in live reef fish, and fraudulent documentation.

Similar to the Philippine framework, the management of fisheries in Indonesia comprises a number of national policies, laws, and regulations directly and indirectly related to fisheries. The primary law governing fisheries is Law No. 31 of 2004 Concerning Fishery (Republic of Indonesia), as amended by Law No. 45 of 2009 (Republic of Indonesia). Other national laws also apply.[3] Governmental regulations, ministerial decrees, and ministerial decisions are adopted to govern aspects of fisheries such as fishing vessel registration and licensing, fisheries business licensing, control of fish transhipment, fish marketing, vessel monitoring system, fisheries surveillance, and port state measures. These laws do not explicitly address transnational criminal activities in fisheries but provide a range of fisheries violations relating to conditions of fishing licences, use of or falsification of licences, fishing during certain seasons and areas, illegal trade of fish and fishery products, failure to comply with aquaculture standards, and other violations (see, for example, Law No. 45 of 2009 (Republic of Indonesia) ss 83A, 85, 93, 94A, 98, 100A–C)).[4]

What distinguishes the Indonesian fisheries law from the Philippine fisheries law is its direct reference to potential criminal acts in fisheries. It goes beyond addressing issues related to overfishing and makes reference to 'theft of fish and other illegal fishing actions, not only inflicting losses on the State, but also threatening the interests of fishermen and fish cultivators, industrial climate, and the national fishery business' (Indonesian Law No. 45 of 2009, Elucidation of Law of the Republic of Indonesia 2009). It recognises the limitations of Law No. 31 of

2004 (Republic of Indonesia) in addressing these concerns and raises the need for a more effective fisheries enforcement and modern fisheries management. It highlights the major legal gaps in the field of fishery in enforcement, application of sanctions, and jurisdiction or relative competence of district courts over criminal acts (Elucidation of Law of the Republic of Indonesia 2009). To address these gaps, Indonesia's Law No. 45 of 2009 provides for the application of the principles of benefit, justice, equality, integrity, transparency, togetherness, partnership, efficiency, preservation, autonomy, and continuous development (Law No. 45 of 2009 (Republic of Indonesia) art. 2). It institutes legal changes in the following key areas to address criminal aspects of fisheries: law enforcement and coordination mechanism between agencies; investigations of criminal acts in fisheries; penal and administrative sanctions; judicial procedures on the determination of time limit for a case investigation; facilities of fisheries law enforcement including possibility of legal actions in the form of sinking foreign vessels operating illegally in the Indonesian fisheries management zones; strengthening port measures; and extension of fisheries court jurisdiction.

Monitoring, control, surveillance and enforcement tools

The Philippines and Indonesia have adopted a number of monitoring, control, surveillance, and enforcement tools to monitor fishing activities in their waters and ports, the activities of vessels flying their flags in other jurisdictions and on the high seas, and foreign vessels authorised to fish or conduct transhipment activities. While this section will not explain the specific application of these MCS and enforcement tools and mechanisms in both countries, the salient features of these tools that are relevant for addressing transnational crime in fisheries will be highlighted. These include fishing vessel registration, vessel and gear licensing, vessel monitoring systems, logbook systems, observer programmes, port state inspection, air and vessel patrols, and catch certification and documentation. Most of these tools apply only to large-scale fishing vessels. Each of these tools has a different scope of application in terms of fishing area, type of vessels, and type of fishing activities. Indonesia is also implementing a 'fisheries control system' and has established a fishery court, both developments that are most relevant to addressing criminal acts in fisheries.

The key fisheries MCS tool for Indonesia and the Philippines, applied mostly to medium to large fishing vessels, is the registration and licensing system. Although fishing vessel registration and licensing are two separate processes usually administered by different authorities, they are connected in that all fishing vessels of a particular size are required to be registered and comply with vessel safety requirements before the vessel can obtain the necessary licences to fish. There are different types of licences: for the Philippines, the commercial fishing vessel and gear licence (CFVGL) is required, while Indonesia issues a number of licences, namely the fishery business licence (SIUP), fishing vessel and gear licence (SIPI), and the licence for fish transporting vessels (SIKPI). The Philippines also issues international fishing permits for its vessels wishing to fish outside national jurisdiction, as well as permits to tranship fish in port for foreign fishing vessels.

In the course of registering, fishing vessel information is obtained, such as proof of ownership and proof of identity of the owner, specification of the vessel, size and tonnage. For foreign vessels intending to change their flag to Indonesia or to the Philippines, the vessel identity is confirmed by the authorities and a deletion certificate is required from the previous flag state. All registered vessels have unique identification numbers to avoid double registration. Registration of vessels may be subject to cancellation or deletion in certain circumstances on grounds of non-compliance with regulations and violations of fisheries law.

After vessels are registered, they are required to obtain fishing vessel and gear licences before they can conduct any fishing activity. Valid certificates of registry, certificates of vessel inspection, and certificates of ownership are required to apply for a licence. Compliance with fisheries laws and regulations, including the submission of fishing logbooks and catch effort reports, is a requirement before obtaining or renewing any license. Licensed fishing vessels and gears are to be clearly marked in accordance with international standards for the marking of fishing vessels and gears. As mentioned above, one of the requirements for fishing vessels is to keep a record of their catch, composition, size of fish, and other data in a logbook, which they submit to national authorities for purposes of data collection. Logbooks, in addition to port sampling, are key sources of fisheries information in the Philippines and Indonesia.

One of the tools to ensure compliance of vessels is the implementation of a vessel monitoring system (VMS). This system, usually satellite-based, requires commercial fishing vessels to install a transponder or mobile transceiver unit which automatically reports the position of the vessel at regular intervals. This allows national fisheries authorities to track vessels through a land-based monitoring centre. Foreign fishing vessels and Indonesian- and Philippine-flagged vessels fishing outside national jurisdiction are the key vessels required to be equipped with VMS. Apart from using this technology to monitor compliance of vessels, traditional methods of monitoring are employed, such as fisheries patrol and air surveillance conducted by the countries' marine police, navy, and coastguard to ensure compliance with fisheries law, investigate possible violations, and deter and apprehend fisheries violators.

The Philippines and Indonesia have also commenced the implementation of national observer programmes, where vessels, particularly those fishing for tuna, are required to accept observers on-board vessels in order to collect biological samples, verify catch size and composition, inspect logbooks, and monitor the general compliance of vessels with fisheries regulations. Because of limitations in capacity, national fisheries authorities may not be able to have 100 per cent observer coverage for all commercial fishing vessels and all types of fisheries; however, they target specific risks – such as fishing activities of foreign fishing vessels, transhipment at sea, and fishing during area and season closures – as priorities for observer inspection. Although observer programmes are quite new in both countries, support infrastructure, facilities, and personnel are now in place to facilitate implementation.

Aside from targeting illegal fishing, port state measures are used to collect data in port and ensure compliance with food sanitary and safety requirements. Various port state measures apply in the Philippines and Indonesia, such as designation of ports for foreign fishing vessels, advanced notice of entry and inspection of fishing vessels, gears, catch, and documents. As port states, the two countries enforce jurisdiction by providing for the denial of port entry, confiscation of catch, and detention of vessels in breach of fisheries regulations.

Catch documentation or certification is a new scheme implemented by both Indonesia and the Philippines in compliance with obligations to regional organisations and as a requirement for trade to key markets such as the European Union and the United States. The main function of catch certification systems is to ensure that only fish obtained through legal means enter the international market. Catch certificates are required to be filled out by the master of the fishing vessel and validated by designated authorities of the two countries. These catch certificates accompany all fish and fish products bound for international trade.

MCS for fisheries provide useful tools to detect and deter illegal fishing activities, primarily by verifying the source and quantity of catch, identifying people and vessels engaged in fishing, and ensuring compliance with fisheries regulations. However, these tools neither monitor nor investigate the involvement of transnational criminal groups in fisheries or the potential laundering of proceeds from illegal fishing activities.

Anti-money laundering in the Philippines and Indonesia

In the realm of combating transnational crime and terrorism, one of the key mechanisms is the adoption of anti-money laundering tools. Both the Philippines and Indonesia have enacted anti-money laundering laws to track proceeds from transnational crime, although such laws do not have specific provisions relating to illegal fishing.

Philippine anti-money laundering law

The Philippines has enacted Republic Act No. 9160 (or the Anti-Money Laundering Act of 2001), as amended by RA No. 9194, which provides for the criminalisation of money laundering from a number of unlawful activities highlighted below. This law covers transactions in cash or equivalent money instruments in excess of PhP500,000 (AU$12,500) within one banking day, which was significantly lowered from the original threshold amount of PhP4 million (AU$100,000) before the amendment of the Act. The law became further restrictive in that RA No. 9194 expanded the reporting requirements to include 'suspicious transactions' regardless of the amount involved. Transactions considered suspicious include those having no legal or trade obligation or economic justification; where the client is not properly identified; in which the amount involved is not commensurate with the business or financial capacity of the client; where the circumstances relating to the transaction appear to deviate from the profile of the client or the past transactions; and where the transaction is structured to avoid reporting requirements (RA No. 9194 s 3(b–1).

Suspicious transactions also include those related to unlawful activities as defined in RA No. 9194 and relevant laws, including kidnap for ransom, drug-related offences, graft and corrupt practices, plunder, robbery and extortion, illegal gambling, piracy on the high seas, swindling, smuggling, hijacking, arson and murder, fraudulent practices, felonies, and qualified theft (RA No. 9160 s 3(i), as amended by RA No. 9194). These predicate offences to money laundering do not include illegal fishing. The closest reference to fisheries is found in article 310 of the Penal Code on 'qualified theft', which includes 'fish taken from a fishpond or fishery'.[5] This definition, however, is neither sufficient nor clarified in interpretation as covering all types of illegal fishing in the country, particularly those that may be associated with environmental crime. In addition, offences under the Anti-Money Laundering Act include any involvement in money laundering, including failure to perform an act that ends up facilitating the offence, failure to report transactions, failure to keep records, malicious reporting, and breach of confidentiality (RA No. 9160 s 14, as amended by RA No. 9194).

Based on available information, there were more than 28 million covered suspicious transaction reports and almost 4,000 suspicious transactions in 2007 (Philippine Anti-Money Laundering Council 2007: 16). These transactions were all subject to enquiry and 50 per cent of the total number were subject to further investigation since they were found to be related to unlawful activities such as kidnap for ransom, drug-related violations, qualified theft, *estafa*, graft and corruption, and terrorism-related activities (Philippine Anti-Money Laundering Council 2007: 17). More than 4,000 cases were filed in 2007 related to money laundering, involving civil forfeiture, criminal cases, administrative cases, and application of freeze orders, the latter of which included most covered transaction cases (Philippine Anti-Money Laundering Council 2007: 17).

An Anti-Money Laundering Council (AMLC) has been established as the financial intelligence unit (FIU) of the Philippines to investigate money laundering matters and cooperate with other countries and FIUs in transnational investigations and prosecutions. The AMLC investigates covered and suspicious transactions, determines the true identity of those involved in such transactions, institutes civil forfeiture and remedial proceedings, imposes administrative fines, applies to courts for orders to freeze monetary instruments or property alleged to be pro-ceeds from unlawful activities, as well as adopt other measures that may be necessary to counteract money laundering (RA No. 9160 s 7, as amended by RA No. 9194). The AMLC has developed a transaction monitoring, tracking, and analysis system, and a transaction complaint mechanism, as well as freezing of assets and civil forfeiture as some of the tools to track proceeds from unlawful activities and to deter such illegal activities.

In addition to cooperating and participating in investigations conducted by foreign governments, the AMLC may also enlist the assistance of other Philippine government departments and institutions in investigating money laundering cases, and in tracking down, freezing, and restraining assets. As part of undertaking its mandate, the AMLC is a member of or supports coordinating mechanisms such as the Anti-Terrorism Council, Presidential Anti-Graft Commission, Presidential Anti-Smuggling Task Force, Presidential Anti-Organized Crime Task Force, and the National Law Enforcement Coordinating Committee. The scope of the Anti-Money Laundering Act and the nature of cases investigated by the AMLC also necessitate strong cooperation with government departments and bureaus, including the Philippine National Police, National Bureau of Investigation, Philippine Center on Transnational Crime, Department of Interior and Local Government, Department of Justice, Department of Finance, Department of Transportation and Communication, Bureau of Internal Revenue, Bureau of Immigration and Deportation, National Intelligence Coordinating Agency, and the Armed Forces of the Philippines.

Indonesia's anti-money laundering law

Similar to Philippine law, Indonesia has criminalised money laundering under Law No. 15 of 2002 on Anti-Money Laundering Law. Money laundering under Indonesian legislation uses a combined list and threshold approach to cover predicate offences. Article 3 of Law No. 15 of 2002 refers to proceeds of crime as assets in the amount of at least Rp500 million (AU$54,000), obtained either directly or indirectly from any of the following criminal acts: corruption; bribery; smuggling of goods, workers and immigrants; banking offences; narcotics- and psychotropic-related offences; slavery and trade in women and children; illegal trading in arms; kidnapping; terrorism; theft; embezzlement; and fraud. Any person involved in any transaction of such assets is punishable under criminal law. Reporting of transactions falling within the ambit of this law is also required. In addition to the Anti-Money Laundering Law in Indonesia, the Criminal Code also deals with limited forfeiture, freezing, and seizing of criminal proceeds and instruments of crime and property intended to be used in the commission of a money laundering or terrorist-financing offence. Articles 38 to 49 of the Criminal Procedure Code contain provisional measures and confiscation procedures for cases involving corruption, fraud, cheating, and illegal logging. These laws do not provide for criminalisation of illegal fishing offences as predicate offences to money laundering.

Various guidelines have been developed for financial providers on how to identify suspicious financial transactions and how to report such transactions. These guidelines are meant for money changers and money transfer services business, as well as financial services providers such as general banks, rural banks, mutual fund managers, securities companies, insurance businesses, pension funds, and financing institutions.

The Indonesian Financial Transaction Reports and Analysis Centre (INTRAC) is the financial intelligence unit of the country. It receives and analyses suspicious transaction reports, cash transaction reports and other information, and also distributes analysed reports to law enforcement agencies. The INTRAC provides input to policymaking and facilitates inter-agency cooperation and collaboration with other governments and FIUs in investigating money laundering cases.

Integrating fisheries MCS, enforcement and anti-money laundering tools

While MCS and fisheries enforcement tools apply primarily to address illegal fishing, such tools are confined within the framework of fisheries management and compliance and are not linked sufficiently to anti-money laundering. MCS tools such as fishing vessel registration and licensing, observer programmes, VMS and catch certification do not specifically address transnational crime in fisheries or activities that are most susceptible to illicit acts, such as use of fishing vessels to transport migrants and drugs or smuggle goods and arms, corruption in licensing, and trade of high-value low-volume species for live reef food fish from the Philippines and Indonesia. Similarly, anti-money laundering legislation in the Philippines and Indonesia does not provide for illegal fishing as a predicate offence to money laundering. One can therefore examine the gaps between fisheries and anti-money laundering legislation and tools to find ways to bridge the gaps, pending the adoption of a more comprehensive framework to address the problem.

The first gap between fisheries and anti-money laundering regimes that needs to be addressed is the lack of sufficient connection between illegal fishing and a predicate offence to money laundering. There are a number of options to address this gap. One option is to expand the definition of unlawful activities under the anti-money laundering law. A legislative bill in the Philippines points towards this direction and proposes the expansion of the definition of 'unlawful activities' to include violations under sections 86 to 106 of the Philippine Fisheries Code, violations of the revised Forestry Code, violations of the Wildlife Resources Conservation and Protection Act, as well as forgeries and counterfeiting (RA No. 9160 s 3(21)). While this legislative initiative may be deemed to be a promising development to address transnational crime in fisheries, careful consideration is needed to identify types of illegal activities that may be considered predicate offences to money laundering. One needs to distinguish between different types of illegal fishing, the gravity of the offence, and the sanction to be imposed on the illegal activity. Clear distinction needs to be made between a pure fisheries management violation and a transnational criminal act in fisheries where the former is usually addressed only as an administrative or a civil offence. A blanket provision linking all types of violations under fisheries legislation as predicate offences to anti-money laundering may lead to inappropriate convictions.

The second option is an amendment in the respective national fisheries laws of Indonesia and the Philippines to include 'trafficking in fish', similar to the fisheries legislation in the Australian State of New South Wales (Fisheries Management Act 1994 (NSW) ss 21A–B). The Fisheries Management Act 1994 (NSW) distinguishes trafficking in fish from other fisheries violations by reference to 'indictable quantity' of fish or indictable species of fish (that is, abalone and eastern rock lobster) (Fisheries Management Act 1994 (NSW) sch. 1C). Trafficking in fish, according to s 21B(2) of the Fisheries Management Act 1994 (NSW), means dishonestly taking, selling, receiving, or possessing fish of an indictable species. The maximum penalty for trafficking in fish is ten years' imprisonment. Additionally, the court may impose a penalty for the offence of up to ten times the market value of the fish (Fisheries Management Act 1994 (NSW) s 21C).

In the case of Indonesia, Law No. 45 of 2009 amending the fisheries legislation of 2004 already contains provisions recognising the link between illegal fishing and other illicit activities, although no specific reference is made to the range of activities that may be considered 'criminal acts in fisheries'. Such references may provide the basis for further amendments developing specific regulations that address transnational crime in fisheries, including the application of sanctions adequate for the severity of the violation. Law No. 45 of 2009 also provides for the investigation, prosecution, and punishment of criminal acts in fisheries. Investigation of criminal acts in fisheries may be conducted by civil fisheries investigators, naval officer investigators, and police investigators (Law No. 45 of 2009 (Republic of Indonesia) art. 73). Indonesia has also established fisheries courts in Jakarta, Medan, Pontianak, Bitung, and Tual to deal with criminal acts in fisheries. Fisheries courts, positioned within district courts, are special courts for the environment within the public court system. A similar system or model of investigation and prosecution for transnational crime in fisheries could be adopted by the Philippines.

Fisheries MCS tools may also be improved in order to ensure that fishing vessels or fishermen are not used by syndicates to engage in transnational crime. One common and key feature of fishing vessel registration and licensing, observer programmes, VMS, port state measures, and catch certification systems is the collection and analysis of information. Information obtained using these MCS tools include the characteristics of a fishing vessel, its owner and operator, fishermen and fish workers, licence number, type and conditions, reported catch (and bycatch), observed actual catch, landed or transhipped catch, fishing location, destination of fish, associated traders and markets, and recorded apprehensions of fisheries violations. Access to this information will assist FIUs in investigating the involvement of criminal syndicates in illegal fishing. Currently, FIUs do not have direct access to fisheries information.

In order to facilitate such access, it would be necessary to develop a data protocol, in the form of regulations or memoranda of understanding between government authorities to allow the retrieval or transfer of such information while protecting confidentiality of fisheries information. Conversely, fisheries observers, VMS officers, boarding and inspection officers, port inspectors, and catch documentation officers would also need to be familiar with the type of activities and information that FIUs require to establish illegal fishing as a predicate offence to money laundering. These MCS tools, if implemented effectively, could be useful in deterring and minimising illegal fishing, as well as fraud and corruption in fisheries.

Catch certification is one of the key tools addressing illegal fishing and may be used to track the illegal trade of high-value low-volume species (i.e. live reef food fish) sourced from Indonesia and the Philippines. Catch certification traces the legality of the source of fish and, as currently used in the international trade of tuna species, is able to detect fraudulent trade documents. This system, supplemented by a proper record of live reef fish trade business interests, including fishing vessel owners, operators, traders, and fishermen, would be an effective tool to prevent illegal international trade of reef fish.

To address corruption affecting fisheries licensing, the simplest and most basic approach is to establish a more transparent system of record keeping and an appropriate system of checks and verification. This may include an electronic repository of vessels authorised to fish, allowed fishing gears, fisheries management areas where such vessels are entitled to fish, and other information. Other measures to deter and prevent corruption in fisheries may also be adopted within the administrative framework and may be dealt with within the anti-corruption legislation of the Philippines and Indonesia.

In addition to proposed improvements of these tools, the Philippines and Indonesia would also need to conduct studies on transnational crime in fisheries within their jurisdiction, focusing on the types of illegal fishing and actors associated with transnational crime, beneficial ownership of fishing vessels, and use of fishing vessels for criminal activities. There is a need for AMLC and INTRAC to increase their familiarity with the nature of fisheries businesses in order to detect illegal fishing activities involving criminal syndicates, possible fraud and corruption. Lastly, these measures will not be effective without strengthened cooperation between relevant agencies, which involve those with fisheries functions and those combating money laundering and transnational crime. Effective collaboration is necessary in using MCS tools to support the work of FIUs, intelligence gathering and integrating fisheries data with relevant information on money laundering cases. The Philippines and Indonesia would also benefit from enhanced participation in regional efforts to address illegal fishing, transnational crime, and money laundering, including through mutual legal assistance between states and exchange of information to track proceeds of crime from fisheries.

Conclusion

This chapter underscores that the fisheries laws and regulations in the Philippines do not directly address possible links between illegal fishing and transnational crime, whereas Indonesian fisheries law recognises criminal acts in fisheries, albeit at a general level. Monitoring, control, surveillance, and enforcement tools for fisheries are undertaken both on land and at sea, and not only prevent unlawful fishing at its source but also identify target destinations of illegally caught fish. However, such tools focus primarily on deterring acts of illegal fishing rather than fraud, corruption, and money laundering.

Although two separate legal regimes address illegal fishing and transnational crime, it can be argued that fisheries MCS tools may be utilised to support the work of financial intelligence units to address money laundering stemming from proceeds of crime. Pending the adoption of legislation that provides for illegal fishing as a predicate offence to money laundering, fisheries MCS tools may be improved in order to address fishing activities that are most vulnerable to trans-national crime, such as the use of fishing vessels for other illicit acts, illegal trade of high-value low-volume species, and corruption in the licensing system. This requires an effective legal and institutional framework merging elements from both fisheries and non-fisheries related measures.

Notes

1 A number of institutions have conducted studies on the protection of the environment by means of criminal law such as the United Nations Interregional Crime and Justice Research Institute (UNICRI), the United Nations Asia and Far East Institute of Crime Prevention and Treatment of Offenders (UNAFEI), Max Planck Institute for Foreign and International Criminal Law, Australian Institute of Criminology (AIC), and International Centre for Criminal Law Reform and Criminal Justice Policy. See Commission on Crime Prevention and Criminal Justice: Report on the first session (21–30 April 1992), UN ESCOR, Supp No. 10, UN Doc E/1992/30, E/CN.15/1992/7, para IV(1)(a).

2 Monitoring, control, and surveillance (MCS) in the context of fisheries refers to a whole range of legal, management, and compliance tools to prevent and deter illegal fishing activities. According to the UN Food and Agriculture Organization (FAO), 'monitoring means the continuous requirement for the measurement of fishing effort characteristics and resource yields; control is the regulatory conditions under which the exploitation of the resources may be conducted; and surveillance is the degree and types of observations required to maintain compliance with regulatory controls imposed on fishing activities' (Flewelling 2004: 3).

3 For example, Law No. 5 of 1983 on the Indonesian Exclusive Economic Zone, Law No. 21 of 1992 on Shipping, Law No. 22 of 1999 Regarding Regional Autonomy, and Law No. 27 of 2007 on Coastal and Small Islands Management.

4 See, for example, Law No. 45/2009, Amendment to Law No. 31 of 2004 Concerning Fishery (Republic of Indonesia) ss 83A, 85, 93, 94A, 98, 100A, 100B, and 100C.

5 It should be noted that there is no definition of 'fishery' in RA No. 8550. The closest definition is 'fisheries', which refers to all activities relating to the act or business of fishing, culturing, preserving, processing, marketing, developing, conserving, and managing aquatic resources and the fishery areas, including the privilege to fish or take aquatic resource thereof (RA No. 8550 s 4(31)). If the term 'fishery' is interpreted as including the catching of wild fish and all fisheries-related businesses, then it may be argued that the Anti-Money Laundering Act covers some acts of illegal fishing.

References

Barber, C.V. and Pratt. V.R. (1998) 'Cleansing the Seas: Strategies to Combat Cyanide Fishing in the Indo-Pacific Region', *Tambuli*, 4: 10–16.

Brack, D. and Hayman, G. (2002) *International Environmental Crime: The Nature and Control of Environmental Black Markets, Background paper for RIIA Workshop, 27–28 May 2002*, London: The Royal Institute of International Affairs Sustainable Development Programme. Available online at www.chathamhouse.org/sites/default/files/public/Research/ Energy,%20Environment%20and%20Development/environmental_crime_ background_paper.pdf (accessed 13 August 2013).

de Jesus, N. (1999) 'Fishing Monsters Eating Small Fishermen', *Greenfields*, September.

Department of Environment and Natural Resources (DENR), Department of Agriculture Bureau of Fisheries and Aquatic Resources (DA-BFAR), Department of Interior and Local Government (DILG), and Coastal Resource Management Project (CRMP) (2001) *Philippine Coastal Management Guidebook Series No. 8: Coastal Law Enforcement*, Cebu City, Philippines: Coastal Resource Management Project of the Department of Environment and Natural Resources.

Elucidation of Law No. 45 of 2009 Concerning Amendment to Law No. 31 of 2004 on Fishery, State Gazette Supplement 2009 (Republic of Indonesia).

Environmental Investigation Agency (2008) *Environmental Crime: A Threat to Our Future*, London: Emmerson Press.

Fisheries Management Act 1994 (NSW).

Flewelling, P. (1999) 'An Introduction to Monitoring, Control and Surveillance Systems for Capture Fisheries', *FAO Technical Paper*, 338.

Ishak, S.N.I.M. and Hooi, T.K. (2008) 'Live Reef Fish Trade: Status, Issues and Opportunities for Action', *MIMA Bulletin*, 15.

Law No. 5 of 1983 on the Indonesian Exclusive Economic Zone (Republic of Indonesia).

Law No. 15 of 2002 Concerning the Crime of Money Laundering (Republic of Indonesia).

Law No. 21 of 1992 on Shipping (Republic of Indonesia).

Law No. 22 of 1999 Regarding Regional Autonomy (Republic of Indonesia).

Law No. 27 of 2007 on Coastal and Small Islands Management (Republic of Indonesia).

Law No. 45 of 2009, Amendment to Law No. 31 of 2004 on Fishery (Republic of Indonesia).

Philippine Anti-Money Laundering Council (2007) *2007 Annual Report*, Manila: Anti-Money Laundering Council.

Republic Act No. 8550, An Act Providing for the Development, Management and Conservation of the Fisheries and Aquatic Resources, Integrating all Laws Pertinent thereto, and for other Purposes, 25 February 1998 (also known as the Philippine Fisheries Code of 1998) (Republic of the Philippines).

Republic Act No. 9160, An Act Defining the Crime of Money Laundering, Providing Penalties thereto and for other Purposes (Republic of the Philippines).

Republic Act No. 9194, An Act Amending Republic Act No. 9160 (also known as the Anti-Money Laundering Act of 2001) (Republic of the Philippines).

Sadovy, Y.J., Donaldson, T.J., Graham, T.R., McGilvray, F., Muldoon, G.J., Phillips, M.J., Rimmer, M.A., Smith, A. and Yeeting, B. (2003) *While Stocks Last: The Live Reef Food Fish Trade*, Asian Development Bank.

Scales, H., Balmford, A. and Manica, A. (2007) 'Impacts of the Live Reef Fish Trade on Populations of Coral Reef Fish off Northern Borneo', *Proceedings of the. Royal. Society B. Biological Sciences*, 274 (1612): 989–94.

Sustainable fisheries, including through the 1995 Agreement for the Implementation of the Provisions of the United Nations Convention on the Law of the Sea of 10 December 1982 relating to the Conservation and Management of Straddling Fish Stocks and Highly Migratory Fish Stocks, and related instruments, GA Res 63/112, 63rd sess, Agenda Item 70(b), UN Doc A/RES/63/112 (24 February 2009).

Ticke, G.P. (2002) '95 Sino Fishers Caught Poaching in Tubbataha', *The Palawan Times*, 14(1).

United Nations Commission on Crime Prevention and Criminal Justice: Report on the first session (21–30 April 1992), UN ESCOR, Supp No 10, UN Doc E/1992/30, E/CN.15/1992/7.

United Nations Office on Drugs and Crime (2011) *Transnational Organized Crime in the Fishing Industry, Focus on Trafficking in Persons, Smuggling of Migrants, Illicit Drugs Trafficking*, Vienna: UNODC.

White, A.T., Vogt, H.P. and Arin, T. (2000) 'The Philippine Coral Reefs under Threat: The Economic Losses Caused by Reef Destruction', *Marine Pollution Bulletin*, 40(7): 598–605.

9 Following the proceeds of bluewater crime

Case studies from an Australian fishery

Ian Parks

Fisheries and other environmental laws are primarily regulatory in nature. The aim of fisheries regulation is to provide access to a community resource in a sustainable manner, and to regulate and reduce the impact lawful fishing activity has on the environment. Because of the regulatory nature of fisheries laws, they are often ill-equipped to deal with serious non-compliance with legislative controls on the utilization of the resource. In this chapter the problem of profit-driven fisheries crime will be discussed, together with a novel approach of utilizing proceeds of crime offences and asset confiscation powers to combat this problem. It will also discuss a range of tools available to follow the proceeds of fisheries crime and demonstrate their workability through a series of case studies. The case studies and legal examples are drawn mostly from the jurisdiction of the Australian State of Victoria but the models are transferable. It will be concluded that agencies combatting profit-driven fisheries crime need to take a holistic approach to the problem, and utilize the vast legislative toolset available to fit the needs of the particular investigation and prosecution.

Profit-driven fisheries crime

Profit-driven fisheries crime is an expanding issue facing fisheries throughout the world as supply decreases due to the collapse of fisheries and demand increases due to population growth. The supply-and-demand issue facing fisheries resources is part of a more general acceptance that there is a severe problem with future global food security (Agnew *et al.* 2009: 1). Profit-driven fisheries crime is also assisted through the overlapping nature of the licit and the illicit markets (White 2008: 172). Profit-driven environmental crime will be discussed in the context of two main categories: harm caused by organized criminal groups operating outside of the regulatory scheme; and harm caused by businesses or individuals operating within the regulatory scheme. The reason profit-driven crime is of particular concern is that its commercial nature and scale provides the potential for significant environmental harm. It also brings greater complexities to fisheries policing activity, such as its transnational nature (White 2008: 283), the resources available to its actors in both the execution of its objects and in resisting social control, and its impact on inter-agency law enforcement relationships (Australian Crime Commission 2009: 5).

Organized criminal groups

Organized criminal groups have many features that make them similar in structure and capability to conventional businesses, with the exception that their activities and profits are illicit (Australian Crime Commission 2009: 5). These groups operate with clear management structures, plan carefully and strategically and are able to adapt to changing law enforcement and regulatory responses. What makes these groups of concern for environmental policing is that they (like many large corporations) need to diversify their business interests in order to maintain growth and increase profits. As traditional illicit markets become saturated or higher risk due to law enforcement activities, organized crime groups increasingly look to other illicit markets where their skills and multi-jurisdictional networks are able to be effectively used (Australian Crime Commission 2009: 6; Mackenzie 2002: 2). One of these illicit markets involves trafficking in fish resources.

Local and international criminal groups have been trafficking in 'environmental goods', such as fish, flora, fauna and hazardous substances, for some time because of their substantial (and lower-risk) profits (Mackenzie 2002: 2; Schmidt 2005: 270). For example, the trafficking of abalone to Asian markets from South Africa and Australia has involved organized criminal groups for some time (Napoleoni 2009: 175; Steinberg 2005; Tailby and Gant 2002). Many experts believe, however, that organized environmental crime will become an even greater problem than it currently is (Putt and Anderson 2007: 11; Schmidt 2004: 270). Natural resources such as fish, wildlife and timber are declining due to over-consumption and habitat destruction (Pauly 2009; Schmidt 2004). For example, the Australian population of 19.5 million people consumed 442,000 tonnes of seafood in the year 2000. It is projected that by 2050 Australia's 25 million population will require 1,150,000 tonnes of seafood (Anderson and McCusker 2005; Kearney *et al.* 2003). This will result in the economics of supply and demand increasing the market value of those resources that remain, creating opportunities for organized crime.

The profitability of trafficking in natural resources is also attractive to criminal organizations for other reasons. First, it is a ready source of venture capital for more traditional criminal activities, such as drug trafficking (Hayman and Brack 2002; Mackenzie 2002). Conversely, capital raised by traditional criminal industries may be used to finance 'legitimate' business interests involving the exploitation of natural resources (Hayman and Brack 2002; Mackenzie 2002). For example, an organized crime enterprise may enter the fishing industry in order to launder the proceeds of other enterprises and/or to provide a legitimate reason for being at sea in order to receive illicit goods from other vessels. Similarly, the transit networks used for trafficking traditional illicit commodities may also be used to traffic natural resources. Smugglers may engage in 'back loading', where drugs are carried in one direction and natural resources on the return journey (Hayman and Brack 2002). In some cases, natural resources may be exchanged for drugs to avoid currency transactions that may trigger anti-money laundering measures (Mackenzie 2002). All of these options offer an incentive for diversification into fisheries and other environmental crimes, and therefore create challenges for environmental policing.

Industry fraud

The fishing industry is regulated to varying degrees in different jurisdictions for the purpose of ensuring that the exploitation of fisheries resources is conducted in a sustainable manner. This includes licensing and approval regimes, input controls such as gear restrictions and closed seasons, together with output controls such as quotas, other catch limits and size limits. As a result of an increasing public concern for the environment flowing from evidence of harm caused by humans, beneficiaries of public natural resources will increasingly confront restrictive regulation designed to serve the interests of the community at large (Cetron and Davies 2008: 102).

Where fisheries are in decline, existing holders of fishing rights are increasingly tempted to obtain a financial advantage over their competitors by defrauding the regulatory regime. For example, a joint operation by the Australian National Crime Authority and Tasmanian Police investigated an extensive criminal syndicate involved in the trafficking of abalone that involved both individuals within the regulated industry and organized criminals from outside the industry (Australian Crime Commission 2009: 6). Similarly, the increasing corporatization of the commercial fishing industry (Baird 2004) and the corresponding decline of owner-operators may lead to a decrease in stewardship by licence holders given the corporation's primary objective of profit rather than of an owner-operator lifestyle. All of these factors may lead to an increase in crime.

Proceeds of crime offences

Fisheries statutes are often not designed to combat serious criminality. Offences are generally classified as regulatory in nature and often only have monetary penalties available. Even where imprisonment is a sentencing option, the maximum period of imprisonment is often at the low end of the scale when compared with general criminal offences such as theft, burglary, fraud and drug trafficking. When dealing with cases of serious profit-driven criminality, an effective approach can be to investigate and prosecute general criminal offences in addition to, or instead of, specific offences in the fisheries statute. This approach has been utilized in the fisheries arena successfully for some time, particularly in the area of conspiracy charges (*R v Hoar* (1981) 51 FLR 231; *Georgiadis v The Queen* (2002) 11 Tas R 137) and fraud charges (*Guillot v Hender* (1999) 86 FCR 294; *R v Turner* (No. 7) (2001) 10 Tas R 219).

In more recent times this approach has been expanded to incorporate proceeds of crime offences. In a number of Australian jurisdictions the offence of dealing in the proceeds of crime is also known as 'money laundering' (Crimes Act 1958 (Vic) s 194; Crimes Act 1900 (NSW) s 193B). These offences are primarily indictable crimes (classified as felonies in some jurisdictions), punishable by up to

20 years' imprisonment (Crimes Act 1958 (Vic) s 194(1); Crimes Act 1900 (NSW), s 193B(1)). In most Australian jurisdictions the crime of money laundering has three parts:

- a specified unlawful activity or predicate offence ('the predicate offence');
- a transaction or act of dealing in money (or other property) that is the proceeds of that specified unlawful activity ('the conduct element');
- a knowledge element, which may involve a sliding scale from actual knowledge to recklessness (and in some cases a reasonable suspicion) ('the fault element').[1]

The predicate offence

Money laundering offences were originally inserted in the statute book to assist in the fight against organized crime and specifically against drug-related crime. To this end, the predicate offence that could be subject to a money laundering offence was originally often limited to drug offences; however, many legislators have broadened the predicate offence category to many and varied offences (Stessens 2000: 11). This is partly because many more profit-driven crimes, such as fisheries, forestry and other natural resource harms, now have a high profile on the international political agenda (Gilmore 2004: 166). As Stessens (2000: 14) points out, 'from an ethical point of view it is hard to understand why the laundering of drug proceeds should be criminalised and not the laundering of, say the proceeds of environmental offences'. Currently, jurisdictions still vary on what underlying offences can constitute a predicate offence for the purposes of money laundering offences. For example, the principal federal money laundering statute of the United States (18 U.S.C. §§ 1956 and 1957) has a specific list of crimes that constitute an predicate offence (of which there are no fisheries or wildlife offences), whereas in Victoria the principal unlawful act can be any indictable offence or one of a number of listed summary offences (Crimes Act 1958 (Vic) s 193; Confiscation Act 1997 (Vic) Schedule 1). The list of specified summary offences includes a large number of offences under fisheries, wildlife, forestry and other natural resource management statutes.

The conduct element of money laundering

Under s 194 of the Crimes Act 1958 (Vic), the conduct element of the offence of money laundering involves dealing with the proceeds of crime.

'Deal with' is defined to include 'receive, possess, conceal or dispose of'. As this is an inclusive definition, it does not define the limits of conduct that the courts may consider to fall within the term (Crimes Act 1958 (Vic) s 193(1)).

The term 'proceeds of crime' is defined to mean property that is derived or realized, directly or indirectly, by any person from the commission of a predicate offence (or unlawful activity that occurred outside Victoria that would be a predicate offence if it had occurred in Victoria). The offence clearly has extraterritorial reach to prohibit the dealing in proceeds of a crime against the law of another jurisdiction that occurred either nationally or internationally. In Victoria, the courts have taken a very wide view of the scope of 'proceeds of crime'. For example, the Victorian Court of Appeal upheld a money laundering conviction of a thief who sold goods she had stolen (*R v Beary* (2004) 11 VR 151). In explaining the application of the offence, Ormiston JA (at [5]) said:

> In technical terms the appellant either 'disposed' of the proceeds of her criminal activities, namely the stolen property, or she 'received' money from the handlers, which was indirectly the proceeds of her own thefts, and she knew, obviously, that the property disposed of or the money she received (as the case may be) was derived directly or indirectly from those unlawful thefts.

The term 'property' is defined in s 193(1) to include 'money and all other property real or personal including things in action and other intangible property'. This is broad enough to cover fish, wildlife, plants and other natural resources.

The fault element of money laundering

The money laundering offences in Victoria contain a sliding scale of penalties, depending on the degree of the fault element that applies to the conduct. These include:

*   knowledge and intention to conceal (s 194(1)): 20 years' imprisonment;
*   knowledge (s 194(2)): 15 years' imprisonment;
*   recklessness (s 194(3)): ten years' imprisonment;
*   Negligence (s 194(4)): five years' imprisonment;
*   strict liability (no fault element) (s 195): two years' imprisonment (summary offence).

Section 195 of the Crimes Act 1958 is a summary offence (not triable by jury) punishable by up to two years' imprisonment. It is a strict liability offence that only requires the prosecution to prove that:

(a)   the accused dealt with property; and
(b)   there are reasonable grounds to suspect that the property was the proceeds of crime.

Under Australian law, 'suspicion' is a lower state of mind than 'probable cause' or a 'reasonable belief' and has been defined as 'a state of conjecture or surmise when proof is lacking' (*George v Rockett* (1990) 170 CLR 104 at 115).

Case studies

The following case studies aim to demonstrate the practical use of proceeds of crime offences to deal with fisheries crime. These offences are utilized where the predicate offence is inadequate in some way, such as having an insufficient penalty available for the impact on the resource or being difficult to detect and prove. Three case studies will be utilized to illustrate how money laundering offences can be effectively used to deal with profit-driven natural resource crime.

Case study 1: Operation Woodstock

The first case study illustrates the advantage of using proceeds of crime offences in circumstances where the predicate offence under the specific fisheries legislation is of insufficient seriousness to address the impact of the unlawful conduct on the natural resource.

From 2004 to 2005 the Fisheries Division of the Department of Primary Industries (DPI), in the State of Victoria, Australia, conducted an investigation into a person suspected of buying illegally taken abalone. Abalone is a highly valuable shellfish that inhabits the inshore reefs along the Victorian coast. The commercial abalone fishery is the most valuable fishery managed by the State and has a strict regulatory regime including a traceability system of documentation, labeling requirements and the licensing of processors (Tailby and Gant 2002).

The man owned two adjoining houses in a suburb of Melbourne. One of the houses was used as the family home, while the other was secretly converted into an illegal abalone processing facility, with an industrial walk-in freezer installed. He then arranged for the commercial printing of thousands of receipts and a number of rubber stamps which falsely contained the details of licensed abalone processors. The man then operated a business from the converted residence and his restaurant, buying illegally taken abalone from poachers and selling it on to retailers, who were provided with the forged receipts to legitimize the abalone. Fisheries officers executed search warrants on the two houses and found 4,698 abalone weighing 556kg and valued at $79,500, as well as thousands of false receipts and miscellaneous other items used to pass off his business as legitimate and licensed.

In a novel approach, the man was charged with the crime of knowingly dealing with property (the abalone) that is the proceeds of crime under s 194(2) of the Crimes Act 1958 (Vic). The maximum penalty for the money laundering offence was 15 years' imprisonment, whereas the maximum penalty for the predicate offence was one year's imprisonment. The relatively minor maximum penalties available in the fisheries legislation were considered inadequate for the gravity of the offending and the level of criminality involved. The charge was laid on the basis that the accused:

- received abalone in contravention of a provision of the Fisheries Act 1995 (Vic) that is prescribed as a predicate offence (the predicate offence);
- possessed that abalone in his converted house (the conduct element); and
- knew that the abalone was the proceeds of crime (the fault element).

The fault element was relatively simple to establish, as the accused was the person who committed the predicate offence.

When the matter was brought before the court, counsel for the accused objected to the money laundering charge on the grounds that it was inappropriate. In rejecting that submission, the trial judge stated:

> Just dealing with Count 1, let me say despite your counsel's submission in criticism of the prosecution for choosing to use this particular offence against s.194 of the Crimes Act, I see no basis for that criticism. The charge is properly brought. Proceeds of crime, as defined in s.103 encompasses property derived from the commission of an offence, inter alia against s.40 of the Fisheries Act; namely, the unlicensed receipt of fish.
>
> (*The Queen v Kha* (Unreported, County Court of Victoria, Williams J, 18 April 2007) at [2]).

The man was subsequently convicted and sentenced to 12 months' imprisonment, suspended for three years, fined $25,000, forfeited all of the processing equipment found at his premises, and paid $100,000 representing his interest in the house used to process the abalone (in lieu of forfeiture) (*The Queen v Kha* (Unreported, County Court of Victoria, Williams J, 18 April 2007) at [23]). The accused's wife was fined $15,000 for her role in the offences (Butcher 2007).

Case study 2: Operation Mint

One of the most serious categories of offence contained in fisheries legislation is unlawful commercial fishing. Prosecution of this type of offence is one of the primary controls to protect fish stocks from overfishing, particularly in limited-entry licensing regimes. To be successful, the prosecution must prove that the fish were unlawfully taken, but evidence to establish the fact that the fish were taken unlawfully can be very difficult to establish, especially when the sale occurs distant in both time and space from the actual unlawful take. This second case study illustrates the advantage of utilizing a specific proceeds of crime offence common in Australian jurisdictions, in such circumstances where it is difficult to prove the fish were taken unlawfully for commercial purposes.

The case study relates to the prosecution of an unlicensed commercial fisher operating on the Bellarine Peninsular near Geelong in the Australian State of Victoria. The principal offender took fish, such as whiting and calamari squid, under the cover of recreational fishing entitlements and illegally sold his catch to restaurants and other seafood businesses. While the investigation discovered sufficient evidence to prove a number of instances of illegal commercial fishing, in some instances there was evidence of a sale of fish by the principal to a seafood dealer, but no direct evidence to prove that the fish were taken unlawfully. To overcome this difficulty, the principal was charged with the offence of dealing with property reasonably suspected of being the proceeds of crime under s 195 of the Crimes Act 1958 (Vic). As outlined above, s 195 does not require proof that the property (in this case, fish) was in fact the proceeds of crime. The prosecution merely had to prove that there were reasonable grounds to suspect the fish were the proceeds of crime. The facts surrounding the transaction giving rise to a reasonable suspicion that the fish were the proceeds of unlawful commercial fishing included:

- no receipts being issued or requested (when this was standard business practice of the buyer);
- the seller was not a licensed commercial fisher or the operator of a legitimate seafood business;
- other evidence that the seller was in the business of illegal commercial fishing.

The principal was convicted and fined a total amount of $4,000 for the fisheries offences and convicted and sentenced to a one-month suspended prison term on the proceeds of crime charge. He was also ordered to pay a pecuniary penalty of $3,790 under the Confiscation Act 1997 (Vic), representing the benefit he obtained from the offences, and was prohibited from fishing for five years. In addition, his vehicle and fishing equipment were forfeited under the Fisheries Act 1995 (Vic).

Case study 3: Operation Fusion

The third case study will be utilized to illustrate another approach to dealing with unlawful commercial fishing in circumstances where specific predicate fisheries offences are difficult to prove. In this case, officers conducted a five-year investigation into alleged illegal commercial fishing conducted in remote inland waters near Mildura in the State of Victoria. For environmental reasons, there is no commercial fishing permitted in this area of the State.

The gathering of evidence of acts of illegal commercial fishing was found to be difficult given the remoteness of the area involved, so the focus of the investigation shifted to the money trail. Evidence was discovered of multiple and consistent cash deposits made into the principal offender's joint bank account with his wife. Financial analysis revealed that there was no obvious legitimate source of the funds, and timelines were used to match the deposits with evidence of fishing activity. Investigators were able to locate the buyer of the illegal fish, who was operating from the car park of the Melbourne Wholesale Fish Market, outside of his employment with a legitimate seafood provider. Investigators traced a total of $74,580 deposited into the bank accounts of the principal offender and his wife as representing the proceeds of illegal commercial fishing involving between five and seven tonnes of native Murray cod and golden perch (Butcher 2010).

The principal offender was charged with knowingly dealing in proceeds of crime from March 2005 to January 2009 under s 194(2) of the Crimes Act 1958. He was convicted and sentenced to 15 months' imprisonment, suspended for two years, and he was ordered to pay a pecuniary penalty of $46,810 (his share of the $74,580) and to pay costs of $1,500. He was also prohibited from possessing fishing equipment or being in any boat on or next to Victorian waters for ten years. A residential property owned by the principal offender and his wife was also restrained to hold against the $75,000 pecuniary penalty order for money obtained from the proceeds of crime. A boat and more than 300 items of commercial fishing equipment and commercial scales valued at several thousand dollars were also forfeited (Butcher 2010).

Analysis

Each case study outlined above had a different factual matrix, which illustrates the power and range of money laundering offences. In case study 1, the fish was the property directly representing the proceeds of crime. In case study 2, it was difficult to prove that the fish were actually the proceeds of crime; however, the offence only required proof that it was reasonable to suspect that the fish were taken for sale unlawfully. In case study 3, the investigators focused on the money trail, with the money received for the sale of the fish representing the proceeds of crime. The case studies demonstrate that investigators have the flexibility to either follow the natural resources, in this case fish, or follow the money.

The benefits and utility of proceeds of crime offences when dealing with fisheries crime in Victoria have been formally recognized through specific legislation. In a novel approach, the Fisheries Act 1995 (Vic) treats proceeds of crime offences under the Crimes Act 1958 (Vic) as if they were offences under the Fisheries Act. The practical effect here is that fisheries officers can utilize their powers of arrest, search and seizure under the Fisheries Act to investigate proceeds of crime offences where the predicate offence is a fisheries offence (Fisheries Act 1995 (Vic), s 98). Similarly, the strong forfeiture provisions under the Fisheries Act will also apply (Fisheries Act 1995 (Vic), s 106(5A(b))).

Asset forfeiture

In any case when dealing with serious criminal activity, prosecution followed by punishment does not sufficiently deter profit-driven crime on its own (Thornton 1992: 13). To be effective, the benefit gained, usually called the proceeds of crime (e.g. fish, cash), and the instruments or means used to facilitate the criminal activity (e.g. boats, nets) must also be forfeited.

Asset (or property) forfeiture is divided into two major legal types: criminal conviction-based forfeiture and civil forfeiture. Conviction-based forfeiture requires a criminal prosecution and finding of guilt to the criminal standard (beyond reasonable doubt) before forfeiture can occur. Civil forfeiture operates independently of the prosecution process and does not require a finding of guilt to the criminal standard. The real distinction between conviction-based forfeiture and civil forfeiture is the manner in which the breach of the law that triggers forfeiture is adjudicated. In conviction-based forfeiture there is a criminal conviction under criminal process, whereas in civil forfeiture there is civil process with a civil standard of proof. Nevertheless, it should be noted that, in the Australian State jurisdiction of Victoria at least, proceedings involving conviction-based forfeiture are civil in nature, with the result that facts are determined on the balance of probabilities and evidence may be adduced using civil processes (such as by affidavit) (Confiscation Act 1997 (Vic) s 133).

Categories of forfeiture

Asset forfeiture involves three broad categories of property seizure, each with a different object (Stessens 2000: 30). The first category involves the forfeiture of the instruments of crime. Instruments of crime are items of property that are used in the commission of, or used to facilitate the commission of, an offence. In the fisheries context, this commonly includes the boat and fishing equipment used to facilitate the unlawful taking of fish. The second category is known as the subject of the crime, which involves goods that are subject to the criminal behavior. In a fisheries context, this commonly involves the fish that are unlawfully taken or sold. The third type is the proceeds of crime. This commonly involves the money obtained from selling the unlawfully taken fish or other illicit goods.

Although each category is theoretically distinct, in practice and in law there is a significant overlap between them. For example, an item of fishing equipment used by an offender may represent both the instrument and subject of different crimes. The equipment may be an instrument of crime when used to take fish in excess of catch or size limits; however, equipment may also be the subject of a crime when the use of that class of equipment is itself unlawful. Similarly, the statutory scheme dealing with confiscation may merge each of the categories into one class, known as 'tainted property' (Confiscation Act 1997 (Vic), s 3(1)).

The other categorization of asset forfeiture involves the mode in which confiscation occurs. According to Stessens (2000: 31), two modes can be distinguished: object forfeiture and value forfeiture. Object forfeiture involves the transfer of property, whereas value forfeiture involves an obligation to pay an amount of money. The first mode has been present in fisheries jurisprudence for some time, particularly in relation to fishing equipment, boats and fish. The second is usually not contained in the fisheries legislation, but rather general asset confiscation laws.[2]

Forfeiture of instruments of crime under fisheries legislation

The seizure and forfeiture of instruments used in breaches of legislation has had a long history in fisheries and customs law within Australia. Its history stems from powerful forfeiture measures originally employed to protect federal revenue (Freiberg and Fox 1992: 106). In the High Court of Australia in *Re Director of Public Prosecutions; Ex parte Lawler* ((1994) 179 CLR 270 at 289), Dawson J observed:

> Confiscation of property connected with the commission of crimes was long part of the common law and had its origin in the doctrines of attainder and deodand. Property could be forfeited even if its owner was not involved in the crime. Forfeiture at common law was abolished in England in 1870 and

thereafter in this country, but statutory powers of forfeiture have remained in certain areas and, indeed, have been introduced in some new areas.

The utility of forfeiture provisions in fisheries legislation has long been recognized by the courts. Also in the Australian High Court in *Cheatley* (1972) 127 CLR 291 at 296, Barwick CJ stated:

> The protection of the fishing grounds of the nation from foreign exploration is somewhat akin to the protection of the country from smuggling. Drastic action in protection of the country's interests in any instance may be regarded as warranted, indeed, if not to be expected. Each is an area where pecuniary penalties are unlikely to provide adequate protection.

Similarly, in *Jetopay Pty Ltd v Dix* (1994) 76 A Crim R 427 at 435, Underwood J said:

> General deterrence looms large upon the assessment of penalty for breaches of fisheries legislation. . . . The offences are difficult and expensive to detect and the rewards are very substantial for those who take fish to which they are not entitled.

It is this need for deterrence that has been the rationale for powerful forfeiture provisions contained in fisheries legislation (Sullivan 1994: 37). Perhaps consistent with an aversion to imprisonment as a primary penalty for fisheries offences, forfeiture of assets has been a primary deterrent measure. In fact, imprisonment is specifically precluded under Article 73 of the United Nations Convention on the Law of the Sea (UNCLOS) for fisheries offences committed by foreign flagged boats in the Exclusive Economic Zone. This has made drastic forfeiture provisions necessary as the only real deterrent against foreign boats and their owners (Gullett 2004: 171). For example, in 1999, following a large number of incursions by foreign fishing boats in the sub-Antarctic, the Australian Parliament introduced a tough forfeiture regime in an effort to increase deterrence of illegal foreign fishers (Parliament of Australia 1999a).

Discretionary conviction-based forfeiture

The most common form of forfeiture under Australian fisheries statutes for boats and vehicles used in the commission of an offence is conviction-based forfeiture. This involves a discretionary power being provided to a court by statute to consider forfeiture as part of the sentencing process following a finding of guilt in a criminal proceeding (Fisheries Act 1995 (Vic) s 106(5); Fisheries Management Act 1994 (NSW) s 269; Fisheries Act 1994 (Qld) s 177; Fisheries Management Act 2007 (SA) s 90; Fish Resources Management Act 1994 (WA) s 218).

The statutes do not provide guidance on the exercise of this discretion; however, the Australian appellate courts have provided some assistance to sentencing judges. In *Caldow v Hemming* ((1991) 55 A Crim R 449), the Supreme Court of South Australia considered the forfeiture discretion under the South Australian fisheries legislation. The appellants pleaded guilty to numerous charges under the Fisheries Act 1982 (SA) concerning illegal fishing. Caldow was convicted and fined $38,793. The presiding magistrate also ordered that Caldow's boat, outboard engine, trailer and equipment found in the boat be forfeited to the Crown. The charges related to the taking of 2,922 abalone weighing 328.6kg and with a wholesale value of $16,430. In reviewing various authorities, Mulligan J considered that the following matters are relevant to the exercise of the discretion:

(a) whether the illegal activity was willful, deliberate or accidental: *Cheatley v R*, per Barwick CJ at 296;
(b) the nature of the goods, the need for a deterrent penalty and the difficulty of enforcing the law: *Cheatley v R* per Mason J at 310; and
(c) the age and antecedents of the offender and the amount of fish taken.

At page 456 he made the following observations:

> . . . upon the application of those principles the order for forfeiture was, in my view, inevitable. The appellant Caldow set about a deliberate and well-planned illegal fishing activity utilising the equipment, which was subject to the (forfeiture) order . . .
>
> It seems to me that where an offence against the Act is of a serious nature, involves the taking of a considerable amount of fish and is deliberately committed, forfeiture of all equipment used should be ordered. The protection of the fishery and the need for deterrence will usually require such an order. It will be no answer to say that forfeiture will cause financial hardship.

Automatic or mandatory conviction-based forfeiture

Another form of forfeiture common under Australian fisheries legislation is automatic forfeiture following conviction. In the State of Tasmania, the Living Marine Resources Management Act 1995 (Tas) s 225 provides that if a court convicts a person of an offence, then any fish related to the offence, any equipment used in or connected with the offence and any vessel, vehicle, aircraft or other thing used in or connected with the offence is forfeited. The Act then provides the court with discretion to order that forfeiture not take place if satisfied that special reasons exist. A similar provision exists under the Northern Territory Fisheries Act (NT) (s 46(1)(b)) which provides that seized items are forfeited unless the court, for special reasons relating to the offence orders otherwise. As the special circumstances must relate to the offence, the personal circumstances of the offender are irrelevant (*Perry v Simlesa* [2002] NTMC 041 at [23]). These provisions essentially set out a presumption that forfeiture will occur automatically on conviction, but allow for discretion in special cases for courts to order that it not occur.

A similar species of forfeiture is found in Victoria, where a court is required to order forfeiture of all seized things where the person is found guilty on a third occasion of a serious offence (Fisheries Act 1995 (Vic) s 106(5A)). Here, forfeiture does not occur automatically by operation of the law, but rather it requires the court to order forfeiture under its 'discretionary' power (*Fisheries Inspector v Turner* [1978] 2 NZLR 233 at 239). Unlike the provisions outlined above, there is no discretion to waive forfeiture for special circumstances. It might be argued that a 'special circumstances' exception is less necessary here, because the person must be a repeat offender for mandatory forfeiture to apply.

Automatic civil forfeiture

While many fisheries statutes provide a discretionary power for a court to order forfeiture of property used in the commission of offences following a conviction, there are other statutory provisions that provide for automatic forfeiture regardless of whether or not there is a conviction. For example, under the Australian federal Fisheries Management Act 1991 (Cth) (s 106A), a foreign boat, its catch, nets and equipment used in the commission of an offence are automatically forfeited to the Commonwealth. Forfeiture occurs once the events which constitute the relevant offence occur (*Olbers v Commonwealth* (2004) 148 A Crim R 547). Once the boat is seized, the owner must claim the boat within 30 days or the boat is automatically condemned as forfeited, effectively preventing any legal action to recover it. Forfeiture under provisions such as this are effected by operation of law rather than by a judicial or executive order (*Olbers v Commonwealth* (2004) 148 A Crim R 547 at 551). If a claim is made, the owner must institute proceedings against the Commonwealth for recovery or a declaration that it is not forfeited (Fisheries Management Act 1991 (Cth) s 106F(1)). Similarly, in Victoria, under the Fisheries Act 1995 (Vic), fish taken or possessed in contravention of the Act (s 106(1A)) and prohibited fishing equipment (s 106(1)) are automatically forfeited on seizure. The rationale for forfeiture here is that possession is unlawful *per se* and therefore forfeiture is necessary and reasonable to prevent a further offence. In any case, fish and other flora and fauna found in Victorian waters are the property of the State until taken lawfully under the Act (Fisheries Act 1995 (Vic) s 10).

As automatic forfeiture occurs by operation of the statute, there is no necessity for the State to institute any proceedings for forfeiture. Where proceedings are instituted, they are not directed to the question of whether forfeiture should occur, but rather they adjudicate and record that forfeiture has already occurred (*Olbers v Commonwealth* (2004) 148 A Crim R 547 at 552). Proceedings are civil in nature, and therefore the court only needs to be satisfied to the civil standard of proof (balance of probabilities) that an offence has been committed (*Olbers v Commonwealth* [2004] FCA 229 at [65] per French J). Although, given the serious consequences that flow, the court must be satisfied to a high degree of proof (*Briginshaw v Briginshaw* (1938) 60 CLR 336 at 368–369).

The policy justification for the Australian federal automatic forfeiture provisions is that drastic action was required to address the ongoing activities of illegal foreign fishing vessels in the Australian fishing zone, particularly in remote areas such as the sub-Antarctic territories and off north-western Australia (Parliament of Australia 1999b: 9,674). The aim of the legislation was to shift the onus to the illegal foreign fishers to establish their legitimacy for being present in the Australian fishing zone without authorization. However, some commentators have criticized the measures as being in breach of Australia's obligations under UNCLOS (Baird 2008; Gullett 2005). For example, Gullett (2004) observed that any rights or remedies of owners under UNCLOS may be unavailable if the owner does not successfully contest the purported forfeiture of their vessel. This is because, under Australian law, the Commonwealth of Australia becomes the owner of the vessel once it is in the Australian fishing zone unlawfully (Fisheries Management Act 1991 (Cth) s 106A). Similarly, Baird (2008) argues that the Australian forfeiture provision is contrary to article 73 of UNCLOS, particularly the requirement that arrested vessels and their crews be promptly released upon the posting of reasonable bond or other security. Notwithstanding these concerns, domestic Australian courts are obliged to follow Australian law as set out in the *Olbers* decision.

Nature of forfeiture

One of the powerful features of forfeiture of instruments of crime under fisheries legislation in Australia is that it operates *in rem* (against the thing). This means that the thing is forfeited irrespective of the offender's ownership or interest (*Re Director of Public Prosecutions; Ex Parte Lawler* (1994) 179 CLR 270). Once forfeiture is completed, it creates an estoppel *per rem judicatam* and is binding on the world at large (*McGovern v State of Victoria* [1984] VR 570).

In *McGovern* the Full Bench of the Supreme Court of Victoria considered the consequences of a forfeiture order under the Fisheries Act 1968 (Vic). The principal offender was convicted in the magistrates' court, but the presiding magistrate, under a discretionary power to order forfeiture as part of the sentencing process, declined to forfeit a boat used in the commission of the offence. The State appealed to the County Court, which on a rehearing (appeal *de novo*) ordered forfeiture of the boat. In the period between the two court proceedings the boat was returned to the offender, who sold it to McGovern. After the forfeiture order was made, Fisheries officers recovered the boat from McGovern, who then sued the State in the Supreme Court for a declaration that the boat was his property. The suit was dismissed by the Supreme Court, which held that once the order for forfeiture was made and the title in the boat vested in the Crown, it could not be challenged.

Accordingly, a consequence of the *in rem* nature of forfeiture under fisheries legislation in Australia is that forfeiture may occur even though the owner of the property may have had no complicity in the offence. The courts have held that this is justified on a number of grounds. First, in the fisheries context, enforcing the law against foreign owners of large fishing boats is difficult and forfeiture is the only real deterrent available (*Cheatley* (1972) 127 CLR 291 at 310 per Mason J).

Second, it has the desirable effect of inducing owners and secured creditors to exercise greater care in transferring possession of their property (*Calero-Toledo v Parson Yacht Leasing Co* (1974) 416 US 663, 686–688). Third, forfeiture serves the aim of incapacitation. As Dawson J observed in *Lawler* (1994) 179 CLR 270:

> A punishment may have more than one aim, but in addition to the common aims of deterrence and retribution, forfeiture by way of penalty has an element of incapacitation, which has no regard to the innocence, or otherwise, of the person who must bear the loss of property. Rather the concern of the law is that the offence will not be repeated by the same means.

The remedy for innocent owners of forfeited property is an action for damages against the accused for wrongfully causing the loss of their property (Glover 1992).

Forfeiture under general confiscation legislation

All Australian jurisdictions have general laws providing for the confiscation of instruments and proceeds of crime. These provisions have traditionally been developed and used in the fight against drug trafficking, terrorism and financial crime. They can involve forfeiture of instruments of crime, such as a vehicle used to transport contraband, and/or an order that the offender pay to the State any benefits obtained as a result of the offence. As with forfeiture under fisheries legislation, confiscation laws can be conviction-based, where the court makes an order following conviction for a relevant offence, or a civil process, where an order can be made independently of any prosecution for the offence. In many cases the general confiscation legislation will overlap with specific fisheries forfeiture provisions, as is the case in Victoria.

Discretionary conviction-based forfeiture

Under the Confiscation Act 1995 (Vic) ('the Confiscation Act'), a court finding a person guilty of a 'Schedule 1 offence' may order the forfeiture of 'tainted property'. Schedule 1 of the Confiscation Act includes any indictable offence and a number of summary offences under the Fisheries Act 1995 (Vic). Tainted property is defined to include property that was used in, or was intended by the accused to be used in, or in connection with, the commission of the offence (Confiscation Act s 3).

A major objective of the Confiscation Act is to balance the aim of confiscation of tainted property with the protection of property rights of innocent third parties. Unlike fisheries legislation, the court can order forfeiture of the property, or an interest in the property (Confiscation Act s 33(1)). An innocent third party can apply to have their interest in the property excluded from forfeiture (Confiscation Act ss 49, 50). The effect of these provisions is that, in practice, when a forfeiture order is made against tainted property, it is only the accused's interest in the property that is actually forfeited.

Tainted property substitution

To better deal with the limitation of forfeiture under the Confiscation Act to the accused's interest in the tainted property, the Act provides for a powerful remedy known as tainted property substitution (Confiscation Act 1997 (Vic) s 34C). This remedy is available where property used in the commission of an offence is not available for forfeiture. The court may make a declaration that property of a similar nature or description that the defendant has an interest in be substituted for the unavailable tainted property. This remedy was introduced due to criminals using rental cars and rental properties to avoid confiscation of their own assets (Victoria, Legislative Assembly 2003: 1313–1314). Now if an offender uses a rental car in the commission of an offence, their personal car can be forfeited in substitution of the rental car.

Automatic forfeiture

In addition to discretionary forfeiture provisions for 'Schedule 1 offences', the Confiscation Act also has a species of automatic forfeiture for more serious offences ('Schedule 2 offences'). These offences include serious drug matters and fraud, and proceeds of crime offences involving a value of $50,000 or more for a single offence or $75,000 for multiple offences forming part of a series. Relevantly, Schedule 2 also includes indictable offences under the Fisheries Act 1995 (Vic) where the quantity of fish involved is five times the commercial quantity prescribed under that Act[3] or more. If a person has been convicted of a Schedule 2 offence, all property restrained under the Confiscation Act is forfeited 60 days after the conviction. As with automatic forfeiture under the fisheries legislation, forfeiture occurs under the statute and does not require a forfeiture order.

The owner of the property (including the accused) may apply to the court for an order excluding their interest in the property within 30 days of the restraining order being made (Confiscation Act s 20). The applicant must satisfy the court, on the balance of probabilities, that the property was lawfully obtained, is not tainted property, will not be the subject of a tainted property substitution declaration, and is not derived property (Confiscation Act s 22(1)(a)). In the case of an applicant for exclusion who is not the accused and the property is tainted property or 'derived property', the court must be satisfied that the person was not involved in the commission of the offence and did not know the property was going to be used in connection with the offence (Confiscation Act s 22(1)(b)).

Derived property is defined to mean property used in, or in connection with, any unlawful activity by the accused or the applicant for an exclusion order, or derived or realized, or substantially derived or realized, directly or indirectly, from any unlawful activity (Confiscation Act 1997 (Vic) s 7B). The term 'unlawful activity' is defined to mean an act or omission that constitutes an offence against any law punishable by imprisonment (whether Australian or foreign) (Confiscation Act 1997 (Vic) s 3(1)). The effect of these provisions is that the applicant must establish that the property is not only not tainted in connection with the offence charged, but also not used in the commission of, or proceeds of, any other offence.

The court must also be satisfied that if the person acquired the property after the offence was committed there were no grounds for them to reasonably suspect that the property was tainted or derived. The applicant must also establish that the property is not in the effective control of the accused and that it was acquired for sufficient consideration. As can be seen, the Confiscation Act in Victoria is more sensitive to innocent third parties than the forfeiture provisions of the Victorian fisheries legislation, as demonstrated in McGovern's case.

Pecuniary penalty orders

The forfeiture provisions outlined above provide for confiscation of objects or property linked either to the offence or to the offender. In contrast, pecuniary penalty provisions operate to disgorge the benefits obtained from the commission of the offence. A pecuniary penalty order is an order that an offender pay to the State a pecuniary penalty equal to the value of any benefit derived by the offender from the commission of the offence (Confiscation Act 1997 (Vic) s 59). A pecuniary penalty order is a debt due to the State, and is enforceable under normal judgment debt recovery procedures.

In Victoria, if a person is convicted of a Schedule 1 offence, the State may apply to the relevant court for a pecuniary penalty order (Confiscation Act 1997 (Vic) s 58(2)). On an application for a pecuniary penalty order, the court may assess the value of the benefits derived by the defendant in relation to the offence and order the defendant to pay a pecuniary penalty equal to the value as assessed (Confiscation Act 1997 (Vic) s 59(1)). Applications are civil in nature and determined on the balance of probabilities (Confiscation Act 1997 (Vic) s 133). In assessing the benefits, the court is not required to engage in calculating or setting off against the value of property derived from the offence, the expenditures incurred or sharing arrangements made between the convicted persons or between themselves and others (*DPP v Nieves* [1992] 1 VR 257 at 262). In practice, applications for pecuniary penalty orders are commonplace, and occur as a matter of course for most serious fisheries offences.

Case study 4: Tat Sang Loo

Tat Sang Loo was the first case of a pecuniary penalty order being made in Victoria under the confiscation legislation for a fisheries offence. Loo was charged in September 1998 with offences against the Fisheries Act 1995 (Vic) relating to the unlawful dealing in abalone between October 1997 and September 1998. On 17 March 1999 he pleaded guilty to 14 charges and was sentenced to a period of imprisonment. An order was also made for the forfeiture of abalone-processing equipment and a motor vehicle. Subsequently he was ordered to pay to the State a pecuniary penalty of $978,275, representing the benefits he received from the offences (*DPP v Tat Sang Loo* [2002] VSC 231).

'Super' pecuniary penalty orders

In addition to provisions allowing the court to make an order that the accused pay a sum equal to the benefits obtained from the commission of the offence, some jurisdictions have powerful provisions that deem all property of the accused at the time of the offence and all expenditure during a specified period as benefits obtained unlawfully. For example, in Victoria, on an application for a pecuniary penalty order with respect to a serious (Schedule 2) offence, the court must treat all property in which the accused had an interest at the time of the first application under the Act (restraining order or pecuniary penalty order), and expenditure of the accused within the period of six years immediately before that date, as benefits obtained from the commission of the offence (Confiscation Act 1997 (Vic) s 68(3)). The burden of proof then shifts to the accused to establish that the property was lawfully acquired, is not tainted property and is not derived property. In the case of expenditure, the accused must satisfy the court that the funds that were expended were lawfully acquired and were not derived or realized by any person from any unlawful activity.

Case study 5: Perkes & Anor v R

Similar provisions have been used to great effect in the United Kingdom to deal with fisheries crime. In *Perkes & Anor v R* ([2010] EWCA Crim 101) two English fish dealers lost an appeal against a proceeds of crime order made under the 'criminal lifestyle' provisions of the Proceeds of Crime Act 2002 (UK). The order was made following their prosecution for offences relating to a failure to keep records of the origin of fish received by them. On 11 May 2007, at Newcastle Crown Court, they pleaded guilty to five counts of failing to submit sales notes and landing declarations relating to purchases of fish that they made. They pleaded guilty and were sentenced to fines of £400 on each count. What was unusual about this case is that the judge also imposed confiscation orders in the sum of £188,195 against Ian Perkes and in the sum of £150,000 against Sean Perkes. It was these orders that were the subject of the appeal.

The confiscation provisions utilized in *Perkes* are conviction-based – but extend beyond the crime(s) for which the defendant has been convicted. Under section 6 of the Proceeds of Crime Act 2002 (UK) the prosecutor may request that the court proceed to confiscation. The court must then decide whether the defendant has a 'criminal lifestyle' (as defined by s 75 and schedule 2 of the Act) if one of the following conditions is satisfied:

- they have been convicted of at least one offence listed in schedule 2 of the Act;
- they have been convicted of conduct forming part of a 'course of criminal activity' from which, in total, they have obtained a benefit of at least £5,000; or
- they have been convicted of an offence of any description committed over a period of at least six months from which they have obtained a benefit of at least £5,000.

Where the accused falls within the criminal lifestyle definition, the court is required to make the following assumptions:

1. any property transferred to the accused at any time after the 'relevant day' was obtained by them as a result of his general criminal conduct and was obtained at the earliest time he appears to have held it;
2. any property held by the accused at any time after the date of his conviction was obtained as a result of his general criminal conduct;
3. any expenditure incurred by the accused at any time after the 'relevant day' was met from property obtained as a result of his general criminal conduct; and
4. for the purpose of valuing any property obtained (or assumed to have been obtained) by the accused, he obtained it free of any other interests in it.

The burden of proof then shifts to the defendant to show that, on the balance of probabilities (preponderance of evidence), the assumption is incorrect or there would be a serious risk of injustice if the assumption were made. In *Perkes*, investigators conducted a detailed financial analysis of invoices recording cash purchases of fish. These did not contain the name of the sellers in any identifiable form. The appellate court held that the only realistic way the presumption of illegal provenance could be rebutted would be for the accused to identify the sellers of the fish and call them to support their case. When interviewed in relation to the identities of the people who sold them the fish, Sean Perkes was evasive and Ian Perkes walked out of the interview.

Although the appeal did not deal with any significant legal issues (it is difficult to appeal a consent order), it serves to highlight the use of confiscation proceedings in the fight against environmental crime.

Restraining orders for 'freezing' assets

A key component of asset confiscation legislation is the provision of power to make a restraining order. Orders for forfeiture or the payment of pecuniary penalties are ineffective if the accused is able to dispose of their assets. Restraining orders may be obtained from a court under the Confiscation Act 1995 (Vic) s 11 if a person is charged with a Schedule 1 offence, or will be charged within 48 hours. A restraining order is an order that no property or interest in property to which the order applies may be disposed of or otherwise dealt with except in accordance with the order. The purpose of a restraining order is to preserve the property for a forfeiture order, automatic forfeiture, or to satisfy a pecuniary penalty order under the Act (Confiscation Act 1995 (Vic) s 15). The restraining order may also be made to preserve property for restitution or compensation ordered under the Sentencing Act 1991 (Vic).

The restraining order is a key legislative tool that helps overcome some limitations inherent in physical seizure powers under the fisheries or other criminal legislation. For example, powers of seizure granted to law enforcement officers are generally limited to moveable property. They do not allow the seizure of real estate, shares or other intangible proprietary interests such as funds in a bank account. Similarly, in a federal nation such as Australia, seizure powers in State fisheries acts are only exercisable within the State's jurisdiction. However, under a cooperative scheme, restraining orders under each State or Territory's confiscation legislation is enforceable in other jurisdictions (Confiscation Act 1995 (Vic) s 126). Another benefit of the restraining order is that its purpose is not limited to securing forfeiture of the restrained property, but it may also secure property to satisfy debts that arise out of compensation orders and pecuniary penalty orders.

Conclusion

Profit-driven crime is an expanding issue threatening the sustainable use of fisheries and other natural resources. The threat of profit-driven crime comes from two major sources: organized criminal groups operating outside of the regulatory scheme; and businesses or individuals operating illegally within the regulatory scheme. Profit-driven crime is of particular concern because its commercial nature and scale provides the potential for significant environmental harm.Fisheries legislation alone is ineffective in dealing with this threat as it is often aimed at lower-level criminality. It is for this reason that some agencies dealing with serious fisheries offences have resorted to general criminal offences such as fraud and conspiracy, and, in more recent times, proceeds of crime offences. Proceeds of crime offences in Australia provide a flexible regime of indictable offences that are well equipped to deal with serious fisheries crime in circumstances where specific fisheries legislation is an inadequate deterrent.

The confiscation provisions available to deal with profit-driven fisheries crime represent a wide and overlapping 'ecosystem'. Specific fisheries forfeiture provisions are well tailored for dealing with moveable property, such as fish, fishing equipment, boats and vehicles. They are a necessarily blunt remedy to deter and incapacitate offenders. General criminal asset confiscation legislation is well tailored for dealing with real estate and intangible property such as shares and money in bank accounts. It is also provides tools through restraining orders and pecuniary penalty orders to allow the disgorging of the benefits achieved by offending to ensure that 'crime does not pay'. Agencies need to take a holistic view of the system and view it as a toolset that can be assessed and, where necessary, utilized to fit the needs of the particular investigation and prosecution.

Notes

1 For some offences a further act of concealment is required: Crimes Act 1958(Vic) s 194(1).
2 See, however, the Fisheries Act (R.S.C., 1985) (Canada), s 79.
3 The Fisheries Act 1995 (Vic) prescribes a commercial quantity for the purposes of triggering indictable offences, such as trafficking a commercial quantity of a priority species (s 111A) or possessing a commercial quantity without authority (s 111C).

References

Agnew, D.J., Pearce, J., Pramod, G., Peatman, T., Watson, R., Beddington, J. R. and Pitcher, T.J. (2009) 'Estimating the worldwide extent of illegal fishing', *PLoS ONE*, *4*(2).

Anderson, K.M. and McCusker, R. (2005) *Crime in the Australian Fishing Industry: Key Issues*, Trends and issues in crime and criminal justice, No. 297, Canberra: Australian Institute of Criminology. Available online at www.aic.gov.au/publications/current%20series/tandi/281-300/tandi297.aspx (accessed 10 August 2013).

Australian Crime Commission (2009) *Organised Crime in Australia: 2009*, Canberra: Australian Government.

Baird, R. (2004) 'Illegal, unreported and unregulated fishing: an analysis of the legal, economic and historical factors relevant to its development and persistence', *Melbourne Journal of International Law*, *5*(2), 299–334.

Baird, R. (2008) 'Australia's response to illegal foreign fishing: a case of winning the battle but losing the law?', *The International Journal of Marine and Coastal Law*, *23*(1), 95–124.

Butcher, S. (2007) 'Abalone business nets large fine', *The Age*, 8 November 2007, Melbourne. Available online at www.theage.com.au/news/national/abalone-business-nets-large-fine/2007/11/08/1194329387771.html (accessed 10 August 2013).

Butcher, S. (2010,) 'Plunder of endangered river fish exposed', *The Age*, 15 May 2010, Melbourne. Available online at www.theage.com.au/national/plunder-of-endangered-river-fish-exposed-20100514-v4n8.html (accessed 10 August 2013).

Cetron, M. and Davies, O. (2008) *55 Trends Now Shaping the Future of Policing*, Proteus Trends Series, Carlisle: Proteus.

Freiberg, A. and Fox, R. (1992) 'Forfeiture, Confiscation and Sentencing', in B. Fisse, D. Fraser and G. Coss (eds) *The Money Trail: Confiscation of Proceeds of Crime, Money Laundering and Cash Transaction Reporting*, Sydney: Law Book Company.

Gilmore, W.C. (2004) *Dirty Money: The Evolution of International Measures to Counter Money Laundering and the Financing of Terrorism*, Strasbourg: Council of Europe.

Glover, J. (1992) 'Restitutionary principles in tort: wrongful user of property and the exemplary measure of damages', *Monash University Law Review*, *18*(2), 169–93.

Gullett, W. (2004) 'Developments in Australian fisheries law: setting the law of the sea convention adrift?', *Environment and Planning Law Journal*, *21*(3), 169–76.

Gullett, W. (2005) 'Smooth sailing for Australia's automatic forfeiture of foreign fishing vessels', *Environment and Planning Law Journal*, *22*(3), 169–73.

Hayman, G. and Brack, D. (2002) *International Environmental Crime: The Nature and Control of Environmental Black Markets*, London: Royal Institute of International Affairs.

Kearney, B., Foran, B., Poldy, F. and Lowe, D. (2003) *Modelling Australia's Fisheries to 2050: Policy and Management Implications*, Canberra: Fisheries Research and Development Corporation.

Mackenzie, S. (2002) *Organised Crime and Common Transit Networks*, Trends and issues in crime and criminal justice, No. 233, Canberra: Australian Institute of Criminology.

Napoleoni, L. (2009) *Rogue Economics: Capitalism's New Reality*, Westminster: Seven Stories Press.

Parliament of Australia (1999a) Fisheries Legislation Amendment Bill (No. 1) 1999: Explanatory Memorandum. Available online at http://parlinfo.aph.gov.au/parlInfo/search/display/display.w3p;query=Id%3A%22legislation%2Fems%2Fr914_ems_6223ee11-612d-424c-8858-8d49cf3af2a8%22 (accessed 10 August 2013).

Parliament of Australia (1999b) Fisheries Legislation Amendment Bill (No. 1) 1999: Second Reading, *Parliamentary Debates (Hansard)*. Available online at http://parlinfo.aph.gov.au/parlInfo/search/display/display.w3p;query=Id%3A%22chamber%2Fhansards%2F1999-10-14%2F0021%22 (accessed 10 August 2013).

Pauly, D. (2009) 'Aquacalypse now: the end of fish', *The New Republic*, 28 September 2009.

Putt, K. and Anderson, J. (2007) *A National Study of Crime in the Australian Fishing Industry*, Research and Public Policy Series, No. 76, Canberra: Australian Institute of Criminology.

Schmidt, C. (2004, February) 'Environmental crimes: profiting at the earth's expense', *Environmental Health Perspectives*, *112*(2).

Schmidt, C.-C. (2005) 'Economic drivers of illegal, unreported and unregulated (IUU) fishing', *International Journal of Marine & Coastal Law*, *20*(3/4), 479–507.

Steinberg, J. (2005) *The Illicit Abalone Trade in South Africa*', Pretoria: Institute for Security Studies.

Stessens, G. (2000) *Money Laundering: A New International Law Enforcement Model*, Cambridge: Cambridge University Press.

Sullivan, M. (1994) 'Forfeiture of fishing vessels in Australia and New Zealand', *Maritime Law Association of Australia and New Zealand Journal*, *14*(1), 35–66. Available online at www.austlii.edu.au/cgi-bin/sinodisp/au/journals/ANZMarLawJl/1999/4.html?stem=0&synonyms=0&query=fishing%20vessels%20forfeiture (accessed 10 August 2013).

Tailby, R. and Gant, F. (2002) *The Illegal Market in Australian Abalone*, Trends and issues in crime and criminal justice, No. 225, Canberra: Australian Institute of Criminology. Available online at www.aic.gov.au/publications/current%20series/tandi/221-240/tandi225.aspx (accessed 10 August 2013).

Thornton, J. (1992) 'Confiscating Criminal Assets: The Proceeds of Crime Act and Related Legislation', in B. Fisse, D. Fraser and G. Coss (eds) *The Money Trail: Confiscation of Proceeds of Crime, Money Laundering and Cash Transaction Reporting*, Sydney: Law Book Company.

Victoria Legislative Assembly (2003) Confiscation (Amendment) Bill 2003, Second Reading. *Debates*, *55*(1), 1312–17.

White, R. (2008) *Crimes Against Nature*. Cullompton: Willan.

Part V

Illegal logging

Combating corruption
and following the proceeds

10 Monitoring illegal logging at the national level

Lessons from Indonesia

Ahmad Dermawan, Krystof Obidzinski, and Salwa Amira

Indonesia's timber industries

Since the early 1970s the forestry sector has become a major contributor to Indonesia's economy. Initially, the focus of Indonesia's forestry was on the extraction of logs and in the late 1970s Indonesia became the global leader in the export of roundwood (Ruzicka 1979; Ross 2001), and timber export contributed as much as 18 per cent to the total exports (Ruzicka 1979; Ross 2001). Following the imposition of a log export ban in 1982, the emphasis shifted to the development of downstream processing, particularly plywood (Dauvergne 1997; Manurung 1997). By the late 1980s, Indonesia had become the largest exporter of tropical timber products. Indonesia was a major exporter of tropical plywood on the global scene and plywood production was a key contributor to national revenues (Guizol and Aruan 2004). Between 1980 and 1989, the number of plywood mills increased from 29 to 116 (Fenton and Neilson 1998). Within a decade, annual plywood production surged from one to nine million cubic metres. Since the mid-1990s, the further reshaping of the sector has featured the emergence and ascent to prominence of the pulp and paper industries and timber plantations (Barr 2001).

In 2012, the forestry sector, led by the pulp and paper industries, continued to generate significant export earnings which amounted to US$9 billion or 5.89 per cent of all export earnings excluding oil and gas (Bank Indonesia 2013). The total value of the output generated by forest sector was 207.5 trillion rupiah (about US$21 billion) or 2.52 per cent of the Indonesian gross domestic product (GDP) (Ministry of Forestry and BPS 2009). The forestry sector has also been an important source of employment. At the height of plywood production in Indonesia in the early 1990s, the Indonesian Wood Panel Association (APKINDO) estimated that timber extraction and processing supported about 2.6 million jobs or 2 per cent of national labor force (Fenton and Neilson 1998). The Ministry of Forestry reported that logging and timber plantation concessions absorb approximately 49,500 jobs. In 2010, the Indonesian Central Statistical Agency reported that forest industries absorb approximately 708,000 jobs in the large- and medium-scale industries (BPS 2011). These figures do not take into account employment in micro- and small-scale industries. BPS (2011) reported that the number of micro- and small-scale establishments in the timber and timber products, paper and paper products and furniture industries in 2010 was approximately 753,500. BPS (2011) reported that the amount of employment absorbed by micro- and small-scale forest industries could reach approximately 1.48 million.

Declining earnings in Indonesia's forestry sector is in part linked to the longstanding imbalance between the high demand for timber and increasingly limited legal supplies. Two key processes have influenced this trend. First, in the early 1980s the government of Indonesia decided to support the expansion of local wood processing, particularly in plywood. This policy shift did succeed in making Indonesia a leading producer and exporter of tropical plywood, but it was not accompanied by measures that would have ensured that the raw timber supplies needed are legal and sustainable (Barr 2001; Dauvergne 2001; Guizol and Aruan 2004). Second, the proportion of different types of wood processing in the export sector changed significantly over 30 years. As discussed, until the mid-1990s plywood was the main product, but since then the pulp and paper sector has emerged as the dominant segment of the forest-based economy (Barr 2001; Sunderlin 2002). In order to support the emergent pulp and paper industry, the government of Indonesia encouraged the development of timber plantations by providing large areas of the forest estate for conversion. However, the development of these plantations has lagged, adding to the supply–demand gap (Ross 2001; Guizol and Aruan 2004; Barr *et al.* 2009).

The widening gap between the high demand for timber and the limited available supply has long been considered the main structural cause of illegal logging in Indonesia (Barr 2001; Brown *et al.* 2005). Although it is common knowledge that such a gap exists, there is as yet no commonly agreed estimate nor a replicable approach to measure and monitor it. At least five studies have been undertaken to assess the supply–demand gap in the timber sector in Indonesia, with seemingly similar empirical approaches (Brown *et al.* 2005; Human Rights Watch 2009; Manurung *et al.* 2007; Scotland, Fraser and Jewell 1999; Tacconi 2007). Yet the results they have produced differ significantly. This chapter aims to assess why this is the case. It does so by comparing the analytical approaches employed in these studies and sources of data used in order to understand the reason for discrepancies. Subsequently, building on the lessons from earlier studies, we present a more refined assessment of the supply–demand gap. In the discussion section we reflect upon the difficulties associated with generating precise estimates of illegal logging which stem from contradictory data at multiple levels. We conclude that improved estimates of illegal logging at the national level are useful for policy-making and preventive measures, and provide recommendations for the methods to be used to improve the reliability of future assessments. We also emphasize the need to examine the reasons for wide-ranging data discrepancies between national agencies and international organizations.

The first section of the chapter reviews five analyses of the supply–demand gap in Indonesia's forestry sector. We compare them in terms of data sources, assumptions about the volume and origin of timber, level of timber consumption and conversions and calculations performed. We assess similarities and differences, and pinpoint areas in the five studies which can be improved. Subsequently, we present a more comprehensive analysis of the supply–demand dynamics in Indonesia's forestry sector over the last decade. As the reliability of various sources of information emerges as an important determining factor, we compare the data sources available in order to assess the range of differences and underlying causes. Discovering a wide range of differences in the available data, we decided to use the national forestry statistics rather than international figures as the former represent fewer interactions of rounding and modification.

In order to collect and analyze the necessary information, we have conducted key informant interviews, reviewed mainstream literature on timber supply and demand in Indonesia, collected government and private sector forestry statistics and undertaken policy document review.

The quantitative data about the production and consumption of timber in Indonesia was obtained from the Ministry of Forestry (MOF) and the Ministry of Industry. These agencies compile the most comprehensive datasets available on forestry production and trade in Indonesia. In addition, we use data from different ministries to enable triangulation of information which will help to better understand and cancel out potential discrepancies.

Review of the available supply–demand studies

There are five main studies that attempt to estimate the supply and demand dynamics in Indonesia's forestry sector (Scotland *et al.* 1999; Brown *et al.* 2005; Manurung *et al.* 2007; Tacconi 2007; Human Rights Watch 2009). All the studies estimate the gap between the supply and demand, and thereby assess the extent of illegal logging. Table 10.1 summarizes key features of these studies such as the timeframe of the analysis, sources of data, whether domestic consumption is included in calculations, whether export is considered and the extent of the supply–demand gap.

Timeframe

All five studies use different timeframes. Three of the studies cover less than five years. Four studies overlap but only marginally (1–2 year periods). The different timeframes employed make it difficult to view the studies as a combined body of knowledge. Rather, they are stand-alone pieces of analysis. The short timeframe of the majority of studies limits the reliability of the results as short-term anomalies or recording mistakes are not evened out.

Sources of data

To a varying extent, all studies used data from MOF. MOF datasets were augmented with data from other sources such as Indonesia's National Statistics Bureau (BPS), Pulp and Paper Industry Association (APKI), Ministry of Industry and Trade, as well as international organizations such as the United Nations Food and Agriculture Organization (FAO) and the International Tropical Timber

Table 10.1 Key characteristics of five supply–demand analyses

Issues	Scotland et al. 1999	Brown et al. 2005	Manurung et al. 2007	Tacconi 2007	Human Rights Watch 2009
Timeframe	1997–1998	2006–2025	1980–2005	2000, 2003	2003–2006
Data sources	MOF[a], APKI[b], BPS[c], own estimates	MOF, own estimates	FAO[d], MOF, APKI	FAO, MOF, own estimates	MOF, ITTO[e]
Domestic markets	Yes	Yes	Yes	Yes	Yes
Foreign markets	Yes	No	No	Yes	No
Extent of supply–demand gap (million m^3)	41.2–56.6	25–30	4.0–42.2	19.1–24.0	20.0–45.0

Notes: a. Ministry of Forestry, b. Asosiasi Pulp dan Kertas Indonesia (Indonesian Pulp and Paper Association), c. Badan Pusat Statistik (Central Statistics Agency), d. Food and Agricultural Organization of the UN, e. International Tropical Timber Organization

Organization (ITTO). At least three studies used their own estimates for different variables – for example, domestic consumption of timber (Scotland *et al.* 1999), capacity of timber industries (Brown *et al.* 2005), and illegal log export (Tacconi 2007).

Scope of analysis

Studies by Scotland *et al.* (1999) and Tacconi (2007) take into account domestic and international markets to estimate the supply and demand dynamics. These studies include export and import of timber to calculate the overall supply and demand, although they use different estimation methods. Scotland *et al.* (1999) included roundwood and processed timber imports in the supply–demand equation, whereas Tacconi (2007) included only roundwood imports. In contrast, studies by Brown *et al.* (2005), Manurung *et al.* (2007) and Human Rights Watch (2009) cover domestic markets only.

Timber supply sources

Table 10.2 summarizes the supply sources discussed in these studies. All of the studies focus on natural forest concessions, forest conversion concessions, timber plantations and other legal logging operations as major sources of timber. Scotland *et al.* (1999) added domestic wastepaper and the import of roundwood and processed products (plywood, sawnwood, pulp and paper) into the supply equation. Tacconi (2007) included only log imports as an additional timber supply source. Manurung *et al.* (2007) added timber volumes from Perusahaan Umum Kehutanan Negara (Perhutani), a state-owned forest company operating in Java and Madura, as a distinct source of roundwood.

Demand sources

Table 10.3 summarizes the sources of timber demand or consumption, using the assumption that demand comes from the operations of timber-based industries. Demand estimates are derived from production levels of timber-based industries

Table 10.2 Sources of timber to estimate supply

Supply sources	Scotland et al. 1999	Brown et al. 2005	Manurung et al. 2007	Tacconi 2007	Human Rights Watch 2009
Concession logging	✓	✓	✓	✓	✓
Forest conversion	✓	✓	✓	✓	✓
Timber plantations	✓	✓	✓	✓	✓
Perhutani			✓		
Other legal sources		✓	✓	✓	✓
Wastepaper	✓				
Imports of roundwood	✓			✓	
Imports of processed wood	✓				

Table 10.3 Sources of demand estimates

Demand commodities	Scotland et al. *1999*	Brown et al. *2005*	Manurung et al. *2007*	Tacconi *2007*	Human Rights Watch *2009*
Plywood	✓	Full capacity use assumed across all industries	✓	✓	✓
Sawnwood	✓		✓	✓	✓
Veneer			✓	✓	✓
Blockboard			✓	✓	
Particleboard			✓	✓	
Woodchips			✓		
Pulp	✓		✓	✓	✓
Paper	✓		✓		
Woodworking			✓		

and converted into their roundwood equivalent. Scotland *et al.* (1999) calculate timber consumption using three main sources only: plywood mills, sawnwood mills and pulp and paper mills. In the case of the pulp and paper industry, both pulp volumes and paper volumes are converted to roundwood equivalent. Since paper is produced from pulp, double counting is possible. Brown *et al.* (2005) do not attempt to estimate actual demand. Instead, the study assumes a likely level of installed capacity of timber industries in the time period of interest and seeks to establish whether legal sources of timber can meet this demand. Manurung *et al.* (2007) cover all major industries to estimate demand. The Human Rights Watch (2009) timber demand estimate is based largely on ITTO data that focuses on plywood, sawnwood and veneer. The authors have also added estimates about timber consumption by pulp and paper industries.

Estimation techniques

Table 10.4 presents the estimation techniques used in the studies. As Table 10.4 indicates, all of the studies apply the general procedure of tallying and comparing supply and demand volumes. All studies include domestic timber consumption in timber supply. The studies by Scotland *et al.* (1999) and Tacconi (2007), however, also take into account timber imports when estimating supply volumes, whereas other studies do not.

Extent of timber supply–demand gap

Due to different data sources, different data ranges for supply and demand analysis, as well as some differences in estimation techniques, the results of the timber supply–demand gap vary across the studies (Table 10.5). The highest and lowest estimates presented in Table 10.5 could not be compared directly because the data is from different time periods. The year 2003 is the only period covered in common by three studies (Human Rights Watch 2009; Manurung *et al.* 2007; Tacconi 2007). Their estimates for 2003 are 24 million cubic metres, 41 million

Table 10.4 Estimation techniques of timber supply and demand

Study	Estimation technique
Scotland *et al.* 1999	Roundwood supply + total imports (of roundwood and timber products in roundwood equivalent) – exports (roundwood and timber products in roundwood equivalent) = net roundwood balance on external trade Net roundwood balance on external trade – domestic consumption = net roundwood balance *Negative net roundwood balance indicates illegal logging*
Brown *et al.* 2005	Timber supply: production of roundwood (from logging concessions, conversion, timber plantations and other legal permits), based on area, productivity and growth Timber demand: assumed constant at industrial capacity *The gap indicates 'unsustainable harvest' or potential for illegal logging*
Manurung *et al.* 2007	Timber supply: production of roundwood (from forest concessions, timber plantations and forest conversions, Perhutani, other legal sources) Timber demand = production of timber products (sawnwood, plywood, veneer, woodworking, blockboard, particleboard, chipwood and pulp) in roundwood equivalent *Illegal logging occurs when demand is higher than supply*
Tacconi 2007	Timber supply = legal supply (forest concessions, timber plantations and forest conversions) + illegal supply Timber demand = production of timber products (sawnwood, fiberboard, particle board, plywood, veneer, and pulp in roundwood equivalent) + (log exports + illegal log exports – log imports) *Illegal supply = production of all timber sectors – legal supply*
Human Rights Watch 2009	Legal timber supply = production of roundwood from logging concessions, clear-cuts, timber plantation harvest, imports Timber demand = production of timber industries including plywood, sawnwood, veneer and pulp in roundwood equivalent *Illegal supply = total timber demand – legal wood supply*

cubic metres and 45 million cubic metres respectively. The implications of using different data sources, data types and estimation techniques translate into high discrepancies between estimates by Tacconi (2007) and the other two studies.

Building on previous analyses

The review of past estimates of illegal logging in Indonesia reveals a number of shortcomings. First, most studies have limited timeframes. Manurung *et al.* (2007)

Table 10.5 Estimates of timber supply–demand gaps

Issues	Scotland et al. (1999)	Brown et al. (2005)	Manurung et al. (2007)	Tacconi (2007)	Human Rights Watch (2009)
Extent of supply–demand gap (million m³)	41.2–56.6	25–30	4.0–42.2	19.1–24.0	20.0–45.0

cover a long time period as do Brown *et al.* (2005), but the study by Brown *et al.* (2005) is a projection based on their most recent data, not an analysis of existing data. Reviewing data covering at least a decade when estimating timber supply and demand in the forestry sector is preferable. It facilitates subsequent updates, enables comparability and also guards against data abnormalities in any given year. Finally, longer-term studies can produce insights about trends that are unattainable from short-term studies.

Second, the existing studies rely on seemingly slight but significant differences in calculation methods. They use different ranges of timber products in the analyses of demand, disparate sources of timber for the analysis of supply and different conversion factors.

Third, these studies use data sources that are not easily compared. Different organizations use different methods of data collection and processing which result in different figures. As an illustration, Table 10.6 presents data on sawnwood production published by MOF, FAO and ITTO. In all years in Table 10.6, the estimates are different and, except for 2000 and 2005, FAO and ITTO figures are on average more than five times higher than the statistics from MOF. ITTO's *Annual Review and Assessment of the World Timber Situation* explains that their data is either duplicate estimates taken from FAO data or ITTO's own estimates (cf. ITTO 2008). FAO explains that its forestry data originates from three information sources: official country data, FAO estimates and unofficial estimates (cf. FAOSTAT 2010). FAO and ITTO figures are the same from 2004 onwards. However, getting clarity on the differences between national and international agencies requires a study of its own.

Learning from the past analyses of illegal logging, this chapter builds on these studies by: (1) constructing a supply–demand model that covers at least ten years;

Table 10.6 Sawnwood production data by different sources

	Sawnwood production (m³)		
	MOF	ITTO	FAO
2000	2,789,543	6,500,000	6,500,000
2001	674,868	6,750,000	6,750,000
2002	623,495	6,230,000	6,230,000
2003	762,604	7,620,000	7,620,000
2004	432,967	4,330,000	4,330,000
2005	1,471,614	4,330,000	4,330,000
2006	679,247	4,330,000	4,330,000
2007	587,402	4,330,000	4,330,000
2008	530,688	4,169,000	4,330,000
2009	1,292,579	4,169,000	4,169,000
2010	1,611,474	4,169,000	4,169,000
2011	934,757	4,169,000	4,169,000

(2) covering comprehensively all timber products to calculate demand and supply; and (3) employing multiple sources of information at the national level (national forestry, industry and trade statistics, and private sector reports).

Timber supply

Data on timber supply is presented in Table 10.7. The approach used by Manurung *et al.* (2007) will be followed because it is the most comprehensive study available in terms of the range of timber products in estimating timber demand and the range of sources of timber in estimating the supply. Timber supply in our estimate comes from the roundwood production from natural forest concessions, forest conversion, timber plantations, Perhutani (state-owned forestry enterprise in Java) and other licenses (for example, community-based forest management concessions). Since the late 1990s, total roundwood supply in Indonesia has experienced a sharp decline from 29.1 million cubic metres in 1997/98 to 9 million cubic metres in 2002. The reason for this is the government policy of lowering the annual allowable cut from natural forest that was introduced in 2000. After 2002, the reduction of annual allowable cut was discontinued. At the same time, increasing volumes of timber were produced by timber plantations. In 2007, timber production from plantations nearly doubled from the year before (Table 10.7).

The sudden jump in timber production from plantations, while being good news, yet again raises questions about the veracity of data, this time in connection with the national statistics. Assuming timber plantations use fast-growing species with seven-year rotations, the sudden jump in timber production from plantations in 2007 should, in principle, correspond to a commensurate increase in timber plantation establishment in 1999/2000. However, Table 10.8 indicates that this is not the case. In fact, plantation establishment figures for these years show a decline. MOF and forestry sector practitioners indicate the increase is a result of the accumulation of productive plantation area over time and rising yields. Verification of these assumptions is a major research undertaking in its own right.

Timber demand

The roundwood equivalent figures of timber demand are presented in Table 10.9. The timber industries included in the demand estimation are sawnwood, plywood, woodworking, blockboard, veneer, particleboard, molding, woodchip, pulp and other products. To estimate the demand for wood based on the output of wood-processing industries, product-specific conversion factors must be used. We applied standard conversion factors used by the Ministry of Forestry (MOF 2003) and the Forestry Research and Development Agency, known as FORDA (Prahasto and Nurfatriani 2001). Table 10.9 shows that the plywood industry led the timber demand up until 1998, but has been on the decline since then due to shrinking timber supplies from natural forest concessions. In contrast,

Table 10.7 Log production in Indonesia, by sources (in m³)

Year	Natural forests		Perhutani (SOE)	Timber plantations	Other licenses	Total
	Concession	Conversion				
1997/98[a]	15,597,546	10,038,228	1,821,297	425,893	1,266,455	29,149,419
1998/99	10,179,406	6,056,174	1,682,336	480,210	628,818	19,026,944
1999/00	10,373,932	7,271,907	1,890,901	187,831	895,371	20,619,942
2000	3,450,430	4,564,592	1,511,001	3,783,604	488,911	13,798,538
2001	1,809,100	2,323,614	1,455,403	5,567,282	–	11,155,399
2002	3,019,839	182,708	1,559,026	4,242,532	–	9,004,105
2003	4,104,914	956,472	976,806	5,325,772	59,538	11,423,502
2004	3,510,752	1,631,885	923,632	7,329,028	153,640	13,548,937
2005	5,720,515	3,614,347	757,993	12,818,199	1,311,584	24,222,638
2006	5,586,722	3,434,181	337,797	11,451,249	982,185	21,792,134
2007	6,437,685	3,063,607	48,034	20,614,209	1,328,050	31,491,585
2008	4,610,077	2,764,105	96,954	22,321,885	2,191,511	31,984,532
2009	4,857,150	6,619,247	87,828	18,953,930	3,802,381	34,320,536
2010	5,251,576	14,488,152	98,003	18,556,254	3,720,785	42,114,770
2011	5,088,695	600,598	112,858	19,840,679	21,786,505	47,429,335

Source: Ministry of Forestry

Note: a. Before 2000, Indonesian government accounting and activity reports follow the fiscal year from April 1 to March 31. Starting in 2001 the fiscal year has coincided with the calendar year, from January 1 to December 31. Year 2000 was the transition.

Table 10.8 Timber plantation establishment

	Production of timber plantations (m³)	Timber plantation establishment (ha)
1997/98	425,893	269,109
1998/99	480,210	182,578
1999/00	187,831	138,662
2000	3,783,604	82,317
2001	5,567,282	67,472
2002	4,242,532	118,508
2003	5,325,772	124,691
2004	7,329,028	131,914
2005	12,818,199	163,125
2006	11,451,249	231,954
2007	20,614,209	334,839
2008	22,321,885	291,984
2009	18,953,930	279,959
2010	18,556,254	457,239
2011	19,840,679	346,607

Source: Ministry of Forestry

pulp production has been increasing. By 2008, about 70 per cent of all timber supplies were destined for pulp production, a significant increase from about 30 per cent in 1997/98. Total timber demand measured in roundwood equivalent (RWE) has been oscillating between the low of 31.2 million cubic metres RWE in 2001 to the high of 48 million cubic metres RWE in 1998/99.

Timber supply–demand balance

Based on the total timber supply and demand presented in Tables 10.8 and 10.9, the estimate of supply–demand balance is presented in Table 10.10. Table 10.10 shows that timber demand (that is, actual production of timber industries) has been significantly in excess of timber supply throughout the period of time under consideration. This gap is commonly taken as an indication of illegal extraction of timber. The biggest gap was 33.0 million cubic metres in 2003 and the smallest was 5.3 million cubic metres in 2008. The average gap since the period 1997/98 was 20.3 million cubic metres. It is interesting to see that the sudden jump in the production of plantation timber contributed to the narrowing of the supply–demand gap.

Discussion

This study has sought to examine why, in the existing body of literature on Indonesian forestry, precise figures on illegal logging are difficult to come by. The review of five key studies attempting to measure the supply–demand gap in Indonesia's forestry sector as a proxy to assessing illegal logging indicates basic similarities in terms of calculation. However, there also are significant differences in the range of products covered to obtain RWE of timber demand. There are also differences in the sources of timber taken into consideration for supply analysis, different conversion factors, and so on. Among the key limitations of the existing studies is their relatively short timeframe. This chapter builds on the earlier studies and produces a more refined analysis by employing a more comprehensive approach in estimating both the demand as well as the supply of timber (covering a greater range of variables) and extending the analysis over a longer time period.

Using official MOF data, cross-checked with information from other government sources (Ministry of Industry and Trade) and private sector agencies (Plywood Producers Association and Pulp and Paper Producers Association), it was found that the supply–demand gap in Indonesia's forestry sector was on-going from 1997/98 to 2008. The analysis has found that between 1997/98 and 2008 about half of all timber consumed by wood-processing industries came from undocumented sources which are commonly understood to be illegal. The dataset shows the prominent role the pulp and paper sector plays in sustaining the demand for timber. In 1997/98, the pulp and paper industry accounted for approximately one-third of the overall timber demand. Over the ensuing decade, this increased to over 70 per cent. At the same time, the consumption of timber by the plywood

Table 10.9 Timber demand in Indonesia, in roundwood equivalent

	Production (m³ RWE)										Total Timber demand
	Sawnwood	Plywood	Woodworking	Blockboard	Veneer	Particleboard	Molding	Other processed	Woodchip	Pulp	
1997/98	4,756,483	15,432,623	404,540	1,381,688	2,144,517	885,062	2,627,460	1,346,634	523,065	13,763,025	**43,265,097**
1998/99	4,927,142	16,455,877	1,860	1,522,494	2,496,720	564,694	2,794,394	2,271,443	1,487,946	15,435,000	**47,957,570**
1999/00	3,749,497	10,607,319	29,920	982,321	1,966,498	376,108	1,812,757	1,851,011	609,975	16,625,835	**38,611,241**
2000	5,076,968	10,218,291	855,463	738,588	1,270,800	400,068	458,103	0	59,655	18,402,975	**37,480,911**
2001	1,228,260	4,833,416	794,537	892,409	179,033	593,754	397,526	106,811	1,154,409	20,996,640	**31,176,795**
2002	1,134,761	3,897,132	204,803	27,959	8,285,984	13,462	462,380	0	66,072	22,360,500	**36,453,053**
2003	1,387,939	14,054,279	462,326	1,003,761	549,463	187,284	919,009	2,075,720	382,131	23,374,395	**44,396,307**
2004	788,000	10,383,102	1,107,151	638,011	295,211	488,140	682,123	2,189,717	950,019	23,439,060	**40,960,534**
2005	2,678,337	10,427,623	375,134	92,727	1,923,190	249,536	779,051	1,029,423	1,056,234	24,603,930	**43,215,185**
2006	1,236,230	8,767,126	111,714	434,716	485,942	81,310	341,131	65,886	1,670,901	25,524,945	**38,719,901**
2007	1,069,072	7,945,005	0	469,352	568,484	0	0	0	3,310,518	28,270,485	**41,632,916**
2008	965,852	7,713,002	0	0	811,788	0	0	0	834,960	26,982,765	**37,308,367**
2009	1,292,579	6,911,385	4,034	27,982	1,306,269	0	54,934	8,360,531	3,038,112	29,362,946	**50,358,772**
2010	1,611,474	7,647,245	43,020	281,230	1,399,635	0	1,186,554	898,134	3,811,953	31,711,982	**48,591,227**
2011	1,701,258	7,596,539	0	0	1,550,581	0	0	0	5,365,305	32,132,417	**48,346,099**

Sources: For pulp, Ministry of Industry and Indonesian Pulp and Paper Association; for others, Ministry of Forestry. The pulp production estimate does not use MOF data because up until 2007 the permit to establish pulp plantations was issued by the Ministry of Industry, after which it was issued by MOF.

Notes: Conversion factor used in the analysis are sawnwood: 1.82m³ of roundwood per m³ of product; plywood: 2.30; woodworking: 2.86; blockboard: 2.30; veneer: 1.90; particleboard: 2.00; molding and other processed are assumed to have similar conversion factor as woodworking (2.86); woodchip: 3.00m³ of roundwood per ton of woodchip, and pulp: 4.5. Conversion factors for sawnwood, plywood, blockboard, veneer and particleboard are from Ministry of Forestry (2003), conversion factors for woodworking and pulp are from Prahasto and Nurfatriani (2001).

Table 10.10 Timber supply – demand balance

	Timber demand (m³)	Timber supply (m³)	Demand – Supply (m³)
1997/98	43,265,097	29,149,419	14,115,678
1998/99	47,957,570	19,026,944	28,930,626
1999/00	38,611,242	20,619,942	17,991,300
2000	37,480,910	13,798,538	23,682,372
2001	31,176,795	11,155,399	20,021,396
2002	36,453,052	9,004,105	27,448,947
2003	44,396,307	11,423,502	32,972,805
2004	40,960,533	13,548,937	27,411,596
2005	43,215,185	24,222,638	18,992,547
2006	38,719,901	21,792,144	16,927,757
2007	41,632,915	31,491,584	10,141,331
2008	37,308,367	31,984,442	5,323,925
2009	50,358,772	34,320,536	16,038,236
2010	48,591,226	42,114,770	6,476,456
2011	48,346,099	47,429,335	916,764

and sawn timber industries has declined from nearly 50 per cent to 23 per cent during the same time period.

The study shows that since 2003 there has been a clear trend for illegal logging in Indonesia to decline. However, there is uncertainty as to the extent of this decline. If MOF data are used, between 2003 and 2008, illegal logging declined by 27 million cubic metres from nearly 33 million cubic metres in 2003 to 5.3 million cubic metres in 2008. Over the last eight years, a discernible decline in illegal logging in Indonesia has occurred, primarily due to greater international scrutiny, improved forest law enforcement and rising market demand for legal timber products (Lawson and MacFaul 2010). However, these promising signs require at least two caveats.

Data inconsistencies

Detecting illegal logging and assessing its scope requires a careful analysis and a thorough understanding of the data. There are at least three points in time where reported data require explanation. First, as indicated in the previous section, the supply–demand gap decreased in 2006/2008 and again in 2009/2010 due to sudden increases in timber supply. In 2006/2007, the production of timber plantation increased by 80 per cent from 11.4 million cubic metres to 20.6 million cubic metres. While this seems like good news, this sudden growth needs more explanation because it does not correspond with the data on the timber plantation establishment cycle seven years earlier (in the period 1999/2000).

One possible explanation could be that sudden increases in timber supply have been caused by accumulated timber stock from the previous years of timber plantation development. However, there are two challenges to this explanation.

First, the condition of timber plantations during these time periods was generally poor. This happened to be because at that time pulp and paper companies did not support timber plantation productivity at a high level because they could source cheap timber from land clearing permits (Barr *et al.* 2009). Second, Table 10.7 and Table 10.9 show that timber demand by the pulp industry was greater than what was available from timber plantations plus land clearing since 1997/1998, so the theory of accumulated timber plantation stock during this time period does not seem convincing.

The second sudden increase that needs explanation is a 119 per cent increase (from 6.6 to 14.5 million cubic metres) in the timber supply from land clearing in 2009/2010. This shows that the reduction of the timber demand–supply gap comes from an unsustainable source. The third dramatic change in timber supply–demand balance is the sudden decrease in timber produced via land clearing, from 14.5 million cubic metres in 2010 to a mere 0.6 million cubic metres in 2011, although this is offset by an increase of timber supply from 'other licenses' from 3.7 to 21.8 million cubic metres. Of 21.8 million cubic metres, 2.8 million cubic metres came from smallholder forests and 0.4 million cubic metres from timber from plantations (Ministry of Forestry 2012). However, the remaining 18.5 million cubic metres of timber under the category 'other licenses' require further explanation.

Large-scale vs. small-scale actors

The previous section has established that at least a part of timber supply from smallholders is accounted for in the timber supply data. This is possible because the Ministry set out regulation on timber transport permits. The data of the use of letter is reported by district and provincial government to the Ministry of Forestry, including data on the amount of timber from smallholder forests which are transported; thus they are reported in the Ministry's statistics.

However, timber data does not include the timber produced by small and medium-sized industries. In Indonesia, the permits for timber industries at these scales are the responsibility of the district and provincial governments. The production of timber-based industries presented in the Ministry of Forestry's statistics cover industries with an annual capacity of 6,000 cubic metres of timber. The authority to issue permits for industry with annual capacity between 2,000 and 6,000 cubic metres lies with the provincial government, and those with annual capacity below 2,000 cubic metres lies with the district government. The Ministry does not publish the data on the performance of small and medium-sized industries in the annual statistics.

Although the capacity and production of these industries are relatively small, their role is not negligible. As an illustration, there are approximately 15,000 furniture companies in Jepara, one district in Central Java. These companies in total require approximately 0.9 million cubic metres of timber annually (Achdiawan and Puntodewo 2011). More generally, Central Statistical Agency data shows that there were 639,000 small-scale timber industries in 2010 (BPS 2011). Since they are largely unaccounted for in the Ministry of Forestry statistical reports, this would potentially make the official figures for timber demand a significant underestimate.

Conclusions and recommendations

The review of existing timber supply–demand assessments in Indonesia carried out over the last decade provides important lessons for methodological design of future estimates. It also brings to the fore the question of data veracity and reliability, which has important policy implications.

In terms of methodological implications, limited and disjointed timeframes among the available analyses prevent meaningful comparisons and verifiability. Ideally, such studies should assess at least a decade's worth of data to enable a glimpse at year-on-year relationships, ensure greater consistency and show trends. Estimation techniques should cover the widest possible range of timber products to account for demand and timber sources to account for the supply. Conversion factors need to clearly account for roundwood equivalent of wood products.

This study has sought to remedy the above limitations by tracking the supply–demand dynamics in Indonesia's forestry sector over the period of ten years between 1997/98 and 2008. The longer timeframe was the first step in improving the quality of the assessment. The second major advance is in covering the widest possible range of variables for estimating the demand for timber as well as the sources and volumes of timber supply.

The results of the analysis show that illegal logging has been a problem in each of the ten years under study, although in more recent years it has declined significantly. The more refined analysis of the supply–demand dynamics shows this declining trend very clearly.

However, obtaining precise figures on illegal logging remains elusive. The primary reason for this is unreliable and incompatible data – both at the national level and from international sources. Poor data had been a major problem in earlier studies of the supply–demand dynamics in Indonesian forestry and it is primarily responsible for the limitations of these studies. Problems with data have had a major impact on the current analysis as well.

There are major differences between the national forestry statistics and similar data at FAO/ITTO. A closer examination of the national statistics reveal worrying inconsistencies, such as the rapid growth of timber supplies from plantations which is not supported by annual increments in plantation development. International data is several times higher than that reported by MOF, but it is the same from one year to the next and it is not clear how these estimates have been obtained.

This chapter deals with data limitations by using both national and international data, but it does so by utilizing them separately. Doing so results in the formulation of the low range of illegal logging (national data) as well as the high range (international data). The resultant range is broad, but it is still useful as an indication of trends. It also can provide information on the role of specific segments of the wood-processing industry in the consumption of illegal timber.

In addition, since the Ministry of Forestry statistics do not include timber-based industries which operate under annual capacity of 6,000 cubic metres, there is a possibility that its timber demand data will be lower than actual. With this in mind, the demand–supply gap will potentially be larger, and thus the level of illegal logging would be higher than reported.

As it stands, however, exact figures for illegal logging are impossible to establish and this has important policy implications. Not knowing exactly the levels of illegal logging presents a major obstacle to monitoring and verification requirements under international agreements which the Indonesian government is about to sign – that is, a VPA (Voluntary Partnership Agreement) with the European Commission, and a REDD+ (Reduced Emissions from Deforestation and Degradation) agreement with the government of Norway. Both agreements require effective means to monitor and verify legality (in the case of VPA) and effectiveness of the forest conversion moratorium (under the agreement with Norway). While remote sensing is expected to facilitate much of the monitoring effort, statistical verification has an important complementary role as well. However, given current data limitations, the statistical analysis is unlikely to contribute any time soon.

It is therefore a matter of the highest urgency for MOF to take steps to improve the quality of its national forestry data in Indonesia. To this end, the first step would be to understand why there are wide inconsistencies between various data sets and what can be done to improve the reporting system to ensure greater consistency. At the same time, it is also important to investigate the large differences between the national and international forestry figures, and seek clarification on why such large discrepancies exist and how they can be resolved. Understanding underlying causes behind these data problems would go a long way towards improving the reliability of forestry assessments and would enable more effective policy-making.

Acknowledgments

This chapter is the result of a collaborative research project titled 'Strengthening Rural Institutions to Support Livelihood Security for Smallholders Involved in Industrial Tree-planting Programs in Vietnam and Indonesia'. The project was financed by the Gesellschaft für Internationale Zusammenarbeit (GIZ) on behalf of the government of the Federal Republic of Germany. The authors would like to express their gratitude for the financial support received and would like to convey their thanks to project partners in Indonesia and Vietnam for their kind participation. The chapter was thoroughly reviewed by a CIFOR editor, Imogen Badgery-Parker, whose help is gratefully acknowledged.

References

Achdiawan, R. and Puntodewo, A. (2011) *Livelihood of Furniture Producers in Jepara. Annex 12, FVC Annual Report*, Bogor, Indonesia: CIFOR.

Antaranews (2006) 'Kontribusi Sektor Kehutanan Dalam Memantapkan Ketahanan Nasional (The contribution of the forestry sector in strengthening national resilience)', 11 September. Available online at www.antaranews.com/berita/42002/kontribusi-sektor-kehutanan-dalam-memantapkan-ketahanan-nasional (accessed on 10 August 2013).

Bank Indonesia (2013) *Value of Export by Group of Commodities*. Available online at www.bi.go.id/en/statistik/seki/terkini/eksternal/Contents/Default.aspx (accessed on 5 February 2014).

Barr, C. (2001) *Banking on Sustainability: Structural Adjustment and Forestry Reform in Post-Suharto Indonesia*, Washington, DC, and Bogor: WWF and CIFOR.

Barr, C., Dermawan, A., Purnomo, H. and Komarudin, H. (2009) 'Financial governance and Indonesia's reforestation fund during the Soeharto and post-Soeharto periods, 1989–2009: A political economic analysis of lessons for REDD+', *CIFOR Occasional Paper*, 52.

Brown, T. (2002) 'Whose "official" data should we believe?', in C.V. Barber, E. Matthews, D. Brown, T.H. Brown, L. Curran and C. Plume (eds) *The State of the Forest: Indonesia*, Bogor and Washington, DC: Forest Watch Indonesia and Global Forest Watch.

Brown, T.H., Simangunsong, B.C.H., Sukadri, D., Brown, D.W., Sumarta, S., Dermawan, A. and Rufi'ie (2005) *Restructuring and Revitalization of Indonesia's Wood-based Industry: Synthesis of Three Major Studies*, Jakarta: Ministry of Forestry, CIFOR and DFID-MFP.

Dauvergne, P. (1997) *Shadows in the Forest*, Cambridge, MA: MIT Press.

FAOSTAT (2010) *Sawnwood Production*. Available online at http://faostat.fao.org/site/626/DesktopDefault.aspx?PageID=626#ancor (accessed 10 August 2013).

Fenton, R. and Neilson, D.A. (1998) *The Forest Industry Sectors of Malaysia and Indonesia*, Rotorua: Dana Publishing.

Guizol, P.H. and Aruan, A.L.P. (2004) 'Impact of incentives on the development of forest plantation resources in Indonesia, with emphasis on industrial timber plantations in the outer islands', in T. Enters and P.B. Durst (eds) *What Does it Take? The Role of Incentives in Forest Plantation Development in Asia and the Pacific*, Bangkok: FAO.

Human Rights Watch (2009) *'Wild Money': The Human Rights Consequences of Illegal Logging and Corruption in Indonesia's Forestry Sector*, New York, NY: Human Rights Watch.

International Tropical Timber Organization (ITTO) (2008) *Annual Review and Assessment of the World Timber Situation 2008*, Yokohama: ITTO.

Lawson, S. and MacFaul, L. (2010) *Illegal Logging and Related Trade Indicators of the Global Response*, London: Chatham House.

Manurung, E.G.T. and Buongiorno, J. (1997) 'Effect of the log export ban policy on the forestry sector of Indonesia', *Journal of World Forest Resource Management*, 8:21–49.

Manurung, E.G.T., Simangunsong, B.C.H., Sukadri, D., Widyantoro, B., Justianto, A., Ramadhan, S., Sumardjani, L., Rochadi, D., Permadi, P., Priyono, B.M. and Supriyanto, B. (2007) *Road map revitalisasi industri kehutanan Indonesia (Road Map for Revitalizing Indonesia's Forestry Industry)*, Jakarta: Departemen Kehutanan.

Ministry of Forestry (2003) *Data dan informasi kehutanan 2003 (Forestry Data and Information 2003)*, Jakarta: Departemen Kehutanan.

Ministry of Forestry (2009) *Eksekutif data strategis 2009 (Executive Data Strategies 2009)*, Jakarta: Departemen Kehutanan.

Ministry of Forestry and Badan Pusat Statistik (BPS) (2009) *Penyusunan kontribusi industri primer kehutanan terhadap produk domestik bruto tahun 2005–2007 (Preparation of Primary Forestry Industry Contribution to Gross Domestic Product in 2005–2007)*, Jakarta: Dephut and BPS.

Prahasto, H. and Nurfatriani, F. (2001) 'Analisis kebijakan penyediaan kayu dalam negeri (Analysis of the domestic wood supply policy)', *Jurnal Sosial Ekonomi*, 2(2): 111–38.

Ross, M.L. (2001) *Timber Booms and Institutional Breakdown in Southeast Asia*, New York, NY: Cambridge University Press.

Ruzicka, I. (1979) 'Rent appropriation in Indonesian logging: East Kalimantan 1972/73–1976/77', *Bulletin of Indonesian Economic Studies*, XV: 45–74.

Scotland, N., Fraser, A. and Jewell, N. (1999) *Roundwood Supply and Demand in the Forest Sector in Indonesia*, Jakarta: Indonesia–UK Tropical Forest Management Programme.

Sunderlin, W. (2002) 'Effects of crisis and political change, 1997–1999', in C. Colfer and I.A.P. Resosudarmo (eds) *Which Way Forward: People, Forests, and Policymaking in Indonesia*, Washington, DC: Resources for the Future.

Tacconi, L. (2007) 'Verification and certification of forest products and illegal logging in Indonesia', in L. Tacconi (ed.) *Illegal Logging: Law Enforcement, Livelihoods and the Timber Trade*, London: Earthscan.

11 An integrated law enforcement approach

Targeting the proceeds of forest crime in Indonesia

Anna Christina Sinaga and Sofi Mardiah

Introduction

Forest cover in Indonesia in 1950 was estimated to be 162.3 million hectares (Forest Watch Indonesia/Global Forest Watch 2002) but by 2008 had fallen to 93.9 million hectares, a loss of 68.4 million hectares (Ministry of Forestry). The rate of deforestation in Indonesia has been estimated at between 500,000 and 1.5 million hectares per annum in the last three decades to 2010 (Food and Agriculture Organization 2010). Even in the period 2000–05 the rate of deforestation was estimated at 1.8 million hectares per year (FAO 2007). The Indonesian Ministry of Forestry (MOF) announced that the deforestation rate during the period was lower, approximately 1.08 million hectares per year (MOF 2007), although the subsequent period 2003–06 was assessed by it to be slightly higher, at 1.17 million hectares per year (MOF 2008).

This loss of 42 per cent – almost half of national forest cover – was accompanied by heavy financial losses for the Indonesian government. The 2008 audit of forest management by the State Audit Board (BPK) in four provinces (Riau, Central Kalimantan, West Kalimantan and East Kalimantan), for example, showed State losses due to unlawful forest activities to have reached US$26.17 million per year (BPK 2008). Nationally, the average State loss from illegal logging and forest corruption, estimated for the period 2003–06, was US$2 billion per year (Human Rights Watch 2009). The latter amount is as large as the country's spending for health. An even higher State loss due to deforestation and illegal logging was asserted in 2007 by the former Minister of Forestry, M.S. Kaban, at US$3.3million per year (Indonesian Corruption Watch 2010).

Illegal logging is a major cause of deforestation, as are also forest conversion and destructive logging (Applegate, Chokkalingam and Suyanto 2001; Koyuncu and Yilmaz 2009; Sunderlin and Resosudarmo 1996; Tacconi, Obidzinski and Agung 2004). Another significant cause of deforestation is corruption in the forestry sector, which has many manifestations ranging from fraudulent logging concessions and smuggling of illegal timber, to the laundering of illicit proceeds, fraud, tax evasion and illegal trade. Corruption itself is embedded in forest governance systems (Contreras-Hermosilla 2002; FAO 2001; Gupta and Siebert 2004; Indrarto et al. 2012). These systems are confusing, complex and expensive, and provide numerous opportunities for corruption (Dermawan *et al.* 2011). For example, to obtain a logging permit, there are many parties involved in the authorization process, which tends to be corrupt (Indrarto *et al.* 2012; Tanzi 1998). The large State losses have impacts on the environment as well as the economy (World Bank 2006).

Various administrative efforts to tackle illegal logging have been conducted by the government to little avail. The most widely known were the Sustainable Forest Operations (Operasi Hutan Lestari – OHL) I, II and III, which were conducted from 2004 to 2006. In addition, administrative instructions (which are neither laws, regulations nor decrees) have included the issuance of Presidential Instruction No. 4 of 2005 on coordination among agencies in combating illegal logging, and the Home Affairs Minister Instruction No. 3 of 2005 to Provincial Governors and the Heads of Districts (Bupati) throughout Indonesia to accelerate these efforts. However, these efforts have yet to show significant results. A report by Indonesian Corruption Watch, for example, mentions that from the number of cases resulting from the Sustainable Forest Operation II, only about 33 per cent eventually went to court and had a sentence passed (Yuntho, Sari and Diansyah 2009).

The government of Indonesia has also initiated an alternative legal means to tackle illegal logging – the inclusion of forest crimes in predicate crimes of money laundering. This provides opportunities to use other legal instruments to tackle illegal logging problems. Moreover, the government has also initiated the use of anticorruption measures in the forestry sector to tackle forest-related crimes such as bribery, tax evasion and fraud. Although they are not being primarily used to combat forest crimes *per se*, the two laws are gradually also being used against forest-related crimes. A study conducted by Corruption Eradication Commission (Komisi Pemberantasan Korupsi – KPK) in 2010 on regulations regarding the forest estate found that there were four main conflicting regulations for forest zones that create legal uncertainty as to forest status and that often lead to corruption (Dermawan *et al.* 2011). As a result of this study, in 2013, KPK led the signature of a Memorandum of Agreement between 12 Indonesian ministries and agencies. Its three main objectives are: (a) harmonization of regulations regarding the forests, (b) technical and procedural alignment, and (c) conflict resolution (Anti Corruption Clearing House n.d.).

'Follow the wood' approach

Article 50 of Law No. 41 of 1999 defines forest crimes as activities including: occupation of forest land without a permit, encroachment, cutting the trees without a permit, burning forests and transporting logs without a permit. In general, these violations require field investigations to find hard evidence such as illegal wood or unauthorized equipment and the actors who conducted the illegal logging. Therefore, this can be called the 'follow the wood' or 'follow the suspect' approach.

Police data from the three large illegal logging prevention operations conducted by the government, called Sustainable Forest Operations I, II and III, and conducted between November 2004 and June 2006, show that 4,178 crime cases were uncovered, together with 4,680 suspects (Yuntho *et al.* 2009). In addition, 822,296 cubic metres of timber were confiscated. However, despite the number of suspects and illegal logs found in the operation, the law enforcement efforts were not able to apprehend the masterminds of these illegal logging operations. Indonesian Corruption Watch (ICW) reported that during the period 2005–08, only 18 persons (6.7 per cent) among 205 defendants in illegal logging cases were high-level perpetrators, such as directors, managers, law enforcement officers or forestry officials. The others were low-level perpetrators such as field operators, truck drivers or farmers (Yuntho *et al.* 2009). This phenomenon is due to the law enforcement agencies' focus only on perpetrators caught red-handed or proved to be directly related to the cases, in accordance with Law 41/1999 (Santoso *et al.* 2011). This renders law enforcement efforts ineffective in pursuing the masterminds who gain the most from the crime.

Moreover, ICW found that 137 of 205 defendants were acquitted. Forty defendants were sentenced to less than one year, and 14 were sentenced to between one and two years' imprisonment. The remaining ten defendants were sentenced to more than two years' imprisonment (Yuntho *et al.* 2009). While the numbers differ, MOF also found similarly lenient sentences when examining cases of forest crime: of 92 cases in the Supreme Court during the period 2005–09 concerning illegal logging, in 36 cases the defendants were acquitted. In 24 cases the Supreme Court sentenced the defendants to less than one year's imprisonment, and in 19 cases the sentences were between one and two years' imprisonment. The rest of the cases were still undecided by the Supreme Court in 2009 (Ibrahim 2009).

As described above, the law enforcement results from the 'follow the wood' approach do not provide maximum results, either in terms of the perpetrators that are caught or the punishment they receive. The limitations of Law No. 41 of 1999 for illegal logging crimes make it near impossible to apprehend the masterminds, the real players. It is only their pawns who are apprehended. By using 'follow the wood', State losses are rarely if ever recovered. The reason for this is that the maximum fine for this crime, as regulated in Law No. 41 of 1999 art. 78, is US$1 million. This, of course, does not reflect the amount the State loses as a result of illegal logging (Santoso *et al.* 2011).

As a result, illegal logging continues because the main actors are not touched at all and can still control illegal logging activities. Moreover, the proceeds of crime, the lifeblood of this crime, are neither targeted nor recovered. Therefore, a more effective law enforcement approach to tackle illegal logging is urgently needed to catch the higher-level perpetrators and to recover State losses.

'Follow the money' approach

The inspiration for the 'follow the money' approach comes from the system used to combat trafficking crimes (e.g. drugs, humans, weapons). Because these crimes are more organized and global, law enforcement is likely to be more effective if it 'follows the money' instead of focusing on apprehending the perpetrators.

In Indonesia, the development of this approach is supported by the revision of Law No. 15 of 2002 in Law No. 25 of 2003 on Money Laundering. In that revision, illegal logging and other forest-related crimes were categorized as predicate crimes for money laundering (Setiono and Husein 2005). This provides opportunities for the use of anti-money laundering tools to deal with forest-related crimes. Law No. 25 of 2003 was replaced by Law No. 8 of 2010, which includes a broader range of settings for handling money laundering.

In addition, Law No. 30 of 2002 regarding the establishment of the Corruption Eradication Commission (Komisi Pemberantasan Korupsi – KPK) and Law No. 46 of 2009 establishing the Anti-Corruption Court also provide a strong legal basis to develop a 'follow the money' approach in the forestry sector. Anti-corruption instruments are already being used in handling criminal cases related to the forestry sector in Indonesia, described below.

Anti-corruption law enforcement

There are at least two examples of successful anti-corruption cases in the Indonesian forestry sector that revealed the masterminds behind forestry crimes. Not only were the government officials involved apprehended but also the company directors. These cases used Indonesian anti-corruption laws to investigate cash flows, with the support of the Indonesian Transaction Reporting and Analysis Center (INTRAC) (Pusat Pelaporan dan Analisis Transaksi Keuangan – PPATK).

East Kalimantan case[1]

The East Kalimantan case involved SAF,[2] a former governor of East Kalimantan (2003–08), and MAR, the Presidential Director of SDG. The essence of this case was the fraudulent issuance of permits to open one million hectares of forested land for oil palm plantation in Berau, East Kalimantan, Borneo.

SAF was charged and found guilty of a number of offences. These included providing recommendations for issuing the principal permit to open the forest area, as well as a Timber Utilization Permit (Izin Pemanfaatan Kayu – IPK) and a temporary forest plantation concession for oil palm (Hak Pengusahaan Hutan Tanaman Perkebunan – HPHTP) to 11 companies under SDG owned by MAR. SAF also gave SDG dispensation for providing to these same 11 companies a bank guarantee for Forest Resource Provision (Provisi Sumber Daya Hutan – PSDH) and for the Reforestation Fund (Dana Reboisasi – DR), which was the precondition for obtaining a Timber Utilization Permit. MAR, after obtaining the permit, then exploited the timber without even planting the oil palm plantation.

SAF was proven guilty under the anti-corruption law in the Supreme Court. He was found to have abused his power and authority to substantially increase the financial gain of the timber concession companies under SDG. Their logging of 697,000 cubic metres of timber resulted in a loss to the country of up to US$35.4 million.

The court sentenced SAF to four years in prison and a fine of US$23,530 or two months in prison. MAR was sentenced to 18 months in prison and fined US$35.4 million. After finishing his sentence, MAR paid US$35.4 million to KPK and, on 18 March 2008, KPK handed over the money to the State Treasury (Antaranews 2008; ICW n.d.).

Riau case[3]

TAJ, a former Head of Pelalawan District, in Riau Province, Sumatra, was charged with corruption related to the issuance of 15 plantation concessions (Ijin Usaha Pemanfaatan Hasil Hutan Kayu-Hutan Tanaman – IUPHHK-HT) in Pelalawan district, during the period 2001–06. The land for which the permits were issued was not designated plantation concession land. The 15 recipients were not legally qualified to carry out timber utilization activities (MOF Decree No. 21/Kpts-II/2001). Seven of them were companies directly affiliated to TAJ – that is, established by his cronies and subordinates, with the purpose of transferring their IUPHHK-HT to other companies. TAJ received money from the transfer of these permits.

The State suffered a loss of US$128 million as a result of this crime. TAJ allegedly received at least US$176,472. He was charged under arts 2(1) and 18 of Law No. 31 of 1999 as amended by Law No. 20 of 2001 on Corruption Eradication and arts 55(1) and 64 of the Criminal Code. The Supreme Court found TAJ guilty and sentenced him to 11 years in prison and fined him US$58,823 or six months in prison. He was also ordered to pay US$1.236 million as restitution to the State.

Analysis of cases

In these two cases, it is clear that high-level perpetrators who were politically exposed persons were successfully targeted. In handling the two cases, law enforcement officers did not have to catch the perpetrators red-handed and could avoid the shortcomings of the 'follow the wood' approach.

The law enforcement agencies used the national anti-corruption commission and the financial intelligence unit, the roles and functions of which are regulated in the anti-money laundering laws. Moreover, the use of anti-corruption and anti-money laundering laws provided opportunities for the law enforcement agencies to estimate and recover the State losses. This also was not possible using 'follow the wood' approach.

However, in spite of the opportunities provided by this approach, it is new and unfamiliar to Indonesian law enforcement agencies, particularly to the Indonesian police and forestry police. This is shown by the fact that, since its introduction to the Indonesian judicial system, there have not been many anti-money laundering cases in Indonesia, let alone a case of money laundering in the forestry sector. Thus, this 'follow the money' approach may take a lot more time and effort for law enforcement agencies to get used to and to fully implement.

The second challenge is the implementation of asset recovery mechanisms. Although asset recovery is identified in the anti-corruption law, implementing regulations and the capacity of the law enforcement officers are still lacking. The lack of solid international mutual legal assistance hampers the recovery of assets even further. In SAF's case, the law enforcement agencies were actually successful in recovering the State loss from MAR. However, in TAJ's case, efforts to recover State loss are still struggling.

The third challenge in implementing this 'follow the money' approach is the lack of solid mutual legal assistance that is needed if the proceeds of crime are deposited offshore. Mutual legal assistance provides the means for law enforcement agencies to trace funds or suspects and to bring one or both of them back to Indonesia if they are offshore. It needs to be supported by adequate regulations and institutions, and requires international treaties or arrangements and, particularly, dual criminality. Moreover, the central institution for mutual legal assistance in Indonesia still faces problems of limited authority. At the moment, the central authority, as regulated in the Mutual Legal Assistance Law, is the Ministry of Law and Human Rights. Unfortunately, this Ministry does not have law enforcement authority but is simply an administrative institution for mutual legal assistance applications. Meanwhile, mutual legal assistance is heavily related to law enforcement authorities and agencies.

Integrated law enforcement approach

Indonesia is now looking to combine anti-corruption and anti-money laundering instruments to deal with forest crimes, especially illegal logging. The method developed by the Center for International Forestry Research (CIFOR), known as the 'integrated law enforcement approach' applies similar principles to 'follow the money'. With its emphasis on the proceeds of crime, this approach is more likely to be effective in combating organized forest-related crimes and recovering State losses resulting from organized forest-related crimes. It facilitates the arrest of any perpetrators involved in forest crimes and crimes related to forestry, ranging from the perpetrators in the field to the masterminds of these crimes.

Integrated use of legal instruments

Integrated law enforcement needs to be supported by legal instruments. Currently, the main ones are as follows:

1. Law No. 41 of 1999 on Forestry
2. Law No. 31 of 1999 amended in Law No. 20 of 2001 on Corruption Eradication
3. Law No. 8 of 2010 on the Prevention and Eradication of Money Laundering
4. Law No. 32 of 2009 on Environmental Protection and Management
5. Law No. 17 of 2006 on Customs.

Both forestry and non-forestry instruments are needed and additional relevant legislation includes the following areas of law (Santoso *et al.* 2011):

1. Asset recovery: a new innovation in the context of international cooperation in combating organized crime. In Indonesia, asset recovery is regulated by Law No. 31 of 1999 as amended by Law No. 20 of 2001 regarding Corruption Eradication. Provisions for asset recovery are also regulated in Law No. 7 of 2006 on the Ratification of the Convention against Corruption.
2. Know your customer (KYC): the principle applied by the bank to identify its customers and their customers' profiles, to monitor their transactions and report suspicious financial transactions to INTRAC in order to prevent and combat money laundering effectively (Setiono and Husein 2005). In Indonesia, KYC is regulated, based on the Central Bank of Indonesia Regulation (PBI) No. 3/23/PBI/2001 and PBI No. 5/21/PBI/2003. These two regulations were revised in PBI No. 11/28/PBI/2009 on the Implementation of Anti-Money Laundering and Combating the Financing of Terrorism Program for Commercial Banks. This is implemented using the Bank of Indonesia Circular Letter No. 31/11/2009 on Standard Guidance for the Implementation of Anti-Money Laundering and Combating the Financing of Terrorism Program for Commercial Banks. In 2012, PBI No. 11/28/PBI/2009 was replaced by PBI No. 14/27/PBI/2012 with the same title but with additional requirement for banks in conducting due diligence.
3. Politically exposed persons (PEPs): the prevention of financial crime by monitoring in more detail customers who are a greater risk to a financial institution's reputation. Currently, the PEPs mechanism requires financial institutions to conduct enhanced due diligence (EDD) when dealing with PEPs, as stipulated in PBI No. 14/27/PBI/2012 and BI Circular Letter No. 15/21/2013.
4. Mutual legal assistance (MLA): necessary to trace the proceeds of transnational crime and to catch the perpetrators and recover the assets. MLA is regulated in Indonesia by Law No. 1 of 2006 on Mutual Legal Assistance. To ensure that tracing, freezing, seizure, confiscation and return of assets can work effectively, MLA needs to be based on the available treaties and conventions.
5. Geographical information system (GIS): a computer system, capable of entry, retrieval, data analysis and display of geographical data, is useful for providing information on the location, size and type of forests being deforested. This can help the forest management units, the law enforcement agencies, the audit agencies and civil society to monitor forest cover. Based on Law No. 11 of 2008 on information and electronic transaction, the results of GIS analysis can be used as evidence in court. Evidence in the form of maps or the results of GIS analysis are included as legal evidence in accordance with arts 1(1), (4), 5(1), 5(2) and 5(3) of the Law.

Integrated institutional roles

The implementation of an integrated law enforcement approach involves six institutional components which are: law enforcement agencies, a financial intelligence unit, the forest related-sector, audit agencies, civil society and financial institutions. More details regarding these components are as follow (Santoso *et al.* 2011):

1. Law enforcement agencies take the lead in law enforcement efforts to combat illegal logging and related crimes. This includes the anti-corruption commission (KPK) and civil servant investigators, particularly from the Ministry of Forestry, in addition to the regular law enforcement agencies.
2. A financial intelligence unit has the role of processing the data of suspicious transaction reports provided by financial institutions. In Indonesia, this is the Indonesian Transaction Reporting and Analysis Center (INTRAC).
3. Forest-related agencies include the Ministry of Forestry (Central and Regional), forestry businesses and professionals in the forestry sector (e.g. forestry business lawyers). This component has the role of providing information, related to forestry, to law enforcement agencies.
4. Audit agencies provide information related to indications of corruption in forest management and also information on State losses resulting from forest-related crimes. This component consists of the Supreme Audit Board (BPK), the Government Internal Audit (BPKP), the Inspectorate General Unit of MOF and independent auditors.
5. Financial institutions have the role of providing information on suspicious transactions. This component includes the Central Bank of Indonesia, commercial banks, community banks, Islamic banks, the Indonesian Capital Market and Financial Institutions Supervisory Agency (Bapepam), security companies, investment management funds, custodians, trustees, insurance companies, pension funds and financing agencies.
6. Civil society has the role of providing any information related to forest crimes, or any indication of forest crimes, to law enforcement agencies, including NGOs, international organizations and donors.

In practice, implementation of the integrated law enforcement approach is based on Indonesian criminal procedures, from the investigation phase until the final phase of the execution of the court decision, wherein implementation of each of the Forestry Law, Anti-Corruption Law and Anti-Money Laundering Law are combined.

The first step, as regulated in the Criminal Procedures Code and related laws and regulations, involves an investigation that assesses the information about the occurrence of an alleged crime, generally including the size of the area illegally logged, the volume of illegal logs and the location. At this stage the information can be obtained by civil society or by law enforcement agencies. Using anti-corruption instruments, the initial information can be followed by an investigation of State loss, provided by the Supreme Audit Board (Badan Pemeriksa Keuangan – BPK) in its annual audit report. If there are reports of State loss from the forestry sector, then, according to the law, law enforcement agencies are required to investigate.

Using customer due diligence and enhanced due diligence principles, financial service providers (FSPs) identify customers who are politically exposed persons and their financial profile. Furthermore, through BI Circular Letter No. 11/31/2009, FSPs are also encouraged to identify customers who are connected to forestry-related businesses as high-risk customers. When FSPs find irregularities in these customers' profile transactions, they must report this to INTRAC, which will analyse it for any indication of corruption and report their findings to law enforcement agencies (Indonesia 2010).

The second step is based on reports obtained. In general, the police will need to go to the field to obtain evidence of the loss of timber and illegal logging activities and also for evidence of corruption relating to the illegal logging. Based on the Anti-Corruption and Anti-Money Laundering Law, the police can collaborate with the Anti-Corruption Commission (KPK), INTRAC and the Supreme Audit Board. In this step, asset tracing and asset freezing can be used to pursue the proceeds of crime.

The third step is for the prosecutor to build an indictment after the evidence has been collected. The indictment itself can be developed to deal separately with illegal logging, corruption and money laundering. However, it may also combine any of the three, either layered or alternately. When sufficient evidence has been found, as regulated in arts 65, 70 and 71 of Law No. 8 of 2010, the court may freeze the account or temporarily suspend the transactions that have been associated with the crime in question. Freezing or suspension will certainly help prevent the disappearance of the proceeds of crime, which are in fact the State's loss and will be returned to the State. The freezing and suspension of assets is not possible when handling cases of illegal logging using only Forestry Law.

The fourth step is the trial, where the indictment needs to be proven before a judge who decides whether the defendant is guilty of the charges, how long the sentence will be, the amount of the fines and the State loss that should be returned by the defendant.

The fifth step continues recovery of the State loss due to the crime. The asset recovery mechanism may engage international treaties or mutual legal assistance (MLA) if the proceeds of the crime are offshore. Stolen asset recovery is the only instrument provided by the anti-corruption regime.

The five steps are shown in Figure 11.1.

Challenges and opportunities

Despite the opportunities provided by the 'follow the money' approach, Indonesia lacks capacity in using it, particularly within its law enforcement agencies. This is not limited to police officers or prosecutors; forestry officers also need to better understand these instruments. Furthermore, to 'follow the money' requires

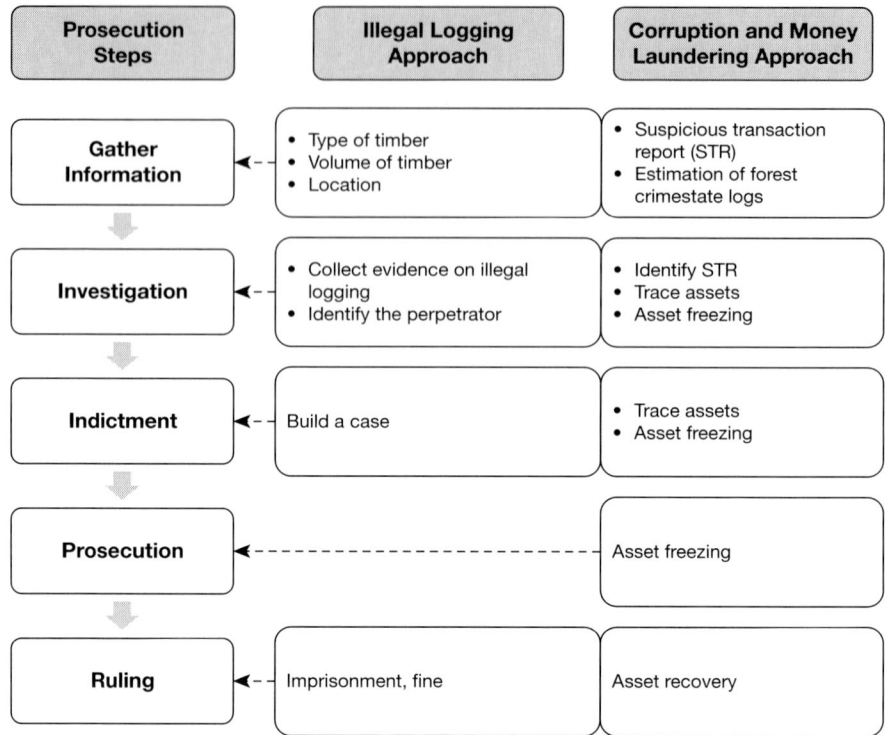

Figure 11.1 Steps in the implementation of ILEA on forest crimes

cooperation among various agencies and actors, both national and international. At the national level, there is little history of cooperation amongst law enforcement agencies (police, prosecutors, KPK) or between these agencies and the Ministry of Forestry. This magnifies the challenges of building international legal cooperation.

Despite the challenges, there are opportunities for KPK and INTRAC, for example, to provide the initial infrastructure support and for the issuance of supporting government regulations. One important development in implementing this approach was the issuance of Circular Letter No. 11/31/DPNP/2009 for the implementation of PBI No. 11/31/DPNP/2009 by the Bank of Indonesia. This Circular Letter is specifically intended for customer due diligence (CDD) for banking customers, with particular attention on those in the forestry sector. One of the provisions for CDD requires banks to request their forest-based business clients to provide documents related to their business. The provisions also provide a list of documents to be requested and recommend that banks conduct field verification using GIS analysis (Sinaga, Setiono and Mardiah, forthcoming). The two regulations were recently replaced with new regulations (PBI No. 14/27/PBI/2012 and Circular Letter 15/21/DPNP/2013) on the same topic with further requirements for banks in conducting CDD and enhanced due diligence. The new regulations maintain particular attention on banking customers in the forestry sector.

Predicate crime investigators, namely the Indonesian police, prosecutors, Corruption Eradication Commission (KPK), National Narcotics Agency (BNN) and the Directorate General of Tax and Directorate General of Customs, from the Ministry of Finance, now have the authority to investigate money laundering under Law No. 8 of 2010 (which revised Law No. 25 of 2003) on the Prevention and Eradication of Money Laundering Crimes (INTRAC 2010). It provides INTRAC with more authority to entirely or partly suspend transactions with assistance from financial institutions. KPK and BNN can now receive and request analysis reports from INTRAC in addition to other law enforcement agencies (Dermawan *et al.* 2011).

Conclusions and recommendations

The forest law enforcement approach in Indonesia, which emphasizes following the suspect, does not work effectively in catching the masterminds of forest-related crime.

The high rate of deforestation in Indonesia cannot be reduced simply by addressing illegal logging using only 'follow the wood'. This approach lacks instruments to combat these crimes effectively and efficiently. Not only is this approach ineffective but it also only catches small players in the big scheme of illegal logging.

Forest-related crimes also need to be urgently addressed, since illegal logging is not the only crime in deforestation. 'Follow the money' is an approach that has been tried and tested with other crimes (e.g. drug trafficking) that have high levels of organization and that cross international borders. The characteristics of forest-related crimes are similar to these and 'follow the money' is an approach more likely to lead to the masterminds and to the proceeds of crimes. In order to be successful in catching the masterminds, law enforcement needs to follow the proceeds of crimes, which are their lifeblood, by combined use of anti-money laundering and anti-corruption instruments. It requires the support of instruments and agencies to integrate 'follow the wood' and 'follow the money' to ensure that each of the actors involved in forest-related crime is apprehended.

However, there are several enabling conditions needed to ensure the effective implementation of this approach in the cases of forest-related crimes. The first is to increase the knowledge and skills of the Indonesian police and state prosecutors in using the instruments of anti-corruption and anti-money laundering in the forestry sector. The second is the need to build real and strong cooperation among law enforcement agencies, financial intelligence units, financial institutions, forestry agencies and audit institutions. Without real cooperation, this approach will be very difficult to implement, and forestry-related crimes will result in yet further loss of forest cover and will be difficult to reduce. The third enabling condition is international cooperation with countries that are frequently the destination of the proceeds of crime from the forestry sector.

Tangible results can be expected from the implementation of this integrated law enforcement approach, to reduce illegal logging crimes or crimes related to the forestry sector. By focusing on tracing and recovering the proceeds of crime, it is expected that the illicit benefits of crime – and in turn forest-related crimes themselves – can be reduced.

Notes

1 Supreme Court Decision No. 380 K/Pid.Sus/2007.
2 Acronyms have been used to safeguard the names of defendants even though the case has been processed by law.
3 Supreme Court Decision No. 736 K/Pid.Sus/2009.

References

Antaranews (2008) 'KPK handed over Rp. 346,8 billion to the State Treasury', March 18. Available online at www.antaranews.com/print/1205821916 (accessed 10 January 2013).

Anti Corruption Clearing House (n.d.) 'Nota Kesepakatan Bersama: Percepatan Pengukuhan Kawasan Hutan.' *Anti Corruption Clearing House.* Available online at http://acch.kpk.go.id/nota-kesepakatan-bersama-percepatan-pengukuhan-kawasan-hutan (accessed 2 December 2013).

Applegate, G., Chokkalingam, U. and Suyanto (2001) *The Underlying Causes and Impacts of Fires in South-east Asia: Final Report,* Bogor: CIFOR and ICRAF. Available online at www.cifor.cgiar.org/fire/pdf/pdf45.pdf (accessed 10 January 2013).

Bank of Indonesia Circular Letter No. 31/11/2009 on the Standard Guidance for the Implementation of Anti Money Laundering and Combating the Financing of Terrorism Program for Commercial Bank.

Center for International Forestry Research (CIFOR) (2011) *Project Final Report: International Cooperation for Helping Countries Facing an Illegal Logging Crisis Project (Integrated Law Enforcement Approach),* unpublished report.

Center for International Forestry Research (CIFOR) (forthcoming) *Strengthening Indonesia's Forest Law Enforcement with Mutual Legal Assistance,* Bogor: CIFOR.

Central Bank of Indonesia Regulation (PBI) No. 3/23/PBI/2001 on Amendment of Bank Indonesia Regulation No. 3/10/PBI/2001 on the Implementation of Know Your Customer Principles.

Central Bank of Indonesia Regulation (PBI) No. 5/21/PBI/2003 on Second Amendment of Bank Indonesia Regulation No 3/10/PBI/2001 on the Application of Know Your Customer Principles.

Central Bank of Indonesia Regulation (PBI) No. 11/28/PBI/2009 on the Implementation of Anti Money Laundering and Combating the Financing of Terrorism Program for Commercial Bank.

Contreras-Hermosill, A. (2002) *Law Compliance in the Forestry Sector: An Overview,* Washington DC: International Bank for Reconstruction and Development/World Bank. Available online at http://siteresources.worldbank.org/WBI/Resources/wbi37205.pdf (accessed 10 January 2013).

Daniel, T. and Maton, J. (2008) 'Civil proceedings to recover corruptly acquired assets of public officials', in M. Peith. (ed.) *Recovering Stolen Assets*, New York: Peter Lang.

Decree No. 21/Kpts-II/2001 on Criteria and Standard of Permit for Commercial Timber Forest Product Utilization for Plantation Forest on Production Forest.

Dermawan, A., Petkova, E., Sinaga, A., Muhajir, M. and Indriatmoko, Y. (2011) *Preventing the Risk of Corruption in REDD+ in Indonesia*, Bogor: CIFOR. Available online at www.cifor.org/publications/pdf_files/WPapers/WP80Dermawan.pdf (accessed 10 January 2013).

Food and Agriculture Organization (FAO) (2001) *State of the World's Forest 2001*, Rome, Italy: FAO.

Food and Agriculture Organization (FAO) (2007) *State of the World's Forest*, Rome, Italy: FAO.

Food and Agriculture Organization (FAO) (2010) *Global Forest Resources Assessment 2010*, Rome, Italy: FAO.

Forest Watch Indonesia (FWI) and Global Forest Watch (GFW) (2002) *State of the Forest: Indonesia*, Bogor/Washington, DC: FWI and GFW.

Gupta, A. and Siebert, U. (2004) 'Combating forest corruption', *Journal of Sustainable Forestry*, 19(1): 337–49. Available online at http://dx.doi.org/10.1300/J091v19n01_15 (accessed 10 January 2013).

Human Rights Watch (HRW) (2009) *'Wild Money': The Human Rights Consequences of Illegal Logging and Corruption in Indonesia's Forestry Sector*, New York: HRW.

Ibrahim, A. (2009) 'Upaya Pemerintah RI untuk Mempersempit Ruang Gerak Kejahatan Kehutanan' (Government Efforts to Constrain Forest Crimes), paper presented at the Seminar on Integrated Law Enforcement Efforts to Combat Illegal Logging, 29 June 2009.

Indonesian Corruption Watch (ICW) (2008) 'From illegal logging, KPK handed over Rp. 346 billion', 18 March 2008. Available online at www.antikorupsi.org/en/content/dari-illegal-logging-kpk-setor-rp-346-m (accessed 18 July 2013).

Indonesian Corruption Watch (ICW) (2010) *KPK harus memimpin pemberantasan korupsi dan mafia kehutanan*. Jakarta: ICW. Available online at http://antikorupsi.org/id/content/kpk-harus-mempimpin-pemberantasan-korupsi-dan-mafia-kehutanan (accessed 27 June 2013).

Indonesian Transaction Reporting and Analysis Center (INTRAC) (2010) *Important Stipulations in the Law of Prevention and Eradication of Anti Money Laundering*, Jakarta: INTRAC.

Indonesia Supreme Audit Board (BPK) (2008) *The Examination Result of Second Semester of 2008: Forest Management and Industrial Plantation Forest Development*, Jakarta: Indonesian Supreme Audit Board.

Indrarto, G.B., Murharjanti, P., Khatarina, J., Pulungan, I., Ivalerina, F., Rahman, J., Prana, M.N., Resosudarmo, I.A.P. and Muharrom, E. (2012) *The Context of REDD+ in Indonesia: Drivers, Agents and Institutions*, Working Paper 92, Bogor: CIFOR.

Koyuncu, C. and Yilmaz, R. (2009) 'The impact of corruption on deforestation: a cross-country evidence', *The Journal of Developing Area*, 42(2): 213–22.

Law No. 1 of 2006 on Mutual Legal Assistance (Republic of Indonesia).

Law No. 11 of 2008 on Information and Electronic Transaction (Republic of Indonesia).

Law No. 15 of 2002 on Money Laundering (Republic of Indonesia).

Law No. 17 of 2006 on Custom (Republic of Indonesia).

Law No. 20 of 2001 on the Revision of Law No. 31of 1999 on Corruption Eradication (Republic of Indonesia).

Law No 25 of 2003 on the Revision of Law No. 15 Year 2002 on Money Laundering (Republic of Indonesia).

Law No. 31 of 1999 on Corruption Eradication (Republic of Indonesia).

Law No. 32 of 2009 on Environmental Protection and Management (Republic of Indonesia).

Law No. 41 of 1999 on Forestry (Republic of Indonesia).

Law No. 8 of 2010 on the Prevention and Eradication of Money Laundering (Republic of Indonesia).

Ministry of Forestry (MOF) (2007) *Indonesia Forestry Statistics of 2007*, Jakarta: Indonesian Ministry of Forestry.

Ministry of Forestry (MOF) (2008) *Calculation of Deforestation Rate in Indonesia in 2008*, Jakarta: Inventory and Forest Mapping Center, Forestry Planology Agency, Indonesian Ministry of Forestry.

Santoso, T., Chandra, R., Sinaga, A. C., Muhajir, M. and Mardiah, S. (2011) *Guidelines on Investigation and Indictment Using the Integrated Law Enforcement Approach*, Bogor: CIFOR.

Setiono, B., and Husein, Y. (2005) 'Fighting forest crime and promoting prudent banking for sustainable forest management: the anti money laundering approach', *CIFOR Occasional Paper*, 44.

Sinaga, A.C., Setiono, B. and Mardiah, S. (forthcoming) *The Role of Banks in Preventing Anti Money Laundering in the Forestry Sector*, Bogor: CIFOR.

Sunderlin, W.D. and Resosudarmo, I.A.P. (1996) *Rates and Causes of Deforestation in Indonesia: Towards a Resolution of the Ambiguities*, Bogor: CIFOR.

Tacconi, L., Obidzinski, K. and Agung, F. (2004) *Learning Lessons to Promote Forest Certification and Control Illegal Logging in Indonesia*, Bogor: CIFOR.

Tanzi, V. (1998) 'Corruption around the world: causes, consequences, scope and cures', *IMF Staff Paper*, 4(4), 559–94.

World Bank (2006) *Strengthening Forest Law Enforcement and Governance*, Washington, DC: World Bank.

Yuntho, E., Sari, I.D. and Diansyah, F. (2009) *Aparat yang Tidak Berpihak pada Pemberantasan Illegal Logging: Hasil Eksaminasi Publik Putusan Pengadilan Negeri Jayapura*, Jakarta: Indonesia Corruption Watch (ICW).

12 Limitations of anti-money laundering techniques

Controlling imports of illegally logged timber

Duncan Brack

Illegal logging and the international trade in illegally logged timber is a major problem for many timber-producing countries, particularly in the developing world. It causes environmental damage, costs governments billions of dollars in lost revenue, promotes corruption and undermines the rule of law and good governance; in some cases it has funded armed conflict. It retards sustainable development in some of the poorest countries of the world.

In recent years, however, governments have paid increasing attention to illegal logging and the associated trade in illegal timber. International attention began to focus on the topic during the late 1990s, and the inclusion of illegal logging as one element of the 1998–2002 G8 Action Programme on Forests in particular helped to trigger widespread international discussions on the issue.

It has always been recognised that consumer countries contribute to the problems of illegal logging by importing timber and wood products without ensuring that they are legally sourced. In fact, until recently, importing countries have had few legal mechanisms available to exclude illegal timber even if they could detect it – with a few exceptions (including the small number of tree species listed under the Convention on International Trade in Endangered Species of Wild Fauna and Flora – CITES), it was not unlawful to import timber products produced illegally in a foreign country.

Illegal logging and the EU FLEGT initiative

In response to the developing international debate, and in recognition of its role as one of the world's largest timber importers, the EU published its Action Plan for Forest Law Enforcement, Governance and Trade (FLEGT) in 2003; it remains the most ambitious set of measures adopted by any consumer country or bloc to date.[1] The Action Plan includes:

- The negotiation of FLEGT voluntary partnership agreements (VPAs) with timber-producing countries. These include a licensing system designed to identify legal products and license them for import to the EU (unlicensed products will be denied entry), combined with capacity-building assistance to partner countries to set up the licensing scheme, improve enforcement and, where necessary, reform their laws.

- Examination of the extent to which existing laws in EU member states – for example, on theft or money laundering – could be applied to imports of timber produced illegally in foreign countries, particularly products originating from countries not participating in VPAs and therefore not covered by the licensing scheme.
- Consideration of additional legislative options to prohibit the import of illegal timber to the EU should existing national legislation prove inadequate.
- Encouragement for voluntary industry initiatives, and government procurement policy, to limit purchases to legal sources.
- Encouragement for financial institutions to scrutinise flows of finance to the forestry industry.

Examination of money laundering legislation

In pursuance of the second component listed above – examination of existing national legislation – studies of legislation in six EU member states (Estonia, Germany, Italy, Netherlands, Spain and the UK) were carried out in 2005–06.[2] In general, the studies analysed the applicability of criminal law, civil law, customs misdeclaration and money laundering laws. A workshop was organised by the German and Dutch governments in 2004 specifically on the potential use of anti-money laundering techniques in the case of timber logged illegally outside the EU and then imported into it.[3]

The analysis in this section rests largely on the UK national study. While British legislation on money laundering is somewhat tougher and more extensive than that in some other EU member states, the conclusions are largely applicable throughout the EU. The UK study itself was informed by a legal opinion commissioned by Chatham House on the applicability of money laundering legislation, and discussion on it at two subsequent meetings.[4]

Money laundering is the processing of the proceeds of crime in order to disguise their illegal origin. National legislation allowing authorities to tackle money laundering and seize the proceeds of criminal activity (financial or physical, i.e. property or goods purchased with the proceeds) has grown in importance with the expansion of the illegal trade in narcotics and of international organised crime more broadly. The main question the studies outlined above sought to address was whether this legislation could be used to seize the proceeds of illegal logging carried out in foreign countries, and thus help to reduce illegal logging and to stem imports of illegal timber into the UK or EU.

Money laundering laws in the UK

In the UK, the Proceeds of Crime Act 2002 (POCA) updated and strengthened previous legislation, creating a single set of money laundering offences applicable throughout the UK to the proceeds of all crimes. It strengthened and consolidated the criminal confiscation regime, provided for a civil recovery scheme to recover the proceeds of unlawful conduct in cases where criminal prosecution could not be brought and established the Assets Recovery Agency (ARA) to improve the recovery of the proceeds of crime.

There are three main routes by which the POCA seeks to target those who benefit from or deal in the proceeds of crime: criminal confiscation (Part 2), civil recovery (Part 5) and money laundering (Part 7).

Under criminal confiscation, if a defendant is convicted of an offence, the court has the power to decide whether the defendant has a 'criminal lifestyle' – that is, is a career criminal who has no legitimate source of income, so that every-thing the defendant has acquired and spent over the preceding six years represents the proceeds of their criminal activity. The burden of proof in disproving these assumptions lies on the defendant. If the court decides that the defendant does have a criminal lifestyle, then it must go on to consider whether the defendant has benefited from their general criminal conduct (all criminal conduct, whenever it occurred); if it does not, it can still consider whether the defendant has benefited from the particular criminal conduct in the case in question.

In this case, criminal conduct is conduct that constitutes an offence in the UK or would constitute an offence in the UK if it occurred there. So if the activity in question is illegal under UK law, then the proceeds of the activity can be subject to recovery, provided they are deposited or disposed of within the UK. The fact that the activity itself may have taken place overseas or be carried out by non-UK nationals is not an obstacle.

The civil recovery regime established by Part 5 of the POCA enables the recovery of the proceeds of criminal activity in civil proceedings even where no criminal convictions have been sought or obtained. The proceedings can be brought against the person holding the property at the time, whether they themselves have acted unlawfully or not. Unlike the criminal confiscation procedure, unlawful conduct in this case is defined as illegal conduct occurring in the UK, or conduct occurring in a foreign country which would be illegal both in the UK *and* in the foreign country. The court has to decide on a balance of probabilities whether any matters that are alleged to constitute unlawful conduct have occurred.

Property remains recoverable even after its disposition by the individual who originally obtained it through unlawful conduct, even if it has been converted into other forms – for example, through purchasing assets with the monetary proceeds of the crime. Property ceases to be recoverable, however, if it passes through the hands of a purchaser acting in good faith and without notice that the property was recoverable.

The money laundering offences specified in the POCA can be broadly divided into the conduct itself and failure to disclose engagement in an activity that might indicate money laundering. The first category includes:

- Concealing, disguising or converting criminal property, or removing criminal property from the UK. This covers any act that conceals or disguises the nature, source, location or disposition of criminal property, or its movement, ownership and any other rights (POCA s 327).

- Participating in an arrangement that a person knows or suspects will facilitate the acquisition, retention, use or control of criminal property by or on behalf of another person (POCA s 328).
- Acquisition, use or possession of criminal property – though the purchase of stolen goods at a fair market value, without knowledge or suspicion of their illegal origin, is a legitimate defence (POCA s 329).

Property is defined as 'criminal property' if it constitutes or represents a benefit from criminal conduct, and the alleged offender knows or suspects that it constitutes or represents such a benefit.

The second category, failure to disclose, is an offence if a person knows or suspects, or has reasonable grounds for knowing or suspecting, that another person is engaged in money laundering; the information came to that person in the course of business in the regulated sector; and that person does not make the required disclosure as soon as practicable after receiving the information. The regulated sector covers all businesses involved in accepting deposits and managing investments, including banks, estate agents, accountants, lawyers, etc.

Section 330 of the POCA creates the obligation on anyone who receives information in the course of a business in the regulated sector to report suspicions of the proceeds of any criminal conduct to the authorities. This is the case where the individual has *reasonable grounds* for knowing or suspecting that another person is engaged in money laundering, even if they did not *actually* know or suspect this to be the case. This is quite an onerous requirement, reflecting the expectation that employees in the regulated sector should be capable of exercising a higher level of due diligence in handling transactions than those employed in other types of business, and should be able to recognise attempts at undertaking suspicious transactions.

The maximum penalties provided for offences under the POCA are 14 years' imprisonment for money laundering offences, and five years' imprisonment for failure to disclose or tipping off a suspect.

Money laundering and illegal logging

It would appear that UK money laundering laws are potentially applicable in the case of illegal timber entering the UK. The legislation is primarily aimed at illegal activities occurring outside the UK but where the proceeds are disposed of in the UK – which is exactly the situation with illegal logging. The illegally logged timber itself does not necessarily have to be tracked; it is the disposal of the proceeds of the illegal logging, or trade in the illegal timber, that is important.

The link between the illegal activity and the money laundering offence does not have to be proved absolutely, and neither does the link between the underlying offence and the money launderer. Clearly, there needs to be *some* evidence that the funds being laundered are of illegal origin, but this can take a wide variety of forms. Similarly, courts have considerable latitude to consider, and reach judgements on the basis of, a wide variety of evidence, including generally suspicious behaviour, the lack of evidence or explanations of genuine sources of funds, the use of false names or documents, and so on. The 'failure to disclose' offence places a duty on businesses handling the proceeds to report any suspicion that the funds they are processing might be the proceeds of criminal activity.

As mentioned above, as part of the study of potentially applicable legislation in the UK, Chatham House commissioned a legal opinion on the applicability of money laundering legislation. Two hypothetical – but plausible – scenarios were considered for the disposal in the UK of the proceeds of illegal logging conducted abroad.

In the first case, a UK importer bought plywood from a foreign exporter sourcing his products from a plywood mill using illegal logs; no investigations had been carried out, but both importer and exporter had been warned that they were dealing with illegal timber. For several reasons, this looked like a promising scenario from the point of view of applying the POCA. The illegal logging would have been a crime if it had occurred in the UK, and the plywood imported into the UK appeared to meet the definition of criminal property. Having been warned that illegal products were mixed into the supply chain, the importer should have suspected that he was dealing with the proceeds of crime.

However, in the importer's defence, the link between the original illegal logging and the plywood is likely to be tenuous and difficult to prove. It is also likely that the illegal timber would have been mixed with legal timber, making it difficult to identify or quantify the benefit. If the importer made enquiries via the exporter, and was provided with apparently convincing documentation showing legality, he might be in the clear, particularly if he operated outside the regulated sector (banks and other financial institutions), where the due diligence requirements are lower. Finally, if he purchased the plywood for an adequate consideration – that is, not for significantly less than the normal market value of the product – he might have a further defence.

The second potential scenario involved a more complex series of links. A British investment bank was part of a consortium of investors providing loan finance for the construction of a large pulp mill overseas. The host country's total existing pulp mill capacity already exceeded the total volume of timber that could be produced legally, and an independent group had warned the consortium of the likelihood of the new mill acquiring its raw material from illegal sources. The consortium received assurances from the mill's owners that government harvesting rights had been secured, but evidence was later uncovered showing the mill to be using illegally sourced logs. The consortium, including the British bank, received interest from the income earned from the mill.

Similar principles applied as in the first scenario. The interest payments received by the bank would represent a benefit from criminal conduct, and even if the payments represented 'adequate consideration' for the loan, this would not be a defence, as providing goods or services to help someone commit a crime, even at fair market value, is not consideration. Furthermore, operating in the regulated sector as it did, the bank should have both made a disclosure to the authorities and carried out its own due diligence procedure. Had the bank made such a disclosure at the time, however, and not been subject to a restraining order by the relevant agency, it would have been free to proceed with arranging the loan.

Our overall conclusion was that the POCA did provide a basis for legal action against imports of illegal timber into the UK and also any investments associated with it – at least in theory.

Practical considerations

An equally important matter, however, is whether the legislation was likely to be used in practice. In reality, there are several constraints to its effective implementation in the case of illegal logging.

As noted above, there remains the problem of showing that the products handled by the UK importer were themselves illegal and that he knew that they were. Operating outside the regulated sector, timber importers are not subject to the same due diligence requirements as banks and other financial institutions. In any case, it may be very difficult for the relevant authorities to detect the fact that products, or money, entering the UK *are* the proceeds of illegal logging. It is not likely to be easy to collect evidence of the original crime from the country of origin, particularly where there is no domestic investigation or prosecution under way; and in some cases enforcement agencies in the countries of origin are themselves prone to corruption or collusion in the crime and in falsifying documentation. The importer may also have a defence if the products were purchased at market value.

In general, there is a low level of awareness, and virtually no experience, within UK enforcement agencies of illegal logging issues and the possible links between illegal logging (or environmental crime more broadly) and money laundering. Enforcement agencies in general, including the Crown Prosecution Service, have competing priorities, including the drugs trade, people trafficking, arms trafficking and terrorism. The Crown Prosecution Service clearly considers illegal logging abroad to be a lower priority than these other offences, and the likely complexity and costs of investigation and prosecution will always be set against the likelihood of securing a conviction.

The sheer volume of reports submitted under the POCA makes detailed scrutiny difficult; in 2004, the National Criminal Intelligence Service estimated that it was processing about 100,000 reports from the regulated sector per year. And in trying to spot money laundering, financial intelligence units (the government agencies dealing with money laundering and other financial crimes) tend to look for abnormal flows of money – cases where an unusual series of deposits or transfers suggest possibly illegal behaviour. In the case of illegally logged timber entering the UK, the pattern of financial flows between the institutions financing and carrying out the logging or processing operations and those selling and purchasing the products may look exactly like the normal series of transactions that would be expected; the fact that the products being imported are illegal may be difficult or impossible to detect just from examining the movement of the associated money.

In general, then, the chance of using money laundering laws successfully to tackle imports of illegal timber into the UK (and, by extension into other consumer countries) seems to be very low. There are, however, three situations under which it might be substantially higher:

- Where the offence is committed by, or involves, banks or other actors in the regulated sector – who have a higher degree of responsibility to apply due diligence procedures.
- Where there is an ongoing investigation or successful prosecution in the country of origin. In this case, the use of the POCA against the profits of the operations disposed of in the UK may provide a valuable reinforcement to the activities of the overseas enforcement agencies, helping to punish not just those carrying out the illegal activities but also those individuals and companies financing them and disposing of the proceeds.
- Where there is good cooperation with the authorities in the country of origin. However, in this case it may be much more fruitful to pursue a FLEGT voluntary partnership agreement (VPA), which covers all imports from the country to the EU (see next section).

Alternative options

Because of these practical limitations, most of those involved in the debates in the EU in 2004–06 concluded that the use of anti-money laundering laws was not likely to be a particularly valuable option in attempting to exclude illegal timber from the EU market. Attention turned instead to a range of alternative measures; similar debates have taken place in the US and other consumer countries.[5] A series of options have emerged.

Bilateral agreements with timber-producing countries specifically aimed at the timber trade have lain at the heart of the EU's FLEGT Action Plan. Six VPAs have now been agreed, between the EU and Cameroon, Central African Republic, Republic of Congo, Ghana, Indonesia and Liberia. Negotiations are currently under way with Côte d'Ivoire, Democratic Republic of Congo, Gabon, Guyana, Honduras, Malaysia, Thailand and Viet Nam, and many other countries have expressed an interest in entering negotiations. These VPAs will establish a licensing scheme under which all exports to the EU will have to be accompanied by an independently verified licence of legality. They are also a vehicle through which to agree improvements in standards of governance in producer countries, and to deliver capacity-building assistance to them, and in these respects have already had positive impacts. They offer one of the best ways of controlling the trade, at least potentially – they are proving slow to establish, and no FLEGT licences have yet been issued.

The US has included provisions on illegal logging and the timber trade in a number of its free trade agreements, most notably that with Peru. This may offer opportunities to restrict the trade in illegal timber, though the outcome in Peru so far has not been particularly encouraging, with evidence of widespread corruption and false documentation being used to undermine the aims of the agreement.[6]

Broader measures to exclude illegal timber from consumer countries lack some of the benefits of specific bilateral agreements, but can be implemented more quickly and with greater coverage. In the US, the extension of the Lacey Act[7] to timber in 2008 (making it unlawful to import or handle timber produced illegally overseas) was a significant development, providing the US with an effective means of encouraging the timber industry to exercise 'due care' and preventing imports of illegal timber. Two enforcement actions have so far taken place, against Gibson Guitar, which was found to have been importing illegally produced rosewood from Madagascar for several years, and also against a single small import of decorative hardwoods from Peru.

The EU's equivalent broader measure is the EU Timber Regulation, which entered into force in March 2013 (this was the 'additional legislative option' deemed necessary after the analysis of national legislation referred to above concluded that existing laws were inadequate). This prohibits the placing of illegally harvested timber and timber products on the EU market and also requires operators to implement a system of due diligence in order to minimise the risk of doing so. In November 2012, the Australian Parliament agreed the Illegal Logging Prohibition Act 2012 (Cth), which contains very similar provisions.

Public procurement policies aimed at purchasing legal (and, usually, sustainable) timber can prove very effective in excluding illegal timber from segments of a consumer-country market. Although, in most countries, government purchasing usually accounts for no more than 10 per cent of the market, it can have a wider impact, through raising the profile of the issue and through importers' desires for relatively simple supply chains. UK timber procurement policy is believed to be partially responsible for the dramatic rise in the proportion of UK timber which is certified as sustainable; in 2008, certified products accounted for more than 80 per cent of the UK market (both domestic production and imports).[8] Thirteen countries around the world now possess timber procurement policies aimed at sourcing legal and sustainable timber: Austria, Belgium, Denmark, Finland, France, Germany, Japan, Mexico, the Netherlands, New Zealand, Norway, Switzerland and the UK; a number of other countries, mostly EU member states, are considering adopting similar policies, and many local and regional governments in these and other countries also possess some kind of timber procurement policy.

Conclusions

The extent to which money laundering legislation can be used effectively in the case of imports of illegally logged timber to consumer countries depends on the objective.

If the aim is to reinforce individual enforcement actions taken in the producer country in which the illegal logging has taken place, seizing the profits of such activities when they are disposed of in foreign countries, then anti-money laundering laws may be helpful – though probably only where a successful court case has actually been brought in the country of origin.

If the aim is systematically to exclude imports of illegal timber from consumer countries, then money laundering laws are not likely to be of much use. The vast bulk of illegal timber entering consumer countries has never been associated with any enforcement action in its countries of origin, whether due to lack of capacity, lack of political will or corruption. Although anti-money laundering techniques could pick off a small proportion of imports, they are never likely to be able to target significant volumes.

For a more comprehensive approach to preventing illegal timber products from entering consumer countries, other options are likely to be much more effective. These include bilateral agreements such as the FLEGT VPAs, broader approaches such as the US Lacey Act, the EU Timber Regulation or the Australian Illegal Logging Prohibition Act 2012 (Cth), and the use of public procurement policy to source legal (and sustainable) timber. An ideal combination of measures would probably be:

- VPAs (or similar) to establish a licensing system with timber-producing countries, covering all exports of timber products; this has the benefits of establishing an identification system for legal timber and also promoting governance reform, which has important implications for the long-term development of sustainable forest management and trade.
- Measures to deal with timber imports from non-partner countries – for example, a measure like the US Lacey Act, EU Timber Regulation or the Australian Illegal Logging Prohibition Act 2012 (Cth), which provides a powerful incentive, or a legal requirement, for importers to scrutinise their supply chains.
- Public procurement policies aimed at legal and sustainable timber, helping to create protected markets in which legal and sustainable timber is not undercut by cheaper illegal and unsustainable products.
- The use of anti-money laundering techniques to follow up enforcement actions in the country of origin of illegal timber.

Notes

1 Commission of the European Communities (May 2003) *Communication from the Commission to the Council and the European Parliament: Forest Law Enforcement, Governance and Trade (FLEGT) – Proposal for an EU Action Plan*, Brussels: Commission of the European Communities. Available online at http://eur-lex.europa.eu/LexUriServ/LexUriServ. do?uri=CELEX:52003DC0251:EN:HTML (accessed 10 December 2013).
2 These studies are all available at www.illegal-logging.info (accessed 10 December 2013).
3 See www.illegal-logging.info for the workshop papers and report (accessed 10 December 2013).

4 See www.illegal-logging.info (accessed 10 December 2013).
5 For more details, see Brack, D. and Buckrell, J. (March 2011) *Controlling Illegal Logging: Consumer-Country Measures*, UK: Chatham House. Available online at www.illegal-logging.info/item_single.php?it_id=1076&it=document (accessed 10 December 2013).
6 See Environmental Investigation Agency (EIA) (2012) *The Laundering Machine: How Fraud and Corruption in Peru's System are Destroying the Future of its Forests*, EIA Global. Available online at http://eia-global.org/news-media/the-laundering-machine (accessed 10 December 2013).
7 16 USC (1990).
8 UK Timber Trade Federation (January 2010) *UK Timber Industry Certification*, London: Timber Trade Federation. Available online at www.illegal-logging.info/item_single.php?it_id=861&it=document (accessed 10 December 2013).

References

Brack, D. and Buckrell, J. (March 2011) *Controlling Illegal Logging: Consumer-Country Measures*, UK: Chatham House. Available online at www.illegal-logging.info/item_single.php?it_id=1076&it=document (accessed 10 December 2013).

Commission of the European Communities (May 2003) *Communication from the Commission to the Council and the European Parliament: Forest Law Enforcement, Governance and Trade (FLEGT) – Proposal for an EU Action Plan*, Brussels: Commission of the European Communities. Available online at http://eur-lex.europa.eu/LexUriServ/LexUriServ.do?uri=CELEX:52003DC0251:EN:HTML (accessed 10 December 2013).

Environmental Investigation Agency (EIA) (2012) *The Laundering Machine: How Fraud and Corruption in Peru's System are Destroying the Future of Its Forests*, EIA Global. Available online at http://eia-global.org/news-media/the-laundering-machine (accessed 10 December 2013).

UK Timber Trade Federation (January 2010) *UK Timber Industry Certification*, London: Timber Trade Federation. Available online at www.illegal-logging.info/item_single.php?it_id=861&it=document (accessed 10 December 2013).

Part VI

Improving environmental enforcement through financial intelligence cooperation

13 Governmental coordination to enforce environmental laws

Perspectives of an Australian regulator

Grant Pink[1]

Introduction

The Australian Government's federal environment department (the Department of Environment, Water, Populations and Communities (DSEWPaC, renamed in late 2013 as the Department of Environment) ('the department')) has more than a decade of experience in the use of networks and networking, as part of governmental coordination as it relates to building capacity to undertake environmental enforcement activities. These experiences mainly relate to the department's increased commitment to and involvement with environmental enforcement networks ('networks') in what could be described as its 'regulatory journey' for the period 2000 to 2011. Focussing particularly on the period from 2004 onwards, it is this regulatory journey that provides the backdrop for this chapter.

This chapter commences with an overview of the department's transition into its increased regulatory role. It also provides a contemporary view of the department's operating environment in respect to environmental enforcement, specific aspects of which include: the general expectation that networking should occur within the public sector; the specific growth and use of networks by environmental enforcement agencies, some examples and experiences of the department in relation to government coordination, principally through existing mainstream law enforcement liaison and networks, and its lead role in one regional network and involvement in other networks; consideration of systems and coordination mechanisms that have been developed and exploited to combat environmental and transnational environmental crime more effectively, including a range of law enforcement responses across the available range of sanctions which could be administrative, civil or criminal in nature.[2]

The chapter then compares the experiences of the department against the experience of others (practitioners and networks) in the context of academic literature relating to networks. It concludes with some observations as to the utility of networks and provides some suggestions for how environmental enforcement agencies might maximise the benefits they derive from their involvement with networks.

Background

The department is the Australian federal government's premier environmental regulator. At 30 June 2011 it consisted of 2,945 staff, most of whom are based in the nation's capital, Canberra. Others are geographically dispersed in locations ranging from the Northern Territory through to Tasmania and as far afield as Antarctica (DSEWPaC 2011: 335). The department administers some 15 pieces of legislation that have offence or penalty provisions. These involve both terrestrial and marine environments, with the marine environment stretching to the 200 nautical mile Exclusive Economic Zone. The department also administers national legislation and is responsible for more than a dozen international treaties and conventions to which the Australian government is a signatory. Table 13.1 lists the department's administered legislation, the activities it regulates and, where applicable, the corresponding international obligations.

The department's transition to a regulatory role

The department had its genesis as a policy, programme and environmental stewardship department. It performed these advisory type functions (in various departments[3] and departmental structures) for a period in excess of a decade from 1990, and as a result developed work practices and a corporate culture which was well aligned with the functions it performed. Significant changes to the department began in 1999 with the passing of the Environment Protection and Biodiversity Conservation Act 1999 (Cth) (EPBC Act). The EPBC Act replaced seven environmental acts[4] and imposed regulatory responsibilities upon the department. This was a significant event, as it changed the 'advisors' into 'regulators'.

A former Federal Environment Minister, the Hon. Peter Garrett AM, referred to the EPBC Act as Australia's central piece of environmental legislation (Garrett 2008: 5) with a focus on those environmental issues that are *matters of national environmental significance* (MNES). The MNES are located in part 3 of the EPBC Act and include: listed threatened species and communities; listed migratory species; Ramsar wetlands of international importance; Commonwealth marine environment; world heritage properties; national heritage places; the Great Barrier Reef Marine Park; and nuclear actions.

The commencement of the EPBC Act in 2000 provided the catalyst for what was the start of the department's regulatory journey. A brief chronology below details the development and refinement of what are now the major components of the department's regulatory infrastructure and capabilities. Specifically:

- 2002 – establishment of a small Compliance Section;[5]
- 2004 – establishment of the department's first dedicated Environmental Investigative Unit (EIU), Compliance Operational Network (CON);[6] and Regulatory Compliance Executive Committee (RCEC);[7]

Table 13.1 Departmental legislation, commodities and activities, and international obligations

Legislation	Typical commodities/activities	International obligations
Aboriginal and Torres Strait Islander Heritage Protection Act 1984	The preservation and protection from injury or desecration of areas and objects in Australia and in Australian waters, being areas and objects that are of particular significance to Aboriginal and Torres Strait Islander people in accordance with their tradition.	None
Antarctic Marine Living Resources Act 1980	Activities in Australia's Antarctic Territories.	Protocol on Environmental Protection to the Antarctic Treaty (1991) (Madrid Protocol)
Antarctic Treaty (Environment Protection) Act 1980		Convention on the Conservation of Antarctic Marine Living Resources (1982)
Australian Antarctic Territory Act 1954		
Heard Island and McDonald Islands Act 1953		
Environment Protection and Biodiversity Conservation Act 1999	Activities in Commonwealth National Parks, Commonwealth Marine Reserves or affecting the environment on Commonwealth land or in Commonwealth waters. Actions having a significant impact on listed protected species, ecological communities, marine species, migratory species, wetlands of international significance, World Heritage Areas, National or Commonwealth Heritage. Nuclear actions.	The Convention on Biological Diversity (1992) The Convention on the Conservation of Migratory Species of Wild Animals (1979) (Bonn Convention) The Japan–Australia Migratory Bird Agreement (1974) (JAMBA) The China–Australia Migratory Bird Agreement (1986) (CAMBA) Convention on International Trade in Endangered Species of Wild Fauna and Flora (1975) (CITES) The Convention on Wetlands of International Importance Especially as Waterfowl Habitat Ramsar (1971) (Ramsar Convention)

(Continued)

Table 13.1 (Continued)

Legislation	Typical commodities/activities	International obligations
		Convention Concerning the Protection of the World Cultural and Natural Heritage (1975) (World Heritage Convention)
		International Convention for the Regulation of Whaling (1986) (International Whaling Convention)
Environment Protection (Sea Dumping) Act 1981	Disposal at sea.	Protocol to the Convention on the Prevention of Marine Pollution by Dumping of Wastes and Other Matter 1972 (1996) (London Protocol)
Fuel Quality Standards Act 2000	Motor fuel contamination.	None
Hazardous Waste (Regulation of Exports and Imports) Act 1989	The export or import of hazardous waste, including electronic waste.	Basel Convention on the Control of Transboundary Movements of Hazardous Wastes and their Disposal (1992) (Basel Convention)
		Convention to Ban the Importation into Forum Island Countries of Hazardous and Radioactive Wastes and to Control the Transboundary Movement and Management of Hazardous Wastes within the South Pacific Region (2001) (Waigani Convention)
Historic Shipwrecks Act 1976	Activities affecting historic shipwrecks including relics previously obtained from wrecks.	Agreement between the Netherlands and Australia concerning old Dutch shipwrecks (1972)
Ozone Protection and Synthetic Greenhouse Gas Management Act 1989	The importation, handling and disposal of ozone-depleting gases and equipment/appliances containing them.	Vienna Convention for the Protection of the Ozone Layer (1988)
		Montreal Protocol on Substances that Deplete the Ozone Layer (1989)

Product Stewardship Act 2011	Encouraging reuse, recycling, recovery, treatment or disposal of products in that class, or waste from such products, in a safe, scientific and environmentally sound way; and requiring purchasers to make product return payments in relation to products in that class.	None
Sea Installations Act 1987	Structures in Commonwealth waters	None
Water Act 2007	Management of the water resources of the Murray-Darling Basin, and other matters of national interest on water and water information.	None
Water Efficiency Labelling and Standards Act 2005	The sale and installation of water-using appliances and plumbing fittings.	None

Adapted: DSEWPaC 2011: 426–8

- 2006 – compliance function grew into two larger Compliance Sections; amendments to the EPBC Act strengthened the compliance and enforcement provisions (Early 2008: 109);
- 2007 – establishment of the first dedicated Compliance and Enforcement Branch, a newly created Monitoring and Audit Section; a Compliance Support Unit (CSU),[8] and a Compliance Management Committee (CMC).[9]

In the five-year period between 2002 and 2007, staff undertaking compliance and enforcement activities increased from around 10 to 60, where they remain at time of writing. Individual sections within the department (see Table 13.2) administer the compliance and enforcement components of legislation relevant to their mandate. Reporting and coordination of compliance and enforcement activities occurs through the CON, recently renamed as the Regulatory Compliance Managers Network (RCMN).

The Regulatory Compliance Executive Committee (RCEC) provides strategic oversight of the department's compliance and enforcement efforts. It is chaired by a Deputy Secretary and its members are around two dozen senior executive staff with compliance and enforcement responsibilities across various pieces of legislation administered by the department. Table 13.2 shows the departmental line areas with functional responsibility against their relevant legislation. The RCEC's role is '[t]o set departmental policy and direction for regulatory compliance activities and enable consistent and effective regulatory compliance and enforcement work by the portfolio' (DSEWPaC 2011: 407).

The department's operating environment

Table 13.2 highlights the fact that the legislation administered by the department covers a myriad of commodities, industries and sectors. The operating environment for these administrative tasks is compartmentalised into offences, priorities and resources, relationships and culture, and coordination mechanisms. The component parts are summarised thus:

- *Offences* – The department is now regulating more Acts, the responses to which enable it to apply administrative, civil and criminal sanctions. To do this effectively, it has required the development of a range of policies, procedures and practices. This work, in turn, has yielded increased interconnectedness with subnational, national, regional and international entities discussed later in this chapter.
- *Priorities and resources* – Like all regulators, the department has finite resources with which to perform enforcement work. It therefore prioritises its enforcement work and that which it refers to other enforcement agencies (typically to the Australian Customs and Border Protection Service (ACBPS) for matters occurring at Australia's international air and shipping ports and to the Australian Federal Police (AFP) for more serious and complex matters).[10]

Table 13.2 Departmental line areas and functional responsibility against legislation

Division	Area	Legislation/Business
Environment Assessment and Compliance	Compliance 1 Section (QLD, VIC, TAS & NT) Compliance 2 Section (NSW, ACT, WA, SA & External Territories) Environment Investigation Unit Monitoring and Audit Section Ports and Marine Section	Environment Protection and Biodiversity Conservation (EPBC) Pt 3 & 13 Environment Protection Sea Dumping (EPSD) Act 1981 Sea Installations (SI) Act 1987 EPBC Pt 7–9 Environment Protection Sea Dumping (EPSD) Act 1981 Sea Installations (SI) Act 1987
Australian Antarctic	Territories Environment and Treaties	Antarctic Marine Living Resources Act 1980 Antarctic Treaty (Environment Protection) Act 1980 Australia Antarctic Territory Act 1954 Heard Island and McDonald Islands Act 1953
Environment Quality	Fuel Quality Management Section Ozone and Synthetic Gas Team National Pollution Inventory & Hazardous Waste Section Resource Recovery & Product Innovation	Fuel Quality Standards Act 2000 Ozone Protection and Synthetic Greenhouse Gas Management Act 1989 National Environment Protection Measures (Implementation) Act 1998 Hazardous Waste (Regulation of Exports and Imports) Act 1989 Product Stewardship Act 2011
Heritage and Wildlife	Heritage Reform and Shipwrecks International Wildlife Trade Section	Historic Shipwrecks Act 1976 EPBC Act Pt 13A
Marine	Regulatory and Operational Policy Section Sustainable Fisheries Section	EPBC Act Part 15 – Marine Protected Areas EPBC Part 10, 13, 13A
Parks Australia	Parks Operational Support Protected Area Policy and Biodiscovery	EPBC Act (Div 4 of Part 15 and Regs terrestrial parks only; Part 13 re Indian Ocean Territories & terrestrial parks only; Regs Parts 9 & 12 (Indian Ocean Territories & terrestrial parks) EPBC Act Part 13 Section 301 & Regs Part 8A
Water Governance	Water Efficiency Labelling	Water Efficiency Labelling & Standards Act 2005
Water Reform	Water Regulation Section	Water Act 2007

Existing governance arrangements enable the RCEC (strategically), RCMN (operationally) and the CMP (tactically)[11] to adjust priorities and move resources about to enable the department to act responsively in regulatory matters.

- *Relationships and culture* – The move to an enforcement role required the department to consider aspects of relationships and culture – that is, relationships with entities such as the regulated community, co-regulators and its own operating culture to determine if they were appropriate and 'fit for purpose' in a regulatory sense.

- *Coordination mechanisms* – The department had to consider the role and significance of networks and networking. It was necessary for the department to develop agreements (e.g. Memoranda of Understanding or 'Exchange of Letters') and put arrangements in place to enable it to participate in joint agency taskforces or to second staff from partner agencies.

Even though the EPBC Act is Australia's cornerstone piece of federal environmental legislation, Australia's Constitution requires that the national and provincial governments share responsibility for the environment (Burnett 2010: 5). Consequently, the EPBC Act complements rather than overrides the environmental laws of local or provincial governments. In fact, '[o]ne of the prime motivations for developing the EPBC Act was to facilitate cooperative approaches between Australian governments for a nationally consistent approach to environmental matters' (Early 2008: 117). Accordingly, the complementary nature of the EPBC Act, coupled with the department's increased regulatory focus, was central to its need to engage (and network) with other enforcement agencies. The department has pursued this engagement through the use of formal and informal networks. Its networking generally and networking with law enforcement and environmental enforcement agencies more specifically are considered in the next section.

Networking in the public sector

Since the mid-1980s, the Australian public sector has undergone significant reform (Briggs 2005: 7; Menzies and Weller 2004: 11). One of the more notable differences has been the effort now devoted by governments to establishing and maintaining relationships with both internal and external stakeholders (Tiernan and Althaus 2005: 37). This focus upon relationships has required public sector managers to undertake the new function of *managing out* (Tiernan and Althaus 2005: 359).

As part of *managing out*, it has been necessary for governments to examine critically how managers operate within, between and outside of government agencies. Not surprisingly, the use of networks and networking has become increasingly important. As Ah Chin (2006: 21) has observed, public sector managers should note that 'the days when governments did everything alone and without consultation are long gone'.

Birchall and Colwill (1996: 124–5) describe networks as a set of relationships that involve 'formal and informal ties between members of a profession or people working in similar jobs'. They consider that some of the benefits associated with networks are that they: improve knowledge as the members of the network can study and learn from successful organisations and individuals; provide the opportunity to get information on how another individual or organisation has handled an issue which you are confronting; allow members to position their organisation (and themselves) in the right situation at the right time; provide support; and help to strengthen existing relationships (and develop new ones) (Birchall and Colwill 1996: 125).

Not surprisingly, public sector agencies see networks and networking as an attractive proposition. This is especially so as Australian public sector reforms of recent decades have resulted in greater demands and expectations being placed upon governments. Governments are now expected to be more outwardly focussed (Tiernan and Althaus 2005: 5) and outcomes-based (Atkins 2005: 11), and to operate more collaboratively (Winkworth 2006: 31).

Globalisation has also resulted in public sector managers, together with the services they provide, being subjected to international benchmarking (Tiernan and Althaus, 2005: 6). Irrespective of whether the government is referred to as interconnected (Atkins 2005: 12), connected, seamless, joined-up (Crowley 2004: 46) or integrated, these terms incorporate the concept of *managing out*. In practice, *managing out* predominantly occurs through partnerships, and it is Fleming and Wood (2006: 47) who suggest that '[p]artnerships, formal or informal, represent the "bones" of the network'. The Advisory Group on Reform of Australian Government Administration (AGRAGA) reviewed the Australian Public Service,[12] releasing its report in March 2010 ('the Moran Review'). When considering how to maintain a highly capable workforce, it suggested that 'professional networks enable employees to draw on a wider range of experiences and perspectives [to assist] when tackling problems' (AGRAGA 2010: 24).

Growth of networks specifically relating to environmental enforcement

The last 25 years have seen a proliferation of networks used by environmental enforcement agencies (Farmer 2007: 249, 261–2). Moreover, as the importance of environmental issues continues to increase, given its interface with a myriad of social, economic and environmental activities, this reliance on networks by environmental enforcement agencies is not expected to diminish – in fact, the opposite is most likely to occur.[13] Tomkins (2009: 517) makes similar observations in relation to networks involving mainstream law enforcement agencies, noting that '[r]ecent years have seen a proliferation of international, regional, national law enforcement organisations working together at an international level' in relation to policing environmental crime. Table 13.3 contains a selection of ten networks that have been established globally since 1990.

Table 13.3 Environmental enforcement networks established since 1990

Established, level, name and website

1990 – Global
International Network of Environmental Compliance and Enforcement **(INECE)**
www.inece.org/overview.html
1992 – Regional (Europe)
Network for the Implementation and Enforcement of Environmental Law **(IMPEL)**
www.impel.eu/about
1992 – Global
Interpol Environmental Crimes Committee **(Interpol ECC)**
www.interpol.int/Crime-areas/Environmental-crime/
Environmental-Compliance-and-Enforcement-Committee
1994 – Regional (Canada, Mexico and USA)
Commission for Environmental Cooperation (CEC)
www.cec.org/Page.asp?PageID=1226&SiteNodeID=310&BL_ExpandID=154
2004 – National (Ireland)
Environmental Enforcement Network **(EEN)**
www.epa.ie/downloads/pubs/enforcement/EPA_enforcement_network_
newsletter_2005.pdf
2004 – Regional (Asia)
Assoc. of South East Asian Nations – Wildlife Enforcement Network **(ASEAN-WEN)**
www.asean-wen.org/index.php?option=com_content&view=article&id=48&Ite
mid=56#2
2004 – Regional (Oceania)
Australasian Environmental Law Enforcement and Regulators neTwork **(AELERT)**
www.aelert.com.au/?page_id=5
2005 – Regional (Asia)
Asian Environmental Compliance and Enforcement Network **(AECEN)**
www.aecen.org/about-aecen
2006 – Regional (Northern Africa)
Network for Environmental Compliance and Enforcement in the Maghreb **(NECEMA)**
www.inece.org/mena/rabat/necema_tor.pdf
2009 – Regional (Middle East)
Arab Network for Environmental Compliance and Enforcement **(ANECE)**
www.inece.org/mena/arabregion/index.html

Note: The website links listed contain further background information on the establishment and/or
purpose of the various networks, with all websites correct and functional as at 5 February 2014.

Departmental experiences in relation to networks and networking

The growth of the department's regulatory role coupled with the depth and breadth of its regulatory responsibilities required that it sought cooperation from other enforcers. For the purpose of this chapter, and in practice, the department's tangible experiences with enforcement networks commenced in 2004. In many ways, Australia's extensive and geographically dispersed environment (terrestrial and marine)[14] provides the department with little choice but to work in partnership with co-regulators at the local, subnational and national level. In this regard, the department has used and continues to use both mainstream law enforcement and environmental enforcement liaison and networks. These various networks and networking activities are now considered in greater detail.

The department's use of existing mainstream law enforcement networks

In the first six months (the first half of 2004) of the department's regulatory journey, it accessed and attempted to utilise existing mainstream law enforcement networks. A number of these agencies, such as the Australian Federal Police (AFP), Australian Crime Commission and the then Australian Customs Service (since renamed as the Australian Customs and Border Protection Service (ACBPS)), were members of the Heads of Commonwealth Operational Law Enforcement Agencies (HOCOLEA).[15] During this period, liaison with these agencies, whilst mostly beneficial, failed to produce the customised or contextualised assistance required by the department which was then very much an emerging regulator. As an emerging regulator, involved in what was esoteric environmental enforcement, operating in a diverse environment, it naturally sought networking opportunities with more comparable regulators.

As a result, and over the next six months (the last half of 2004), the department extended its networking to include agencies such as the Australian Fisheries Management Authority (AFMA) and the Australian Quarantine and Inspection Service (AQIS). These agencies were operating in 'enforcement environments' (and had been for some time) similar to that in which the department was now required to operate. AFMA and AQIS operated within enforcement environments that covered geographically disperse areas and involved partnering with local, subnational, national, regional and international authorities. It is important to note that their work also had a sufficiently scientific interface to resonate with the wider departmental staff which was and remains an important part of the department's operating culture (or psyche).[16]

Around this same time (late 2004), a number of environmental enforcement agencies in Australia were facing similar challenges around regulatory and organisational change management issues. These challenges were associated with their either recently acquired or increased environmental compliance and enforcement roles. There was an unambiguous groundswell of other local, subnational and national environmental regulators who had identified a need for greater coordination and interoperability between co-regulators and partner agencies. The training and up-skilling of compliance and enforcement staff was identified as a clear and shared challenge (Pink 2008: 225; Van der Schraaf 2008: 243).

The department's lead role in a regional network

The Australasian[17] Environmental Law Enforcement and Regulators neTwork (AELERT) was formally established in November 2004 with five foundation member agencies[18] (AELERT n.d.) as a working-level subnational network. By late 2008, with the inclusion of New Zealand central government member agencies, AELERT become a regional network and now is formally recognised as coming under the auspices of the COAG (Council of Australian Governments) framework.[19] AELERT now has 86 member agencies (as at 17 January 2012) and is a network, of environmental regulatory agencies, the aim of which is to 'build relationships between jurisdictions to facilitate the sharing of information and to improve the regulatory compliance capacity of member agencies' (AELERT n.d.).

The department played a lead role in the establishment of AELERT and continues to be committed to its growth and management. For example, it: facilitated a series of precursor meetings with co-regulators and academics during November 2003; organised and managed the inaugural AELERT conference in November 2004; performed the role of inaugural Chair of AELERT;[20] developed, managed and promulgated customised training packages for environmental enforcement officers through the AELERT network in the period 2005–07 (Pink 2008: 229); made successful submissions to the Ministerial Council-level Standing Committees, resulting in AELERT coming formally under its auspices; houses and manages the funded AELERT Secretariat;[21] and actively involves its staff in the majority of the projects and initiatives of AELERT.

The department's involvement in other networks

The department is involved in a number of internal and external networks as part of its regulatory function. These networks (and arrangements) cover the entire spectrum from those that are informal to those that are semi-formal and formal.

Internal networks

As previously mentioned, the department's two major, and formal, internal bodies (a forum and network respectively) are the Regulatory Compliance Executive Committee (RCEC) and Regulatory Compliance Managers Network (RCMN). The work of these bodies has recently been augmented by the creation and establishment of two informal and horizontal networks in 2011.

These networks come in the form of the Compliance and Enforcement Practitioners Network (CEPN) and Communities of Practice (CoP). Both are topic-based forums which provide departmental staff, irrespective of level or placement within the organisation, with an opportunity to come together and learn from colleagues on what are more of the practitioner-based aspects of regulation (Marshall and Pink 2011: 712). More specifically, in broad terms the CEPN: facilitates communication and transmission of guidelines, policies and procedures which are generic or have broad applicability or transference across the department; organises and facilitates non-specialised seminars and presentations; keeps practitioners informed of trends, issues and changes that may affect or influence their regulatory compliance activities; collects and coalesces input from practitioners and then acts as a conduit, elevating issues where necessary, to the RCMN; and acts as an umbrella network for the various Communities of Practice (Marshall and Pink 2011: 712).The Communities of Practice are shaped around the three disciplines of Monitoring and Audit, Compliance and Investigations, as these disciplines are representative of the functions carried out by the majority of practitioners within the CEPN (Marshall and Pink 2011: 712). Given their nature; the CoP are reliant upon participation of the membership, which is self-selecting. Practitioners have been able to focus and share experiences, skills and understanding unique to the particular discipline for mutual benefit with organisational efficiency and effectiveness enhanced. The CoP also have the flexibility, given that they are membership-led and driven, to establish additional CoP relatively quickly and easily. At the time of writing there is interest in establishing two additional CoP around the disciplines of intelligence and regulatory policy.

The various departmental compliance and enforcement bodies (committees, networks and forums) are depicted in Table 13.4.

External networks

The department's external networks include and involve agencies that can be grouped within its shared environmental portfolio, other Australian government bodies and other nations via bilateral or multilateral environmental agreements (MEAs). A non-exhaustive list of such relationships appears in Table 13.5.

Although sitting outside the department's portfolio, general coordination and liaison with the ACBPS – the Australian government's border interdiction agency – has been critical for the department to be able to satisfy its many and varied international obligations. In this role the service is responsible for international and inter-agency cooperation where it plays a vital role in protecting Australia's borders. The ACBPS is focussed on intercepting illicit items which

Table 13.4 Departmental compliance and enforcement bodies

RCEC – Regulatory Compliance Executive Committee – (very formal)
Sets strategic direction for departmental compliance and enforcement effort
Membership: Deputy Secretary, Division and Branch heads by position
RCMN – Regulatory Compliance Managers Network – (formal)
Operationalises RCEC-endorsed compliance and enforcement effort
Membership: Section heads by position
CEPN – Compliance and Enforcement Practitioners Network – (informal)
Provides enabling support for C&E practitioners (includes oversight of CoPs)
Membership: All compliance and enforcement personnel by function
CoP – Communities of Practice – (very informal)
Practitioners determine wants/needs within their CoP
Membership: Voluntarily by interest/identification

Adapted: Marshall and Pink 2011: 714

Table 13.5 The Department's external networks compartmentalised

Network group, agencies involved and websites

Within allied Australian Government Portfolios:
Australian Quarantine and Inspection Service,
www.daff.gov.au/aqis/about/compliance-investigations
Great Barrier Marine Park Authority, www.gbrmpa.gov.au/corp_site/about_us/
legislation_regulations
Murray Darling Basin Authority, www.mdba.gov.au
National Water Commission, www.nwc.gov.au
Within the broader Australian Government:
Australian Customs and Border Protections Service, www.customs.gov.au/site/
page4381.asp
Australian Federal Police, www.afp.gov.au/policing/environmental-crime.aspx
Australian Maritime Safety Authority, www.amsa.gov.au
Australian Pesticides and Veterinary Medicines Authority, www.apvma.gov.au/
compliance/compliance.php
Australian Transaction Reports and Analysis Centre, www.austrac.gov.au/operational_
intelligence.html
Office of the Gene Technical Regulator, www.ogtr.gov.au/internet/ogtr/publishing.nsf/
Content/mc-index-1
**Across multilateral environmental agreements or other international
bodies:**
NB. The multilateral environment agreements (MEAs) form part of the various
international agreements. Refer to the 'International obligations' column in Table 13.1.

Note: Where possible the website links contain further background information on the environmental
enforcement (or associated) activities undertaken by the various agencies, with all websites
correct and functional as at 5 February 2014.

are potentially harmful to the community (ACBPS n.d.). Accordingly, the
majority of seizures made under departmentally administered legislation (and
the various international obligations to which it gives effect)[22] are performed by
the ACBPS. As an example, there were some 5,200 seizure events by the ACBPS
involving specimens under the Convention on International Trade in Endangered Species alone in the 2008–09 financial year (DEWHA 2009a: 241).
Similarly, the AFP assists Australian government departments and agencies with
investigations into:

> serious and complex matters including . . . organised crime, [and] money
> laundering, operational assistance in the course of another department or
> agency's criminal investigation including execution of . . . search warrants
> international liaison and Interpol requests; financial investigation services
> including training, advice and guidance relating to proceeds of crime;
> computer forensics and other forensic services; [and] electronic evidence
> services including training, advice and forensic examination of seized
> computers and electronic items.
>
> (AFP, n.d.)

As the department's regulatory capacity has grown, the nature of the assistance provided by the AFP has changed. Initially, the AFP undertook or substantially led enforcement activity on behalf of the department. The circumstances at time of writing are that the AFP tends to provide a support role through provision of computer forensics analysis as part of an investigation or a coordination role in relation to global enforcement operations in which the department participates. This relationship has also involved discussions around the application of the Proceeds of Crime Act 2002 (Cth) in relation to environmental offences. These discussions have resulted in other agencies such as the Attorney General's Department (AGD) and Australian Transaction Reports and Analysis Centre (AUSTRAC)[23] becoming involved with the department, and in stronger relationships being formed which have led to a greater mutual understanding of how each agency is able to assist the others.

The department meets regularly with the ACBPS, AFP, AQIS and the Commonwealth Director of Public Prosecutions (CDPP).[24] These meetings have increased agency interoperability and assisted in the more effective use of resources, and serious and/or complex crime matters have been able to be elevated in a timely and appropriate manner. Furthermore, any joint operational or enforcement activities (whether prosecutorial in nature or not) are flagged and tracked, and are able to progress more efficiently than was otherwise the case without such communication.

Beyond the Australian Government, the department remains connected with other entities such as the International Network of Environmental Compliance and Enforcement (INECE), INTERPOL's Environmental Crimes Programme (INTERPOL ECP) and the Organisation for Economic Cooperation and Development (OECD), primarily through its Environment Division. The benefits of the relationship with INECE and the OECD is that it has increased the department's knowledge base and provided it with some situational awareness that its efforts are consistent with and benchmarked against those of its international peers.

Liaison with INTERPOL ECP has also reinvigorated the department's relationship with the AFP National Central Bureau (NCB).[25] This relationship has enabled departmental staff to become involved in environmental enforcement projects run under INTERPOL's Working Groups that focus on Pollution Crime and Wildlife Crime (INTERPOL n.d.), and to participate in Global Enforcement Initiatives.[26] As an example, the NCB liaison resulted in an increase in the department's awareness and engagement with the INTERPOL Stolen Works of Arts Programme.[27] This liaison led to significant operational success in 2007[28] when the department and the AFP joined to recover a stolen fifteenth-century world map, by the artist Ptolemy (AFP 2008: 7–9), which was then returned to the Spanish government.

Despite their differing foci, these networks assist the department by providing an awareness of shared regional issues, international better practices and benchmarking, and the coordination of information exchange respectively.

The department's involvement in global and national enforcement initiatives is now considered.

Operation TRAM – conducted in February 2010 – was INTERPOL's first global environmental enforcement initiative and involved 18 countries:

> ... which targeted traditional medicine products containing ingredients prohibited by the Convention on International Trade in Endangered Species (CITES). The department served as National Coordinator for the action, which involved the Australian Customs and Border Protection Service, the Australian Federal Police, the Australian Quarantine and Inspection Service, the Therapeutic Goods Administration and Food Standards Australia and New Zealand.
>
> (DEWHA 2010: 291)

Operation RAMP – conducted in October and November 2010 – was INTERPOL's second global enforcement initiative and involved 51 countries. Once again, the department served as National Coordinator for this intelligence-led operation,. The Australian contribution included:

> [m]ore than 600 operational activities, involving Commonwealth, state and territory authorities and targeting illegal wildlife trade were carried out across Australia under this operation. Operation RAMP's Australian component led to the seizure of 36 animals, inspections and search warrants on 67 premises, and a number of arrests.
>
> (DSEWPaC 2011: 137)

Operation CETUS ran between May 2011 and November 2011. The department coordinated the national operation which saw the Australian government and state conservation and environment agencies come and coordinate their operational efforts under the AELERT banner. The focus of the operation was 'to protect migrating whales from undue disturbance and enforces whale approach limits, particularly at popular whale watching hotspots' (DSEWPaC 2011: 137).

Systems and coordination mechanisms required to combat environmental crime

The department utilises a number of systems and coordination mechanisms in its efforts to combat environmental and transnational environmental crime. Information and intelligence exchanges, coordination and working with non-government and/or non-regulatory partners are now considered further.

Information and intelligence exchanges

With its various permitting and licensing regimes, the department possesses outright and has access to vast amounts of information and intelligence holdings. Though suitable for use in its enforcement efforts, a common challenge encountered by the department and other emerging regulators (especially) is how to share such information lawfully.[29] In response, in 2005, the department developed an internal guideline document which mapped the Commonwealth Information Privacy Principles[30] against those of the Australian states and territories. This research resulted in the development of a document that was able to show that the various privacy principle regimes were not incompatible and in most circumstances permitted the exchange of information for enforcement purposes when certain criteria were met.

Information exchange, and the allied issue of communications, also impacts upon mainstream law enforcement agencies. The AFP considers that its ability to share information is less than optimal. They cite not having a common IT (information technology) platform, combined with the fact that some of the state and territory (provincial) police forces do not have security-rated IT systems,[31] creating challenges when working together.[32]

As the world becomes increasingly transnational in nature, the ability to receive, store and share intelligence holdings nationally and internationally becomes increasingly important. To address this issue, INTERPOL utilises the secure communications system known as I-24/7 which enables users[33] 'to exchange information securely and rapidly' (INTERPOL 2009a: 1). The I-24/7 system provides a model upon which environmental regulators are able to base a system for their use.

Coordination

The department has explored greater coordination of staff and resources as part of its early efforts. In the period between 2005 and 2009, the department seconded ACBPS intelligence staff and AFP investigative staff into its Environment Investigations Unit. The department's decision to establish such a partnership was intended to assist it in establishing its enforcement capacity in a proficient manner (and one that was in keeping with those of other federal-level partner agencies) and to also aid in establishing additional and streamlined networks. The latter was perceived to be important for ensuring that the department was able to move to intelligence and investigative self-sufficiency once the secondments had ended. These secondments were extremely useful during the initial phases of the department establishing its compliance and enforcement capacity. As the department become more capable and self-sufficient as a regulator, the need for secondments passed. Short-term secondments or joint agency taskforces remain a viable option and are considered from time to time. On this issue, White considers that:

> [h]ow best to organise law enforcement activities in regards to different environmental crimes is a perennial issue [and asks] [s]hould specific environmental police units, within police services, be created, as in the case of Israel? Or, should flying squads be created, that are comprised of personnel from different agencies, and that reflect interagency collaboration and expertise?
>
> (White 2008: 202)

Working with non-government, non-regulatory and academic partners

Contemporary environmental regulators are increasingly including and partnering with non-government organisations (NGOs), non-regulatory bodies (NRBs) (INECE 2009: 66–7; White 2009: 491) and civil society organisations (CSOs) (Elliott 2009: 74) as a component of their enforcement effort.[34] The department is no exception. A few examples of partnerships with NGOs (peak bodies and industry associations) are set out below:

- Customs brokers and forwarders – in relation to import and export activities (DEWHA 2009: 37);
- Australian Refrigeration Council (ARC) – appointed to administer the permit schemes in the refrigeration and air conditioning industry (DSEWPaC 2011: 181). More specifically, the ARC is contracted to conduct a compliance audit programme. A range of audits are conducted, including on-site (planned, scheduled audits); remote (paper-based); desktop (telephone-based); drive-by (random drop-in audits). Technical assistance is also provided to the Australian Customs and Border Protection Service where illegal import is suspected, and the ARC follows up on complaints about permit holders (DSEWPaC 2011: 186). It also ensures that the 'handling and purchase of fluorocarbon refrigerant (an ozone-depleting substance) is limited to those who have proven themselves competent and qualified' (ARC n.d.).
- Fire Protection Association of Australia (FPAA) – appointed to administer the permit schemes in the fire protection industry (DSEWPaC 2011: 181). The FPAA checks compliance with the competency-based permit scheme for the fire protection industry in Australia for (fire suppressant) systems using halocarbon-extinguishing agents.
- Australian Acupuncture and Chinese Medicine Association (AACMA) – the Endangered Species Certification Scheme (ESCS) was launched by the then Federal Environment Minister, the Hon. Peter Garrett AM, in May 2008 at the AACMA annual conference (DSEWPaC 2011: 73; James 2009: 29–31). The ESCS enables traditional medicine professionals to obtain official acknowledgement that the products they use or sell do not contain ingredients from threatened species, thus helping reduce illegal international trade. It also provides a prime example of the Australian government working with the community and industry to meet international conservation objectives and to ensure trade occurs within the law, and, when combined with the department's Permit Verification Scheme, forms a part of a regulatory regime which complements Australia's CITES obligations.[35]

The involvement of academic institutions with networks is evidenced by the attendance of academics at conferences run by networks such as AELERT, IMPEL, INECE and INTERPOL's Environment Crime Programme. A prime example of academics partnering with networks, resulting in publications that are underpinned by research to inform environmental enforcement responses, can be seen in the *Electronic Waste and Organised Crime Assessing the Links: Phase II Report for the Interpol Pollution Crime Working Group* which involved Michigan State University (INTERPOL 2009b).[36]

From an Australian perspective, the relationship with academia is expected to grow, and significantly so given the comments of the then Prime Minister, the Hon. Kevin Rudd, during the launch of the Australian National Institute for Public Policy (the Institute) at the Australian National University (ANU) in Canberra on 8 May 2010. During his speech, the then Prime Minister stated that 'one of the Government's key objectives [is] building better links between the expertise in the academic community and the Australian Public Service' (Rudd 2010). He considered that the Institute 'reflect[ed] a new partnership between the public service, ANZOG [Australian and New Zealand School of Government] and the ANU and will ensure Government draws on the wealth of expertise that exists across the ANU and ANZSOG networks' (Rudd 2010). This viewpoint was reiterated shortly thereafter in the Moran Review which recommended that 'agencies should establish more formal links with academic institutions, think tanks and the community and private sectors' (AGRAGA 2010: 43).

Environmental enforcement networks in academic perspective

Fleming and Wood (2006: 6) suggest that '[o]rganisational requirements, international diplomatic relations and global [environmental] crime all provide [the necessary] environments within which networks are established'. This is supported by Raab and Milwaard, who state that:

> the general literature on networks tends to take a positive view with respect to the necessity – as well as the potential – of collaborative approaches to public-sector governance. Networks are seen as superior to hierarchies in tackling the wicked problems that fall outside the mandate of any one public sector organisation.
>
> (Fleming and Wood 2006: 251–2)

An anthology of material exists which has been developed by network practitioners or by academics partnering with or associated with networks. In *Making Law Work*, Zaelke, Kaniaru and Kružíková suggest that:

> [t]he lack of meaningful enforcement and compliance has often been seen as one of the greatest weaknesses of international law, and international environmental law in particular, but new models of cooperation present great promise for effective international action.
>
> (Zaelke *et al.* 2005b: 383)

They argue that much is done beyond the formal international treaties and conventions in regard to environmental law enforcement through 'global webs of "transgovernmental networks"'. They consider network to be a simple concept, described as: 'a form of cooperation involving government or government officials (and under some conceptions, NGOs and the business community as well) that operates without a formal treaty or international institution' (Zaelke *et al.* 2005b: 383).

Similarly, Raustiala (2002: 405) suggests that networks enhance treaties, fill gaps where there are no treaties and facilitate negotiations for future treaties. Not surprisingly, Zaelke *et al.* consider that networks offer greater flexibility and efficiency: 'By working directly peer-to-peer, transgovernmental networks can quickly disseminate and distil information, enhance enforcement cooperation, harmonize laws and regulations, and address common problems from a shared perspective shaped by experience and expertise' (Zaelke *et al.* 2005b: 384).

The old adage suggests that a chain is only as strong as its weakest link. The same can be said of global environmental enforcement, says Slaughter (2004: 57); thus it is no surprise that '[c]apacity building is considered a critical function' of networks (Zaelke *et al.* 2005b: 385). In her book *A New World Order*, Slaughter (2004: 387) suggests that given that organised crime 'operate[s] through global networks', it is appropriate that governments similarly coordinate their efforts. Slaughter (2004: 387) considers that 'government networks are a key feature of world order in the twenty-first century, but they are under appreciated, under supported, and underused' when it comes to global enforcement efforts.

The general discussion on the aims and objectives of networks indicate that they are shaped by 'subject area, membership, and history, but taken together, they also perform certain common functions' (Slaughter 2004: 389). Those common functions can include 'expand[ing] regulatory reach . . . build[ing] trust and establish[ing] relationships among the participants . . . exchang[ing] regular information . . . develop[ing] databases of best practices . . . [and] . . . offer[ing] technical assistance and professional socialisation to members' (Slaughter 2004: 389).[37]

In much the same way, Raustiala (2002: 405) suggests that networks are characterised by 'extensive sharing of information, coordinating enforcement efforts, and joint policy-making activities. These activities plausibly exhibit network effects: the more regulatory agencies that participate in coordinating and reciprocating enforcement efforts, for example, the better off are all the other agencies.'

Whilst not always the case, there is a school of thought that '[e]nforcement networks typically spring up due to the inability of government officials in one country to enforce that country's laws' (Slaughter 2004: 395). This is reinforced by Farmer (2007), who, in his book *Handbook of Environmental Protection and Enforcement: Principles and Practice*, sets aside an entire chapter on networking.[38]

Kaniaru (2002: 52) details the history and development of networks. He cites the United Nations Conference on Environment and Development (UNCED), which took place in Rio de Janeiro, Brazil, in 1992, but more specifically Agenda 21,[39] as somewhat of a catalyst for compliance and enforcement networks. Chapter 38 of Agenda 21 for the first time recognised 'the importance and the role played by international institutional arrangements in the integration of environment and development issues at national, sub-regional, regional and international levels'. Kaniaru (2002: 53) adds that there is a critical need for '[f]ocal points and/or persons hav[ing] been established or designated in many institutions and networks to ensure smooth flow of data and information'.

Observations as to the utility of networks

From the department's perspective there is clear benefit and utility in networks. With networks now playing a key role in its overall environmental enforcement efforts, the department has been able to achieve cooperative outcomes and receive benefits through networks, including: access to entry- and advanced-level training customised for the environmental enforcement practitioner; production and dissemination of policies, procedures and like material across the environmental enforcement (compliance, monitoring, audit and investigation) spectrum; joint enforcement and prosecution outcomes; access to general and after-hours emergency contact details together with an ability to network with likeminded professionals, and access to and involvement in contemporary policy development and academic research.

The utility of networks is supported by the exponential growth of networks in the last 25 years as outlined previously by Farmer (2007: 249, 261–2) and by the sample of networks which appears in Table 13.3. This point is demonstrated in the case of AELERT, which (as previously mentioned) commenced with five foundation member agencies in 2004, grew to 35 member agencies by 2008, and in 2012 had 86 member agencies (AELERT n.d.).[40] Fleming and Wood (2006: 3), among others, draw attention to the fact that '[n]etworks can be insular, difficult to penetrate and at times unaccountable for their actions [and] [t]hey can be conflictual on a number of levels and can be difficult to coordinate'. Mindful of this, and despite the benefits of networks, the department is cognisant of the fact that networks should not be seen as the panacea for all matters of environmental enforcement. Accordingly, the department recognises that there is much work to be done to ensure that there is transparency and accountability within networks. It is for this reason that it has advocated for and integrated increased governance and reporting frameworks into the networks (primarily relating to AELERT (externally) and the RCEC and CON (internally)) it is involved in, as suggested by Slaughter (2004) and Raustiala (2002).

Suggestions for maximising the benefits from association with networks

The department utilises networks at the international, regional, national and subnational level. It does so because it realises that law enforcement agencies, allied entities and environmental enforcement agencies have different experiences and expertise, can share resources to provide a better environmental outcome, and acknowledge that the same incident can contravene a number of laws (across various jurisdictions and areas of interest). As co-regulators and partners, we need to consider who are the most appropriate and best placed to deal with the contravention. The department has been able to increase the benefits derived from networks by being actively involved in those networks. That involvement includes being part of networks' management and governance structure, leading and participating in project and operational initiatives and being a key funder and provider of additional in-kind support.

Farmer (2007) provides a checklist for environmental enforcement agencies already participating in networks. They serve as a reminder of how agencies can maximise benefits from networks and it is equally useful as a prompt for those agencies contemplating participation. The checklist asks:

1   Has the environmental enforcement authority a designated person responsible for coordination with the network?;
2   Is it responsible for part-funding of network activities and, if so, is this fully incorporated in relevant financial planning?;
3   Are effective mechanisms in place to identify staff members who might most effectively participate in relevant network activities?; and
4   Are effective mechanisms in place to disseminate the results of network activities to those in the environmental enforcement authority who would benefit?

(Farmer 2007: 262)

Conclusion

The department, like many new and emerging regulators, faces a number of challenges when seeking to build capacity. It has been the Australian experience that environmental regulators face additional and unique challenges. These include the increasing profile of environmental issues, the speed at which capacity must be built, the esoteric nature of environmental regulation and the relatively small pool of existing specialist knowledge from which to draw. Accordingly, to have the capability to access and utilise networks has been a key factor in organisational success. Indeed, it is an enabler and forms part of the critical path to becoming a competent, capable and credible regulator (Pink 2008: 230). Australian inter-agency collaborations extend from the department to the Australian Federal Police and Australian Transaction Reports and Analysis Centre in relation to matters including financial investigations, proceeds of crime and money laundering investigations related to environmental crimes. As these relationships deepen, the capacity for mutual assistance strengthens.

Overall, this chapter has demonstrated that since the year 2000 when the department inherited substantial regulatory responsibility, but more so in the period between 2002 and 2008, environmental compliance and enforcement went from 'no business, to new business, to core business' (Pink 2008: 227). This has coincided with a significant increase in the department's involvement in networks, so much so that this involvement is now considered an integral part and enabler of much of its enforcement effort. Finally, in the experiences of the department, it has been the combination of the networks, whether internal or external, informal or formal, involving law enforcers, non-law enforcers and environmental enforcers, that has resulted in superior efficiencies of its enforcement effort. All taken together, this has enhanced the department's regulatory reputation.

Notes

1 The chapter represents the views of the author and does not necessarily represent the views or policies of the Australian Government, Department of the Environment, or the University of New England.

2 For example, the EPBC Act 1999 (Environment Protection and Biodiversity Conservation Act 1999), the WELS Act 2005 (Water Efficiency Labelling and Standards Act 2005) and the Product Stewardship Act 2011 contain all three types of sanctions. They are based upon the contemporary model Commonwealth legislation. The remainder of departmentally administered legislation has a combination of one or two of the sanctions (most commonly those that are administrative and criminal).

3 For the period 2000–11, covered in this chapter, the department has been known as EA (Environment Australia), DEH (Department of Environment and Heritage), DEWR (Department of Environment and Water Resources), DEWHA (Department of Environment, Water, Heritage and the Arts) and, most recently, DSEWPaC (the Department of Sustainability, Environment, Water, Population and Communities).

4 The EPBC Act incorporated and replaced the following statutes: the Environment Protection (Impact of Proposals) Act 1974 (Cth); the Australian Heritage Commission Act 1975 (Cth); the National Parks and Wildlife Conservation Act 1974 (Cth); the Whale Protection Act 1980 (Cth); the Wildlife Protection (Regulation of Exports and Imports) Act 1982 (Cth); the World Heritage Properties Conservation Act 1983 (Cth); and the Endangered Species Protection Act 1992 (Cth).

5 This was the first Compliance Section established to focus on the EPBC Act. There were, however isolated pockets of individuals or small teams that were responsible for enforcing other pieces of departmentally administered environmental legislation.

6 The CON is a middle-management (Section Head) forum within the department for staff with compliance and enforcement responsibilities. In June 2011, to reflect a changing role and focus, it was renamed the Regulatory Compliance Managers Network (RCMN).

7 The RCEC is the senior management forum (which is comprised of members of the department's Senior Executive Service) which provides strategic input into the activities of the RCMN. In June 2011, to distinguish the department's (legislatively based) regulatory compliance and enforcement work from its (non-legislatively based) 'programmatic non-compliance and fraud work' which related to instances of non-compliance and fraud against grants and programmes administered by the department, it was renamed the Regulatory Compliance Executive Committee.

8 The Compliance Support Unit (CSU) was established to provide compliance and enforcement support on a whole-of-department basis (intelligence, operational and training) to the various line areas in the department.

9 To more accurately reflect how it operates, the CMC has since been renamed as the Case Management Panel (CMP). The CMP process is a governance framework that provides for senior executive staff oversight at the four critical stages of compliance and enforcement action, namely: commencement, continuation, commitment of substantial resources and response and conclusion. Crucially, the CMP considers use of

coercive powers by departmental officers which can include: execution of warrants, compulsory acquisition of information and answers to questions and, in extreme cases, arrests.

10 Such matters include activities that involve large-scale fraud, have elements of serious or organised crime and crime with trans-national dimensions (AFP n.d.: 1).

11 Refer to note 8.

12 The full title of the review is *Ahead of the Game: Blueprint for the Reform of Australian Government Administration.*

13 The exponential growth of the Australasian Environmental Law Enforcement and Regulators neTwork (AELERT) discussed later in this chapter and the observations of Farmer (2007) attest to this reliance.

14 The Department's terrestrial responsibilities cover all of Australia's eight states and territories, and its seven external territories, pictorially depicted at http:// en.wikipedia.org/wiki/States_and_territories_of_Australia. The Department is responsible for administering an increasing estate of marine protected areas (MPA) which are Commonwealth reserves under the EPBC Act. For further information, see www.environment.gov.au/coasts/mpa/index.html.

15 There are presently some 12 agencies that are HOCOLEA agencies (see ACBPS 2009).

16 The department's psyche refers to the fact that most departmental staff do not readily identify as being regulators. Instead, it is their collective scientific or environmental predilection of staff that has them more readily identifying with environmental stewardship and policy and programmatic activities. The department still has some way to go in relation to organisational change before all parts of the department would identify with or at least accept its regulator status.

17 From 2004 to 2008 the 'A' in AELERT stood for 'Australian'. However, from 2008 it became 'Australasian' after several New Zealand agencies joined the Network.

18 These agencies represent all three levels of government in Australia (local, subnational and national).

19 AELERT reports to the Ministerial Council for Environment and Water which forms part of the Council of Australian Governments (COAG) framework.

20 From 2004 to 2007 AELERT's premier governance body was the National Committee; in 2008, when it was expanded to include New Zealand, it was renamed the Steering Committee.

21 The AELERT Secretariat consists of a Secretariat Project Officer and the position of Secretary.

22 With the most significant seizures relating to: animals and animal-products under the Convention on International Trade in Endangered Species of Wild Fauna and Flora (CITES); hazardous waste shipments under the Basel Convention; and refrigerants (including those contained within imported motor vehicles under the Montreal Protocol on Substances that Deplete the Ozone Layer.

23 AUSTRAC's role is to 'protect the integrity of Australia's financial system and contribute to the administration of justice through our expertise in countering money laundering' (AUSTRAC n.d.). See AUSTRAC (n.d.) for more information.

24 The CDPP is the Australian government's independent prosecuting authority in relation to commencing prosecutions under Australian government legislation. For more information, see www.cdpp.gov.au.

25 The INTERPOL framework relies upon the member countries establishing an NCB. Australia is one of 188 member countries, and the Australian NCB (the portal into INTERPOL headquarters in France) is located in the AFP headquarters in Canberra.

26 For further information on the Global Enforcement Initiative conducted in February of 2010 on illegal trade in traditional medicines containing protected wildlife products, see www.interpol.int/Crime-areas/Environmental-crime/Operations.

27 For further information on INTERPOL's Stolen Works of Art Programme, see INTERPOL (n.d.).
28 At the time, the department was responsible for administering the Protection of Moveable Cultural Heritage Act 1986.
29 The Commonwealth Information Privacy Principles broadly, together with the subject legislation, and when combined with the specific jurisdiction (with whom you want to share information), all affect what information is able to be proactively and reactively shared within the Australian context.
30 The Information Privacy Principles come under the Privacy Act 1988 (Cth).
31 That is, IT systems rated to enable receiving security rated material from the federal system.
32 This observation was made by Mandy Newton, Acting Deputy Commissioner of the AFP, as the keynote speaker on *Evaluation in the AFP*, at the Canberra Evaluation Forum, Canberra, 20 May 2010.
33 Users are restricted, principally to staff attached to the National Police (and allied) Services of its 188 member states (countries). Further information on INTERPOL membership is available at www.interpol.int/About-INTERPOL/Overview.
34 For more information on NGOs and CSOs and the role they play in combating transnational environmental crime, see Elliott (2009: 73–6). It contains specific reference to FLEGT, CAWT and TRACE, on forest law enforcement, wildlife trafficking and forensic services respectively.
35 Which are given effect through Australia's domestic legislation, in this instance by the EPBC Act.
36 Limited copies of this publication were produced and distributed throughout the INTERPOL Environmental Crimes Committee membership; however, electronically copies can be accessed at www.interpol.int/Crime-areas/Environmental-crime/Resources.
37 More broadly and practically, it is recognised that networks are also used to build capacity (through cross-pollination, standardisation of training and sharing development costs (this has been the AELERT experience). There may also be an element of 'peer pressure' in some cases, which creates an imperative for jurisdictions to 'keep up with the Joneses' and also drag developing jurisdictions along.
38 See Farmer (2007: 249–62).
39 The UNCED is also referred to as the World Summit on Sustainable Development and Earth Summit. It is also where the Rio Declaration containing Agenda 21 was drawn up.
40 For a detailed account of the history and growth of AELERT, see Lehane and Pink 2011.

References

Administrative Review Council (ARC) (2008) *Report No. 48 The Coercive Information-gathering Powers of Government Agencies*, Canberra: Commonwealth of Australia.

Advisory Group on Reform of Australia Government Administration (AGRAGA) (2010) *Ahead of the Game: Blueprint for the Reform of the Australian Government Administration*, Canberra: Commonwealth of Australia.

Ah Chin, W. (2006) 'From strategy to reality: a model for community engagement', *Public Administration Today*, 9 (October–December): 21–30.

Atkins, P. (2005) 'Developing transformational leadership capability in the public service', *Public Administration Today*, 3 (March–June): 11–17.

Attorney Generals Department (2009) *Commonwealth Organised Crime Strategic Framework: Overview*, Canberra: Commonwealth of Australia.

Australian Custom and Border Protection Service (ACBPS) (2009) *Annual Report 2008–09*, Canberra: Commonwealth of Australia.

Australian Customs and Border Protection Service (ACBPS) (n.d.) *Protecting Our Borders*. Available online at www.customs.gov.au/site/page5799.asp (accessed 17 May 2010).

Australasian Environmental Law Enforcement and Regulators neTwork (AELERT) (n.d.) www.aelert.net (accessed 8 December 2013).

Australian Federal Police (AFP) (2008) 'One unforgettable journey for a Spanish map', *Platypus*, 98: 7–9.

Australian Federal Police (AFP) (n.d.) *What we do – investigation services for government*. Available online at www.afp.gov.au/what-we-do/investigation.aspx (accessed 17 May 2010).

Australian Refrigeration Council (ARC) (n.d.) *Homepage*. Available online at www.arctick.org/index.php (accessed 8 May 2010).

Australian Transaction Reports and Analysis Centre (n.d.) *About AUSTRAC*, Available online at www.austrac.gov.au/about_austrac.html (accessed on 22 January 2014).

Birchall, G. and Colwill, J. (1996) *Working Relationships: Managing Effective Working Relationships*, Melbourne: Longman Australia.

Briggs, L. (2005) 'Workforce challenges for the Australian public service', *Public Administration Today*, 5(October–December): 6–10.

Burnett, P. (2010) 'The role of impact assessment in: transitioning to the Green Economy', paper presented at the 30th Annual Conference of the International Association for Impact Assessment, Geneva, April 2010.

Crowley, K. (2004) 'Joined up governance: pushing the youth policy boundaries?', *Public Administration Today*, 2(December–February): 46–53.

Department of the Environment, Water, Heritage and the Arts (DEWHA) (2009a) *Annual Report: 2008–2009 Volume 1*, Canberra: Commonwealth of Australia.

Department of the Environment, Water, Heritage and the Arts (DEWHA) (2009b) *Annual Report: 2008–2009 Volume 2*, Canberra: Commonwealth of Australia.

Department of the Environment, Water, Heritage and the Arts (DEWHA) (2010) *Annual Report: 2009–2010*, Canberra: Commonwealth of Australia.

Department of Sustainability, Environment, Water, Population and Communities (DSEWPaC) (2011) *Annual Report: 2010–2011*, Canberra: Commonwealth of Australia.

Early, G. (2008) 'Australia's national environmental legislation and human/wildlife interactions', *Journal of International Wildlife Law and Policy*, 11: 101–55.

Elliott, L. (2009) 'Combating transnational environmental crime: "joined up" thinking about transnational networks', in K. Kangaspunta and I.H. Marshall (eds) *Eco-Crime and Justice: Essays on Environmental Crime*, Turin: UNICRI.

Farmer, A. (2007) *Handbook of Environmental Protection and Enforcement: Principles and Practice*, London: Earthscan.

Fleming, J. and Wood, J.D. (eds) (2006) *Fighting Crime Together: The Challenges of Policing and Security Networks*, Sydney: University of New South Wales Press.

Garrett, P. (Minister for Environment Protection Heritage and the Arts) (2008) 'From the sand hills to the suburbs . . . steps towards a sustainable Australia', media release, 28 July 2008, Canberra. Available online at www.environment.gov.au/minister/archive/env/2008/pubs/sp20080728.pdf (accessed 5 February 2014).

International Criminal Policing Organization (INTERPOL) (2009a) *Connecting Police: I-24/7*. Available online at www.interpol.int/INTERPOL-expertise/Data-exchange/I-24-7 (accessed 5 February 2014).

International Criminal Policing Organization (INTERPOL) (2009b) *Electronic Waste and Organised Crime Assessing the Links: Phase II Report for the Interpol Pollution Crime Working Group*.

Available online at www.interpol.int/Crime-areas/Environmental-crime/Resources (accessed 5 February 2014).

International Criminal Policing Organization (INTERPOL) (n.d.) *Environment Compliance and Enforcement Committee*. Available online at www.interpol.int/Crime-areas/Environmental-crime/Environmental-Compliance-and-Enforcement-Committee (accessed 5 February 2014).

International Criminal Policing Organization (INTERPOL) (n.d.) *Stolen Works of Art*, www.interpol.int/Public/WorkOfArt/Default.asp (accessed 18 May 2010).

International Network for Environmental Compliance and Enforcement (INECE) (2009) *Principles of Environmental Compliance and Enforcement Handbook, April 2009*, Washington, DC: INECE.

James, J. (2009) 'TCM Endangered Species Certification Scheme', *Australian Journal of Acupuncture and Chinese Medicine*, 24(2): 29–31. Available online at http://ajacm.com.au (accessed 5 February 2014).

Kaniaru, D. (2002) 'The role of institutions and networks in environmental enforcement', in *INECE 6th International Conference on Environmental Compliance and Enforcement, April 15–19 2002, San Jose, Costa Rica, Proceedings Volume 2*, Washington, DC: INECE.

Lehane, J. and Pink, G. (2011) 'Evolution of a regional environmental enforcement network: the Australasian Environmental Law Enforcement and Regulators neTwork (AELERT)', in *INECE 9th International Conference on Environmental Compliance and Enforcement, 20–24 June 2011, Whistler, British Columbia, Canada, Proceedings*, Washington, DC: INECE.

Marshall, M. and Pink, G. (2011) 'Internal communication strategies for building capacity among non-inspectors', in *INECE 9th International Conference on Environmental Compliance and Enforcement, 20–24 June 2011, Whistler, British Columbia, Canada, Proceedings*, Washington, DC: INECE.

Menzies, J. and Weller, P. (2004) 'Government in 2020', *Public Administration Today*, 1 (September–November): 10–15.

Pink, G. (2008) 'Building regulatory capacity in environmental agencies: through tailored training', in *INECE 8th International Conference on Environmental Compliance and Enforcement, 5–11 April 2008, Cape Town, South Africa, Proceedings*, London: Cameron May.

Raustiala, K. (2002) 'The architecture of international cooperation: transgovernmental networks and the future of international law', in *Making Law Work: Environmental Compliance and Sustainable Development*, vol. 2, London: Cameron May.

Rudd, K. (Prime Minister of Australia) (2010) 'A new era for the Australian Public Service and the ANU', news release, 8 May 2010, Canberra: Office of Prime Minister. Available online at https://news.anu.edu.au/2010/05/09/prime-minister-kevin-rudd-opens-the-new-crawford-school-building-8-may-2010 (accessed on 5 February 2014).

Slaughter, A.-M. (2004) 'A new world order', in *Making Law Work: Environmental Compliance and Sustainable Development*, vol. 2, London: Cameron May.

Slaughter, A.-M. (2005) *A New World Order*, Princeton, NJ: Princeton University Press.

Tiernan, A. and Althaus, C. (2005) *Managing Out: The Public Sector in the Community*, Canberra: Australian Public Service Commission.

Tomkins, K. (2009) 'Police, law enforcement and the environment', in *Environmental Crime: A Reader*, Devon: Willan.

Van der Schraaf, A. (2008) 'Capacity building in the Dutch inspectorate: bridging the gap', in *INECE 8th International Conference on Environmental Compliance and Enforcement: 5–11 April 2008, Cape Town, South Africa, Proceedings*, London: Cameron May.

White, R. (2008) *Crimes against Nature: Environmental Criminology and Ecological Justice*, Portland, OR: Willan.

White, R. (ed) (2009) *Environmental Crime: A Reader*, Devon: Willan.

Winkworth, G. (2006) 'Ordinary officials – building community capacity through cross-sectoral collaboration', *Public Administration Today*, 9(October–December): 31–8.

Zaelke, D., Kaniaru, D. and Kružíková, E. (eds) (2005a) *Making Law Work: Environmental Compliance and Sustainable Development Volume 1*, London: Cameron May.

Zaelke, D., Kaniaru, D. and Kružíková, E. (eds) (2005b) *Making Law Work: Environmental Compliance and Sustainable Development Volume 2*, London: Cameron May.

14 Integrating intelligence functions into environmental regulatory agencies

Australian experiences

James Lehane[1]

Introduction

> Minds are like parachutes. They only function when they are open.
>
> (Heuer 1999)

Environmental problems have long been noted for their complexity, with cross-cutting social, economic and political concerns linking into environmental issues (Bispham and van Doorn 1996: 1). Introducing a regulatory enforcement regime into that mix does not present a simple task, even for experienced compliance and enforcement practitioners. Therefore, the various forms of an Australian national environment agency have traditionally been policy- or programme-focussed.

In recent years, however, there has been a trend for environmental agencies to deliver broader on-ground operational services (Stanton 2005: 57), including those of compliance and enforcement. Adoption of compliance and enforcement roles has not been a rapid and comprehensive process, with more of a slow build-up approach having been taken (Bispham and van Doorn 1996: 2).

This chapter will explore some of the critical issues surrounding the introduction and integration of an intelligence function within an environmental and regulatory agency. Importantly, it will highlight opportunities for intelligence to be used within an integrated system to aid the identification of risks and priorities, in addition to delivering standard and more traditional intelligence services to enforcement practitioners.

Whilst not solely focussed on any commodity area, the application of an intelligence function is a generic process. Such a process does not require specialist knowledge of any one commodity area *per se*, but is generically applicable across commodities. Crime areas subject to intelligence analysis may range from wildlife to pollution crimes or from the cash economy to digital transactions.

The development and maturation of compliance and enforcement functions within environmental agencies would result in them liaising with financial intelligence units and pursuing, or at least considering, 'proceeds of crime' actions against those choosing not to comply with environmental legislation.

Environmental intelligence emerges

The introduction of compliance and enforcement functions within an environmental agency is not without its challenges. Agency culture can be a major hurdle that impacts on the effectiveness and efficiency of such functions. Significant internal changes are often required for the newly introduced regulatory efforts to be accepted, made effective and form part of everyday operations.

The same may be argued for the introduction of a law enforcement intelligence function within that environmental agency, as internal changes are required of operating procedures, culture and understanding. The introduction of standard law enforcement functions, processes and concepts should be considered as a usual way to improve the effectiveness of regulatory efforts in any regulatory agency. This follows the trend of mainstream law enforcement agencies to better utilise intelligence (Prunckun 2004: 42). However, as a word of caution, it should also be noted that, within the policing environment, 'Intelligence-led policing is in its very early stages' (Osborne 2006: 77). Acknowledging that intelligence-led policing in mainstream law enforcement agencies is in the early stages of development leads to the realisation that intelligence functions will be quite embryonic within emerging regulatory agencies.

Whilst tactical levels of intelligence are seen to deliver real products to front-line investigative staff, higher levels of strategic intelligence services are 'struggling' to gain a foothold and to be utilised and integrated within law enforcement agencies (Ratcliffe 2009 3). Given that not all police organisations have introduced such highly integrated intelligence-led approaches, environmental regulatory agencies are unlikely to take a lead role in introducing such functions. Conversely, without a good model on which to base their intelligence functions, regulatory agencies are also unlikely to introduce them. In addition, the fact remains that environmental agencies, especially smaller agencies, may not have the staff or resources to establish formal intelligence functions (Carter 2004: 2).

Intelligence support factors

Many factors affect the effectiveness of an intelligence function within a law enforcement or regulatory agency, namely, networks, information management systems and appropriate levels of staffing for such functions, along with a clear mandate for operations. Whilst such support factors may not be already in place at the time of introducing an intelligence function into an environmental and/or regulatory agency, their establishment should be a focus for the implementation team, in order to ensure the long-term viability of the function. By establishing a level of short-term effectiveness and producing preliminary sample products, a nascent intelligence function should rapidly establish a degree of credibility within the agency.

Although the mere term 'intelligence' conjures up common misconceptions of secretive operations, heavy coats and dark glasses, the introduction of an intelligence function within any regulatory agency should not be seen as a sinister event. Implementing and applying intelligence processes within a regulatory agency is far removed from such common misconceptions and myths. Intelligence is about applying a process to analyse information to aid understanding of the information being held, and the communication of such analysed and value-added information on to others, namely the *clients* (UNODC n.d.: 5).

Governmental risk management

The effective and integrated use of an intelligence function and product serves as a risk management tool for any host agency. As with any business, a government agency is engaged in risk management on a daily basis. This is recognized as a crucial part of governmental programmes (Australian National Audit Office (ANAO) 2007: 8).

It is the management of identified risks that will guide the compliance and enforcement strategies of a regulatory agency to adapt to and deal with newly emerging regulatory risks and with those risks that can never be eliminated (ANAO 2007: 8). The proactive and responsive management of risks for a regulatory regime, be it environmental, financial or criminal, is a critical component of its regulatory programme.

The risk management sphere is one in which intelligence services can greatly aid and assist government regulatory programmes, including those within environmental agencies, to drive into the future to deliver targeted compliance and enforcement programmes that are based on an understanding of the risks that will be or are being faced (Ratcliffe 2009: 2).

What is intelligence?

In the words of Richards Heuer (1999: 14), 'Intelligence seeks to illuminate the unknown'. Distinguishing information and intelligence, a current United Nations Office of Drugs and Crime (UNODC) document states that 'information' is 'knowledge in raw form'; and 'intelligence' is 'information with added value' and 'information that has been evaluated in context of its source and reliability' (UNODC n.d.: 1).

Intelligence analysis operates at several levels. At base level, tactical intelligence deals with case-specific information to support operational line areas in achieving their business (Grace 2004: 30). Operational intelligence works to assist managers to achieve operational outcomes and to deploy resources to issues as they are identified (Grace 2004: 30). Strategic intelligence provides a higher level of insight into issues and contributes to longer-term strategic or policy decisions (Grace 2004: 30). Whilst separate in some respects, these three levels of intelligence are also integrated to some extent, as each has an influence on the other, as depicted in Figure 14.1.

The application and integration of intelligence functions within military and law enforcement operations is not a new concept by any means. However, after

Figure 14.1 Potential interplay between levels of intelligence

many decades there remain misunderstandings about what intelligence is and how it is carried out (Osborne 2005: 10). Simplistically put, 'in government and private sector alike, analysis is the catalyst that converts information into intelligence for planners and decision makers' (Krizan 1999: 7).

Regardless of whether the intelligence tasking is at tactical, operational or strategic levels, the intelligence cycle comprises a process flow, as depicted in Figure 14.2.

It must be noted that there are many variants on the intelligence cycle, but all cover the same process and guide the explanation of the intelligence process in similar ways.

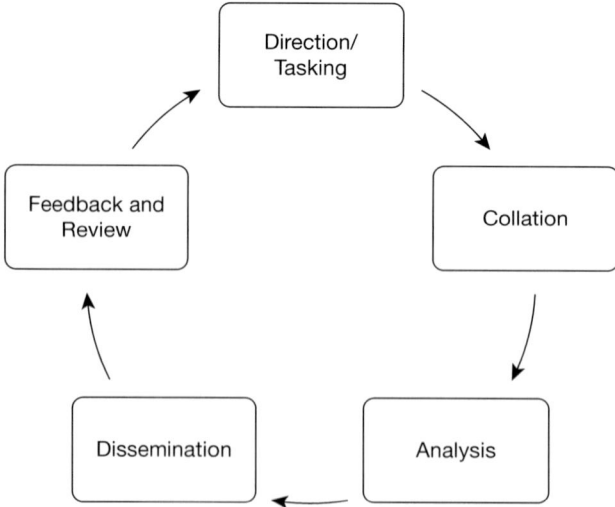

Figure 14.2 General intelligence cycle

Source: Ratcliffe 2009: 7

Table 14.1 Possible crime analysis services

Intelligence tool	Features
Financial analysis	Identification of financial relationships and potentially illegal activity
Market analysis	Identification of the commerce of crime, considering illegal activities and their markets to develop strategies to disrupt and dismantle the markets
Network/association analysis	Identification and visualisation of relationships and activities within a network
Frequency analysis	Counting incidents of non-compliance and crime, comparing counts and analysing trends
Spatial analysis	Mapping to aid analysis to identify patterns of locations of non-compliance/crime
Temporal analysis	Temporal analysis identifies patterns of crime/disorder by time of day, day of week, time of month, time of year, season, special events (holidays, sporting events) as well as the tempo of crime
Problem analysis	Multi-faceted approach to analysing a problems, potentially requiring in-depth research
Communication analysis	Identification and visualisation of relationships evidenced through telecommunications records

Adapted: Osborne 2006: 97–8

Without providing a prescriptive or exhaustive list of what may be expected or delivered by suitably qualified and experienced staff within an intelligence unit, Table 14.1 provides a selection of possible crime analysis services.

The snapshot provided in Table 14.1 of a number of more 'tactically' focussed products that may be produced by a functional intelligence unit provides guidance as to the potential benefits to be obtained by integrating such a function within a regulatory agency.

Keeping the guidance in mind, that 'a systematic, risk-based programme of compliance assessment activities provides a regulator with a cost-effective approach to monitoring compliance, enabling it to target available resources at the highest priority regulatory risks and to respond proactively to changing and emerging risks' (ANAO 2007: 51), the application of a proactive intelligence function could arguably be well placed to aid in the delivery of a risk assessment-based, value-adding programme to the regulatory regime as a whole. As a function, an intelligence area within an agency should be able to deliver accurate, timely and relevant intelligence products to serve the broader purpose of prevention and planning and resource allocation (Carter 2004: 8).

As Foley (2004: 1) notes, 'regulatory theory asserts that the best way to regulate behaviour is by being responsive to the conduct of those who display that behaviour'. Such an approach, when applied across a regulatory agency's risk management programme serves to avoid what Sunstein (1990: 407) referred to as the 'paradoxes of the regulatory state', whereby 'self-defeating regulatory strategies – strategies that achieve an end precisely opposite to the one intended' – are avoided.

Intelligence within an environmental regulatory agency

Protection of the natural environment has been an increasing concern globally for more than 30 years (Brack and Hayman 2002: 3). In some countries, however, environmental enforcement does not hold a very high priority, with the system of government instead tolerating a lower standard such as every country has experienced at some point during its development (Bispham and van Doorn 1996: 3). Even with high concern for protection of the environment, the consistent inclusion of intelligence functions as part of the initial phase of the environmental enforcement function is not usual. An exception occurs in the United States, where the use of strategic targeting by the United States Environmental Protection Authority (USEPA) was reported by Duffy in 1996.

Duffy can be seen as a pioneer in reporting the application of law enforcement intelligence functions within an environmental regulatory agency. He linked intelligence functions to the need to support and enable effective risk management by indicating that:

> targeting of resources is a fundamental activity for any organization regardless of its size, nature of its work, or whether it is a public agency or private enterprise. It can be used by senior managers to inform and direct long-term macro-level strategic decisions looking one or several years into the future, and it can be used to guide short-term field-level decisions (i.e., the next few weeks or months) on how best to allocate resources to meet overall organization-wide goals.
>
> (Duffy 1996: 1)

Duffy (1996) indicates that the USEPA was obviously well advanced in implementing and utilising such a function as early as 1996, leaving other agencies with a decade and a half to catch up.

Mandates and marketing

The internal marketing of the intelligence function within an environmental agency may be considered either standard or a new function or service. However, it is not widely discussed in the general guidelines for intelligence functions that are available across the internet (such as in the US Department of Justice series). This is perhaps because most intelligence functions, units or cells occur only in mainstream law enforcement agencies, especially during the early days of establishing fully environmental regulatory functions. Despite this lack of guiding documentation, McComas (2002: 16) identifies the marketing aspects of an intelligence function as being the second key component indicating the success or failure of such a unit, even going as far as to propose that marketing, alongside political aspects, may be the most critical factor.

As part of establishing the intelligence function, a degree of internal capacity building may have to be undertaken within the host regulatory agency. It must, initially, be centred on the basics: What is intelligence? How can intelligence assist commodity specialists (line areas) in their long-term and day-to-day operations? What can agency staff do to assist or access the intelligence services?

Perhaps even more important is the capacity building of senior executives to enable better appreciation of strategic intelligence product and how it intersects with regulatory operations and policy (Ratcliffe 2009: 8; Krizan 1999: 17). Carter (2004: 14) goes further to require the ability for personnel responsible for intelligence functions to understand different issues, and implement policies and practices to ensure that appropriate types of intelligence product are delivered for client consumption. These strategic-level products, following the definitions provided by McComas (2002: 8), will 'tend to reflect long-term plans, goals and objectives' of the agency and indicate that there needs to be a strong linkage between intelligence professionals and associated policy areas.

More than 50 years ago, Sherman Kent, then a Director of the United States Central Intelligence Agency, noted that the relationship between intelligence analysts and policy officials was not naturally aligned, requiring 'careful thought to set right and constant efforts to keep effective' (Davis 2007: 1).

Accordingly, establishing the intelligence function within a regulatory or environmental agency requires, as an imperative, that a clear mandate be set for the personnel to establish their role and functions. As part of this mandate, they must establish working relations within the agency to educate and to 'demystify' the perceptions of 'intelligence'.

Integration of the intelligence function within an agency

The integration of intelligence functions within environmental agencies has the potential to strengthen relationships between various professional streams within them. Policy professionals of the environmental agency should 'ask probing questions of analysts to make sure they have adequately considered alternatives to their preferred bottom-line judgments, i.e. policymakers are more likely to get quality analysis if they make direct demands for it' (Davis 2007: 5). In a similar vein, intelligence staff also need to better understand the needs of decision makers in order to better serve them (Peppler 2001: 9).

Davis (2007: 7–9) makes five key recommendations for analysts when interacting with policy makers:

1. define the intelligence function's mission realistically;
2. become well informed on policy making;
3. place your trust in intelligence processes and maintain a degree of adaptability;
4. learn and keep up to date with the 'best practices'; and
5. ensure that intelligence products are being understood and acted upon.

The levels of integration between functions, be they policy and law making or intelligence and enforcement, will vary over time and, as the regulatory regime

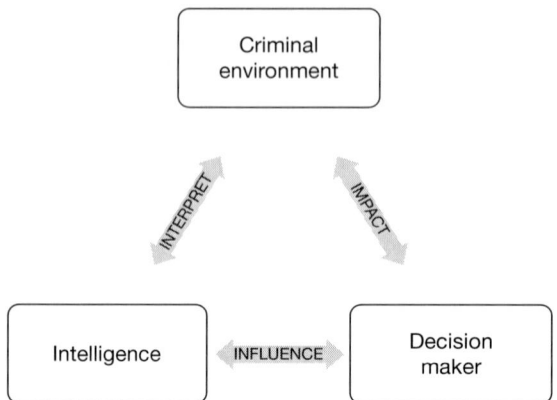

Figure 14.3 Ratcliffe's simplified 'Three-I' intelligence-led policing model

Adapted: Ratcliffe 2003: 3

matures, it would be expected that the internal machinations of that system will become better integrated. Whilst an integrated system may be best placed to serve the needs of those within a regulatory agency, it must also be noted with caution that the use and application of intelligence will not guarantee the 'organisation success or eliminate uncertainty in decision-making' (Peppler 2001: 11).

Ratcliffe (2003: 3) postulated a simplified 'Three-I' (Interpret, Influence, Impact) intelligence-led policing model. The 'Three-I model' (Figure 14.3) is applicable to regulatory agencies and clearly shows how intelligence areas fit well within a simplified structure.

This model is applicable to any regulatory agency. For the 'Three-I' model, the 'Decision maker' role is readily substituted for 'Policy area or decision maker', and 'Criminal environment' readily expanded to encompass the 'Regulated community'.

With regard to how closely integrated intelligence staff should be within a policy area, there is a danger that an analyst may become too close to the policy line area and at risk of losing independence and objectivity (Davis 2007: 2). However, Davis (2007: 2) also notes that the failure to integrate risks identified through the intelligence process may lead to the intelligence function being excluded from feedback, contemporary events and activities, and falling outside of the knowledge base.

The level of integration for the intelligence function within the environmental agency, like all regulatory and enforcement agencies, needs to consider critical aspects, including access to agency databases:

> Regulatory intelligence is information supplied to a regulator or acquired by regulatory staff through their normal activities that, in isolation, may be inconclusive. However, when it is combined with other pieces of intelligence,

or added to other information held in the regulator's database, there may be sufficient evidence of heightened regulatory risks to warrant investigation by the regulator.

(ANAO 2007: 19)

Linkages to client areas should be considered critical to any regulatory operation as its absence will provide significant risks to establishing an intelligence function.

Extending intelligence functions to provide for 'business intelligence'

The integration of an intelligence function delivers more than tactical and operational intelligence to regulatory staff. Such integration should aid the agency to deliver outcomes and priorities, as well as aiding the identification of risks and impacts of compliance and enforcement activities on those operating in contravention of the regulatory regime. More specifically, the ANAO (2007: 36) recommends the targeting of resources using an 'explicit emphasis on conducting a detailed threat analysis before commencing regulatory activity planning', so as to focus on the issues most important to the regulatory regime. Well-integrated intelligence officers would serve as key drivers of such proactive measures. Detailed analysis of a threat, including 'its components and precursors, its causes and consequences', is required so as to efficiently and effectively use existing resources (ANAO 2007: 36). This lends itself to a 'business intelligence' approach. Conducting threat assessments, as identified above, requires looking further afield – internationally or across similar commodity sectors with comparable features – as the intelligence process is generic, applicable across commodities and areas of interests.

Emerging crime risks identified within an agency area of operations or jurisdiction are most likely also to be occurring elsewhere in the world at the same time (ANAO 2007: 52). For instance, criminal enterprises laundering money to legitimise illegal fisheries operations have a high probability of putting proceeds of the environmental crimes through the same laundering process as proceeds of crime from other enterprises.

As Carter (2004: 45) rightly points out, 'criminal enterprises exist to earn illegal profits through the trafficking of illegal commodities: drugs, stolen property, counterfeit goods, and other contraband where there is a consumer demand'. As such, an agency criminal intelligence function would readily have the capabilities to undertake a professional business intelligence assessment on entities or commodities involved with such criminal enterprises.

Networking the intelligence function beyond the agency

For any environmental intelligence function to be fully effective, it requires a well-established network of internal compliance and enforcement clients, along with a supportive policy client; and a larger external intelligence practitioner network of compliance and enforcement members of partner agencies (Carter 2004: 30). 'Effectiveness in enforcement is best reached by cooperation between all agencies involved' (Bispham and van Doorn 1996: 4) as 'Environmental crimes frequently demand a high level of collaboration with non-police agencies' (White 2007: 5).

Mechanisms and networks already exist to facilitate the free flow of information between regulatory practitioners and the associated intelligence staff. For example, in Australia, the Australasian Environmental Law Enforcement and Regulators neTwork (AELERT) was established in 2004 for environmental regulatory agencies to work together in achieving their regulatory aims (AELERT 2010). The current AELERT Strategic Plan 2009–2013 includes the stated object to 'Improve Operational Effectiveness' through the creation of 'gateways for liaison and cooperation between member agencies' (AELERT 2009). With this object as a key component of the network's operations, both regulatory and intelligence function staff within AELERT member agencies have a mechanism to cooperatively engage with each other to enable the free flow of information (subject to relevant information privacy provisions accorded by various legislative instruments from jurisdiction to jurisdiction). As noted by the ANAO (2007: 25), 'open and responsive relationships are beneficial to all parties'. With a network such as AELERT to utilise as a mechanism to exchange Australasian environmental crime information, cooperation would prove beneficial to all participants over time. Osborne (2006: 52) notes that successful dissemination of information as part of an intelligence role 'depends on the quality of relationships of those involved and their abilities to share information appropriately and effectively'.

Mechanisms and networks such as AELERT (and the ever-increasing list of similar environmental enforcement networks) enable a higher degree of cooperation within and between environmental and other enforcement agencies, at local, national and international levels (Brack and Hayman 2002: 20). This degree of cooperation across all mentioned levels can result in the coordination of information gathering and exchange, in addition to the provision of a consistency in approaches across regulatory agencies (Brack and Hayman 2002: 20). Such benefits of a networked approach to environmental regulation will surely prove beneficial towards achieving the stated aims and objectives of the agency.

Future developments

Whilst yet to be more fully explored as a tool to assist or complement investigations within environmental regulatory agencies, the concept of following the financial proceeds of crime is one that will require more consideration across all commodities by regulatory agencies. The concept is captured by the term 'money laundering' described as:

> ... the activities and financial transactions that are undertaken with the specific aim of hiding the true source of income. Usually the money involved

has been derived from an illegal enterprise and the goal is to give that money the appearance of coming from a legitimate source.

(QCMC 2005: 1)

Illegal activities within an environmental commodity area occur due to the financial benefits to be obtained through those actions. As such, an intelligence-led regulatory response could pursue and recoup such proceeds of crime as they are identified.

Within Australia, the role of intelligence in informing the regulatory agenda is gaining traction. A preliminary review of published documents by the Queensland Department of the Environment and Heritage Protection (QDEHP) indicates that some level of analysis and consideration of current and potential future threats has been undertaken. QDEHP has taken the proactive measure of publishing a series of compliance planning documents, including its Compliance Strategy, Annual Compliance Plan and Annual Tactical Compliance Plan (QDEHP n.d.).

Interestingly, there are similarities between these new developments and those in the USA identifying areas for environmental regulatory interest. In 2005, Shimshack and Ward (2005: 523) reported that the US Supreme Court required the USEPA to base its monitoring activities on 'neutral selection', based on geographic factors and time since last inspections were conducted, thereby prohibiting 'purely random inspections'. Such measures are similar to the risk management approach documented by the Queensland Department of Environment and Natural Resources Management, and go towards elements of the ANAO Better Practice Guide in relation to targeting efforts towards threats and risks. Additionally, this example also serves to consolidate the concept that, despite differences across commodity or location, regulatory agencies worldwide face similar issues and are moving in the same direction in terms of delivering regulatory services.

Duffy concludes with thoughts that serve in some ways as recommendations and are so fitting that to summarise them would not do them justice:

1. Define objective and defensible analytical criteria to ensure that the agency is on solid footing in the selection of enforcement priorities and targets; industries and facilities may take exception to having been targeted as a noncomplier or a potential health risk.

2. Synchronize the analytical process with the agency's annual planning processes to maximize results and to better inform the identification and selection of priorities. Establish baseline compliance and enforcement trend data and use this data to monitor and measure success, results and effectiveness.

3. Make the targeting process inclusive (there isn't a monopoly on good ideas), iterative (macro-level for budget and national guidance, region-specific for local priorities and specific inspection plans), and supple to accommodate emerging priorities, new ideas, or unexpected occurrences (e.g., newly-identified health threats, accidents, spills).

4.   Take maximum advantage of the investment that the government has made in the collection (and automation) of compliance and enforcement data. If the agency is not going to use data, perhaps it should not spend resources to collect it.

(Duffy 1996: 8)

Conclusion

Environmental regulatory agencies with fully integrated intelligence functions will be a common reality in the future, as already established in the USEPA. The application of intelligence processes also to regulatory functions and business planning and risk management will be additional benefits of the introduction of such intelligence functions into an environmental agency. Services will follow through the provision of tactical information to environmental enforcement practitioners, operational reviews and assessments to managers, and subsequently to higher-level strategic assessments for decision makers and managers. With moves towards more open and transparent government and ongoing critical reviews of poorly managed environmental compliance and enforcement programmes, an integrated intelligence function can be seen as part of the insurance policy to guard against various criticisms and reviews heading towards any regulatory programme. In conclusion: intelligence is not purely a law enforcement service set of tools; intelligence can serve as a risk management tool and aid in annual business planning of setting priorities against risks, and networks are one of the most critical components required for good intelligence functions.

Note

1 This chapter represents the views of the author and does not necessarily represent the views or policies of the Australian Pesticides and Veterinary Medicines Authority.

References

Australasian Environmental Law Enforcement and Regulators neTwork (AELERT) (2009) *Strategic Plan 2009–2013*. Available online at https://aelert.net/how-we-work-together (accessed 5 February 2014).

Australasian Environmental Law Enforcement and Regulators neTwork (AELERT) (2010) *Background*. Available online at https://aelert.net/about-us (accessed 5 February 2014).

Australian National Audit Office (ANAO) (2007) *Administering Regulation: Better Practice Guide*, Canberra: ANAO. Available online at www.anao.gov.au/~/media/Uploads/Documents/administering_regulation_.pdf (accessed 21 October 2013).

Bispham, T. and van Doorn, J. (1996) 'Criminal Enforcement Role in Environment', paper presented at INECE Fourth International Conference on Environmental Compliance and Enforcement, Chiang Mai, 22 April 1996. Available online at www.inece.org/4thvol1/cerews.pdf (accessed 21 October 2013).

Brack, D. and Hayman, G. (2002) *International Environmental Crime: The Nature and Control of Environmental Black Markets*, London: Royal Institute of International Affairs.

Available online at www.chathamhouse.org/publications/papers/view/107575 (accessed 20 January 2014).

Carter, D. L. (2004) *Law Enforcement Intelligence: A Guide for State, Local and Tribal Law Enforcement Agencies*, USA: US Department of Justice and Michigan State University. Available online at www.cops.usdoj.gov/default.asp?Item=1404 (accessed 21 October 2013).

Davis, J. (2007) 'Improving CIA Analytic Performance: Analysts and the Policymaking Process', *Sherman Kent Centre for Intelligence Analysis: Occasional Papers*, 1(2). Available online at www.cia.gov/library/kent-center-occasional-papers/index.html (accessed 21 October 2013).

Duffy, R.F. (1996) 'Strategic Targeting for Compliance and Enforcement', paper presented at INECE Fourth International Conference on Environmental Compliance and Enforcement, Chiang Mai, 22 April 1996. Available online at www.inece.org/4thvol1/duffy.pdf (accessed 21 October 2013).

Foley, T. (2004) 'Using a Responsive Regulatory Pyramid in Environmental Regulation', paper presented at Queensland Environmental Law Association Annual Conference: Carrot, Sticks and Toolkits, Cairns, 12 May 2004. Available online at www.qela.com. au/_dbase_upl/2004ConfProceedings.pdf (accessed 21 October 2013).

Grace, G. (2004) 'Executive Expectations of the Intelligence Investment', *The Journal of the Australian Institute of Professional Intelligence Officers*, 12(2): 29–33.

Heuer, R.J. (1999) *Psychology of Intelligence Analysis*, USA: Center for the Study of Intelligence, Central Intelligence Agency. Available online at www.cia.gov/library/center-for-the-study-of-intelligence/csi-publications/books-and-monographs/psychology-of-intelligence-analysis/index.html (accessed 5 February 2014).

International Network for Environmental Compliance and Enforcement (INECE) (1996) *Fourth International Conference on Environmental Compliance and Enforcement*, Proceedings, Chiang Mia, 22 April 1996. Available online at www.inece.org/4thvol1/4toc.htm (accessed 21 October 2013).

Krizan, L. (1999) 'Intelligence Essentials for Everyone', *Joint Military Intelligence College Occasional Paper No. 6*, Washington, DC: Joint Military Intelligence College.

McComas, H. (2002) '"Strategy Lost" Dealing with the Need for a Strategic Intelligence Capability', *The Journal of the Australian Institute of Professional Intelligence Officers*, 11(1): 8–23.

Osborne, D. (2006) *Out of Bounds: Innovation and Change in Law Enforcement Intelligence Analysis*, Washington, DC: Joint Military Intelligence College.

Peppler, B. (2001) 'A Conceptual Framework for Intelligence Management', *The Journal of the Australian Institute of Professional Intelligence Officers*, 10(1): 4–14.

Prunckun, H. (2004) 'Advanced Analytics for Law Enforcement Intelligence', *The Journal of the Australian Institute of Professional Intelligence Officers*, 13(2): 42–50.

Queensland Crime and Misconduct Commission (QCMC) (2005) *Background Intelligence Brief: Money Laundering*, QCMC. Available online at www.cmc.qld.gov.au/research-and-publications/publications/crime/money-laundering.pdf (accessed 21 October 2013).

Queensland Department of the Environment and Heritage Protection (QDEHP) (n.d.) *Compliance and Enforcement*. Available online at www.ehp.qld.gov.au/management/planning-guidelines/enforcement.html (accessed 21 October 2013).

Ratcliffe, J. (2003) 'Intelligence-led Policing', *Australian Institute of Criminology Trends and Issues in Crime and Criminal Justice*, 248. Available online at www.aic.gov.au/publications/current%20series/tandi/241-260/tandi248.aspx (accessed 21 October 2013).

Ratcliffe, J. (ed.) (2009) *Strategic Thinking in Criminal Intelligence*, 2nd edn, NSW: Federation Press.

Shimshack, J.P. and Ward, M.B. (2005) 'Regulator Reputation, Enforcement and Environmental Compliance', *Journal of Environmental Economics and Management*, 50(3): 519–40.

Stanton, M. (2005) 'The Law Enforcement Intelligence Paradigm: A Square Peg in a Round Hole', *The Journal of the Australian Institute of Professional Intelligence Officers*, 14(1): 57–69.

Sunstein, C.R. (1990) 'Paradoxes of the Regulatory State', *University of Chicago Law Review*, 57(2): 407–42.

United Nations Office of Drugs and Crime (UNODC) (2011) *Criminal Intelligence Training: Manual for Managers.* Available online at www.unodc.org/documents/organized-crime/Law-Enforcement/Criminal_Intelligence_for_Managers.pdf (accessed 21 October 2013).

University of Wollongong, papers presented at *Following the Proceeds of Environmental Crime: Fish, Forests and Filthy Lucre International Conference*, Wollongong, February 2010. Available online at http://lha.uow.edu.au/law/UOW072309 (accessed 21 October 2013).

White, R. (2007) 'Dealing with Environmental Harm: Green Criminology & Environmental Law Enforcement', *Tasmanian Institute of Law Enforcemnt Studies (TILES) Briefing Papers*, 5. Available online at www.utas.edu.au/__data/assets/pdf_file/0003/293745/Briefing_Paper_No_5.pdf (accessed 21 October 2013).

Part VII
Looking to the future

15 Combating transnational environmental crime

Future directions

Gregory Rose

How can law enforcement authorities engage more effectively across national borders to combat transnational environmental crimes? In particular, what legal and institutional routes exist or new pathways must be built to follow the proceeds of forest and fisheries crime? This chapter considers these questions by identifying existing legal mechanisms, assessing their gaps and then examining possible new approaches to improve international coordination to combat fisheries and forest crimes.

Existing mechanisms

A substantial series of academic journal articles investigate whether existing 'war crimes' and 'crimes against humanity' commissioned by individuals could be interpreted to include major international crimes against the environment (Orellana 2005; Cho 2001). In preparing a draft Code of Crimes against the Peace and Security of Mankind, the International Law Commission of the United Nations in 1991 adopted a draft article specifically on willful and severe damage to the environment (draft Article 26). The draft article was dropped in 1996, although willful and severe damage to the environment remained a topic for discussion as a form of war crime. It was ultimately incorporated in modified form into the Statute of the International Criminal Court as the 'intentional launching of an attack in the knowledge that such an attack will cause widespread long-term and severe damage to the natural environment which would be clearly excessive in relation to the concrete and direct overall military advantage anticipated' during an international armed conflict (Article 8(2)(b)(iv)) (Sharp 1999).

The question of how a new environmental crime directed against states might emerge has been explored in academic writings concerning whether an international crime of 'ecocide' might be developed (Gray 1996; Higgins 2010) and was also explored in the International Law Commission in draft articles on State Responsibility. The Commission, at an early stage, also adopted a draft article on international crimes by states that included pollution of the environment. The crime was defined as 'a serious breach of international obligation of essential importance to the safeguarding and preservation of the human environment, such as those prohibiting massive pollution of the atmosphere or of the seas' (Article 19(3)(d)). Like the draft article in the Code of Crimes against the Peace and Security of Mankind, this provision was ultimately dropped from the draft articles. Accordingly, there is as yet no direct criminalization under international law of environmental harm.

Where non-compliance with environmental regulations is criminalized under national laws, and such activities have transnational elements, they need to be combated though internationally coordinated response efforts. Transnational environmental crime has received less institutional attention than other major transnational criminal activities, such as drug trafficking and terrorism. United Nations crime prevention institutions first became engaged with the subject matter of environmental crime in the lead-up to and immediate follow-up from the United Nations Conference on Environment and Development held in 1992. The UN Commission on Crime Prevention and Criminal Justice (CCPCJ) has, as one of its four mandated priorities, the promotion of criminal law in protecting the environment but it did not engage substantively in this area until 2007, with work focused on forest exploitation crimes. It expanded this focus in 2013 with its 22nd session dedicated to emerging forms of transnational crime, including environmental crime (CCPCJ). The United Nations Office on Drugs and Crime (UNODC), which acts as CCPCJ secretariat, is also starting to turn its attention to transnational environmental crime.

Forests

Illegal logging is likely the most economically significant transnational environmental crime. In 2005, 5–10 per cent of global timber production valued at about US$17.5 billion was attributable to illegal sourcing within a global timber market estimated at US$150 billion (Jaakko Pöyry Consulting 2005). Illicit production at such volumes over-saturates the timber market, driving down the commodity price and harming the licit industry. It can also cause declines in public revenue, biodiversity, soil, water quality and the rule of law.

Illegal logging is most commonly associated with developing equatorial states, but it occurs in all types of forests throughout Southeast Asia, Central Africa, Eastern Europe, Russia, South America and even North America. At least half of all logging activities in the Amazon basin, Central Africa, Southeast Asia and the Russian Federation are probably illegal. Within the Asia-Pacific, for example, authorized Cambodian annual log production in the 1990s was about 450,000 cubic metres, while estimated harvesting was almost ten times more at 4,300,000 cubic metres. Similarly, it is estimated that illegal logging in Indonesia is worth 60–88 per cent of the total annual log harvest (Schloenhardt 2008) and that over one-third of Indonesia's original forests (43 of 120 million hectares) have been devastated by illegal logging (WWF-UK 2003), with dire consequences for rural populations including income loss and accelerating disease and poverty (Dupont 2001).

International Tropical Timber Agreement (ITTA)

International concern over the dangers faced by tropical forests due to rapid deforestation in the 1970s resulted in the United Nations Conference on Trade and Development convening a Tropical Timber Conference to negotiate an agreement to ensure sustainable tropical forest management to protect forests while ensuring a constant supply of timber for trade and promoting employment in the timber industry. Trade in tropical timber contributes substantially to economic growth in developing countries. Sales worldwide are estimated at US$10 billion a year.

The first International Tropical Timber Agreement (ITTA) was adopted in 1983. The countries that signed the agreement are home to 80 per cent of the world's tropical forests and account for 90 per cent of global trade in tropical timber. The second ITTA was signed in 1994 and, although due to expire on 31 December 2006, was extended until the third ITTA, signed in 2006, came into force in 2011.[1] The Agreement provides a framework for cooperation and consultation among countries producing and consuming tropical timber; seeks to increase and diversify international trade in tropical timber and improve conditions in the tropical timber market; promotes and supports research to improve forest management and ways of using wood; and encourages the development of national policies to protect tropical forests and maintain an ecological balance (ITTO).

Article 31, on 'Complaints and Disputes', provides that any complaint that a member has failed to fulfill its obligations under the Agreement, or any dispute concerning the interpretation or application of the Agreement, shall be referred to the International Tropical Timber Council for decision and that decisions of the Council on these matters shall be final and binding. The treaty contains no criminal provisions and therefore there are no recorded criminal incidences under the treaty.

INTERPOL Project LEAF

Under the auspices of the INTERPOL Environmental Crime Programme, a project to study illegal logging and forest-related crime commenced in 2012. Entitled Project LEAF (Law Enforcement Assistance for Forests), its objectives include providing information concerning the networks involved in corruption, fraud, laundering and smuggling of wood products and illegal logging, as well as supporting countries' national enforcement efforts by providing information, training and operational support, and by developing best practices (INTERPOL). Official corruption can be a major factor in facilitating forest crime (Setiono and Husein). Project LEAF therefore focuses in particular on corruption-related crimes emerging under international programmes to mitigate greenhouse gas emissions under the rubric of Reduction of Emissions from Deforestation and Forest Degradation plus (REDD+).

Fisheries

Oceans produce 15–20 per cent of humanity's food protein and contain the vast majority of the earth's life species. Wild-capture fisheries comprise the component of marine living resources that have the highest direct economic value and which are most commonly extracted from the marine environment.[2] An estimated US$10–23 billion is lost to illegal, unreported and unregulated (IUU) fishing around the world each year, US$134–400 million of it lost in the Pacific. This is up to four times more than Pacific Island countries earn in fisheries income by selling fishing access licenses to non-regional countries (MRAG 2005; Baird 2004).

Legally binding global legal measures to promote compliance with international fisheries conservation standards and to prevent fisheries crime are in place and they include the UN Convention on the Law of the Sea 1982, UN Food and Agricultural Organization (FAO) Compliance Agreement 1993, UN Fish Stocks Agreement 1995, the FAO Port States Measures Agreement 2009 and others too numerous to list here. Among these, the Port State Measures Agreement is the most directly relevant to the prosecution of transnational fisheries crimes. Once its final text had been agreed upon, the FAO described it as the first ever global treaty to be focused specifically on the problem of IUU fishing.[3]

Port State Measures Agreement

On 22 November 2009, the Agreement on Port State Measures to Prevent, Deter and Eliminate Illegal, Unreported and Unregulated Fishing (the PSM-IUU Agreement) was approved by the 91 Members of the FAO.[4] It will enter into force 30 days after a total of 25 FAO members have accepted it (PSMA-IUU Agreement Article 29) but, to date, only five FAO members have done so.[5]

The Agreement is based on the customary powers of a Port State to control the terms of access to its port and, in an attempt to deter IUU fishing, harmonizes use of those powers to implement Port State measures (PSMs) against foreign fishing vessels (Kuemlangan and Press 2010). The PSMs to be implemented by Port States under the Agreement include the requirements to: designate ports for the landing of vessels (Article 7.1); publicize the port to which vessels may request entry (Article 7.1); provide minimum standard fishing vessel information prior to it being granted entry to port (Article 8); deny a fishing vessel access to port if there is sufficient information to prove that the vessel has engaged in IUU fishing (Article 9.4), unless the vessel is allowed entry exclusively for the purpose of other punitive action which is at least as effective as denial of entry (Article 9.5); prohibit the landing and transhipping of IUU fish catch (Article 11.1); prohibit port services to vessels that have engaged in fishing activity in contravention of fishing regulations (Article 11); inspect fishing vessels, particularly where there are reasonable grounds for suspecting involvement in IUU fishing activity (Article 12); notify the Flag State (Article 18.1); and carry out enforcement measures (Article 18.3). In relation to enforcement measures, and noting that Article 9.5 allows that punitive action at least as effective as denial of port entry is permitted, Article 18.3 provides that the treaty does 'not prevent a party from taking measures that are in conformity with international law in addition to those specified'.

If the PSM-IUU Agreement does not enter into force, then the primary international legal instrument governing PSM-IUU measures is the non-binding scheme of recommendations set out in the Model Scheme on Port State Measures to Combat IUU Fishing, adopted by the FAO Committee on Fisheries in 2005. In contrast with Article 18.3 of the PSM-IUU Agreement, the Model Scheme provides that the Port State may take other actions against IUU fishing vessels with the consent of, or upon the request of, the Flag State (Model Scheme, Provision 5). If interpreted as a comprehensive statement of the enforcement options available to the Port State, the Model Scheme would purport to limit the range of enforcement measures available. However, the Model Scheme is not a legally binding document and it also explicitly provides that nothing in it affects the exercise by states of their sovereignty over ports in their territory in accordance with international law (Model Scheme, Provision 10).

The recognized authority of Port States to impose law enforcement measures at least as effective as denial of port entry (but in conformity with international law) provides a legal basis for the exercise of criminal law enforcement powers against the vessels engaged in transnational fisheries crimes. The PSM-IUU Agreement and Model Scheme recognize these powers and provide for enhanced law enforcement cooperation through the exchange of information between state authorities but do not harmonize the national approaches to the prescription of fisheries crimes.

Soft laws that set out non-legally binding standards that directly govern fisheries include UN resolutions on driftnet fishing and on sustainable fisheries, and FAO codes of conduct and guidelines; including the International Plan of Action on Capacity, International Plan of Action on Seabirds, International Plan of Action on Sharks and the 2004 FAO Model Scheme on Port State Measures to Combat IUU Fishing. Most relevant is the International Plan of Action-IUU adopted in 2001, supplementing earlier standards, such as the 1995 FAO Code of Conduct on Responsible Fishing, and itself reinforced by later international instruments, including the 2005 Rome Declaration on IUU Fishing.

Although not legally binding, the International Plan of Action (IPOA)-IUU articulates an accepted international standard requiring the penalization of illegal fishing.[6] The use of judicial or quasi-judicial processes to enforce fisheries laws is implicitly recognized in paragraph 17 of the IPOA-IUU, which requires that national implementing legislation address the admissibility as legal evidence of information from electronic data and new technologies. Most importantly, it provides, in paragraph 21, that a state should penalize both vessels and persons of its nationality under its jurisdiction and that the penalties should be sufficiently severe to deter IUU fishing and deprive offenders of their illicit proceeds.[7]

INTERPOL Project SCALE

In relation to law enforcement cooperation, Project SCALE was launched by INTERPOL through its Environmental Crime Programme in February 2013 to combat fisheries crime by facilitating the conduct of coordinated operations and by institutionalizing cooperation between national agencies and with international partners to suppress fisheries crime. In particular, it is developing a case study on fisheries crime in West Africa, a highly vulnerable area to fisheries crime (INTERPOL). Project SCALE provides a strategic plan for INTERPOL's role in addressing connections with crossover crimes, information and intelligence exchange, facilitation of networks between members and provision of analytical and operational support. Supporting Project SCALE, the INTERPOL Fisheries Crime Working Group was also established in February 2013. The Fisheries Crime Working Group aims to promote capacity building, information exchange and operational support to suppress fisheries crime.

Crime prevention

In contrast to the forest and fisheries regimes, global cooperative efforts to combat transnational crime have produced treaties that require their parties to proscribe specified acts as criminal. As yet, none of these require the proscription of specific acts of environmental harm.

Convention against Transnational Organized Crime

The Convention against Transnational Organized Crime (CTOC), adopted in 2000, addresses both the harmonization of certain criminal laws of its parties and the facilitation of law enforcement cooperation between those parties. It requires that its parties criminalize activities such as participation in an organized criminal group (Article 5), laundering of the proceeds of crime (Article 6), corruption (Article 8) or obstruction of justice (Article 24).

These criminal activities might relate incidentally to environmental crimes – for instance, where an illegal environmental activity is undertaken by an organized group, or when the proceeds of the illegal environmental activity are laundered, or where the activity is facilitated by the corruption of public officials or involves obstruction of the administration of justice. Thus, these offences might pick up environmental crime only incidentally.

The CTOC also extends broadly to 'serious crime' if the offence is transnational and involves an organized criminal group. This could cover transnational breaches of environmental standards by organized crime syndicates, but a substantial amount would fall beyond it, due to failing to qualify as 'serious crime', for which offences must carry a maximum penalty of at least four years' imprisonment.[8]

It should be noted that the CTOC also requires that parties establish corporate liability, whether criminal, civil or administrative, in addition to the criminal liability of the natural persons who are principals of a corporation, for the commission of offences it requires to be proscribed.[9]

In relation to the specified crimes, the CTOC also sets in place a range of obligations for international cooperation in law enforcement. These include requirements that the parties cooperate in the confiscation and seizure of suspect criminal assets (Article 13), extradition of alleged offenders (Article 16), provision of mutual legal assistance in prosecutions (Article 18) and the exchange of information in criminal investigations and in criminal intelligence gathering (Articles 26–28). To enable the parties' ongoing cooperation in implementation of their obligations, the CTOC establishes a Conference of Parties (Article 32) and Secretariat (Article 33), which is provided by the UNODC.

In recent years, the CTOC Conference of Parties has become more engaged in the specific topic of transnational environmental crime. In 2008, it decided to include transnational environmental crime as a form of emerging transnational crime in the work of its next session and noted that this form of crime didn't receive attention at the time of the drafting of the CTOC but that it might be embraced within it. Further discussion drew attention to the need for environmental crimes to be included within predicate offences to the crime of money laundering.[10] The sixth and most recent Conference of Parties, held in 2012, elaborated upon the importance of environmental crime as a category of emerging crime (CTOC 2012).

OECD Convention on Combating Bribery of Foreign Public Officials in International Business Transactions

Any enterprise involving exploitation of or impact on natural resources is usually subject to the issue of a governmental permit. For example, permits are required to construct and develop industrial or residential buildings, to discharge or dispose of wastes, to access forests for the logging of timber, to harvest seafood in fishing grounds, to graze livestock in bushland or to access samples of biological resources.

The OECD Convention on Combating Bribery of Foreign Public Officials in International Business Transactions ('Bribery Convention') is open to OECD non-members.[11] It addresses active bribery – that is, actively offering, promising or giving a bribe, regardless of whether it was requested (Article 1). The actual bribe itself is defined as:

> Any undue pecuniary or other advantage whether directly or through intermediaries . . . in order that the official act or refrain from acting in relation to the performance of official duties in order to obtain or retain business or other improper advantage in the conduct of international business.
>
> (Article 1)

The meaning of a foreign country in the context of the Bribery Convention includes 'all levels and subdivisions of government, from national to local'

(Article 1.4.b). A foreign public official then means 'any person holding a legislative, administrative or judicial office of a foreign country, . . . any person exercising a public function for a foreign country, . . . and any official or agent of a public international organisation' (Article 1.4.a).

The Bribery Convention has incidental relevance to environmental crime as its applicability is limited to circumstances that involve transnational bribery. Therefore, as a law enforcement tool it would likely not apply to most instances of forest and fisheries crime.

United Nations Convention against Corruption

The United Nations Convention against Corruption (UNCAC) preamble refers to the connection between sustainable development and the fight against corruption.[12] Despite this, Article 62 of the UNCAC is the only one that specifically mentions sustainable development. It calls upon the parties to take into account the negative effects of corruption on sustainable development, in particular when taking measures for implementation of the Convention through economic development and technical assistance. At its first session, the Conference of Parties to the UNCAC again acknowledged that the fight against corruption is an essential element of sustainable development,[13] but the Conference of Parties has not yet addressed the nexus between corruption and environmental crime. Not all forms of bribery are required to be criminalized. Like the Bribery Convention, the UNCAC applies only incidentally to environmental crimes, in circumstances that involve forms of bribery that the parties have taken the option to criminalize.

Gap analysis

Three substantial gaps impede the ability of international laws and institutions to combat transnational environmental crime. These are (1) conceptual gaps in our understanding of the phenomenon, (2) gaps between national laws that need to be harmonized in order to work cooperatively, and (3) gaps in international law enforcement cooperation. The most debilitating among these is the disharmony between national laws, which obstructs cooperation and also obscures understanding.

Harmonization of criminality elements

Environmental crime is a relatively new category of crime that typically lacks common legal approaches among states (Elliott 2007; Environment Investigation Agency 2008).[14] Studies performed by the Council of Europe and by the European Commission have found that definitions of environmental crimes are diverse and disharmonious. To cooperate in law enforcement, national jurisdictions require comparable legislation against the same crime (i.e. 'dual criminality') (Faure and Heine 2005).

Harmonized national laws are a condition precedent to international cooperation to enforce them. However, approaches to penalties for environmental crimes are varied and environmental crimes are often subject only to minor fines that fall below the threshold for definition as 'serious' crime. States usually require that a crime be classified as 'serious' for it to be considered the subject of transnational law enforcement cooperation. Most international law enforcement cooperation frameworks are designed to address serious criminal offences, rather than administrative or civil offences. Similarly, environmental crimes are not usually treated as 'predicate offences', the proceeds of which would be subject to anti-money laundering measures. Therefore, environmental crimes do not currently cross the threshold set by most jurisdictions for criminal law enforcement cooperation or anti-money laundering action.

In addition to the matter of seriousness of offences, issues remaining to be clarified include the criminal penalization of corporations and their principal officers, which is less usual in civil law system countries, the extension of environmental criminal jurisdiction beyond the geographical boundaries of the sovereign state, which is less usual in common law countries, and appropriate penalties for similar crimes, which presently range widely (Michalowski and Bitten 2005).

International forests and fisheries standards demonstrate that, at the global level, no regimes concerning the criminal punishment of forest or fisheries crimes have been established. Global forests lack a treaty framework that is comprehensive, and there is nothing that addresses forest crime. Many more treaties and institutions are in place governing fisheries management and are designed to combat illegal fishing. However, fisheries treaties tend not to require criminalization of breaches by individuals of their prescribed standards. Instead of engaging with criminal justice systems, they address breaches through managerial and administrative capacity-building mechanisms. International bodies that address forests and fisheries are primarily concerned with standard setting rather than criminal law enforcement, and breaches of internationally prescribed standards of conduct are therefore treated as non-compliance problems rather than as crimes. In contrast, treaties potentially applicable to forest and fisheries crimes have been developed within the legal frameworks for general crime prevention and criminal justice but apply only incidentally to environmental crimes that involve specified circumstances of bribery, money laundering, obstruction of justice and transnational organized crime.

Therefore, despite the recent growth in international norms relating respectively to environment and crime, there is no global understanding about their nexus, no harmonization of legal standards and no agreement on cooperation to combat environmental crime. International environmental law has not yet meshed with transnational criminal law (or international criminal law).

Cooperation in enforcement efforts

Cooperative mechanisms for environmental law enforcement established by INTERPOL are still in the early stages of development. Environmental crime is not one of the organization's six priority areas. However, its Environmental Crime Programme has a rapidly growing staff due to external secondments and funding.[15] The Environmental Crime Programme's work was guided by an Environmental Crime Committee, established in 1992 and which held a biennial conference that served as a forum for environmental crime enforcement information exchange concerning emerging trends, new strategies and practices, expertise and international cooperation. In March 2012, an INTERPOL/UN Environment Programme 'International Chiefs of Environmental Compliance and Enforcement Summit' decided to restructure and rename the committee as the Environmental Compliance and Enforcement Committee, which held its first meeting in November 2013.

The Environmental Compliance and Enforcement Committee is supported by open-ended working groups which each meet annually. Currently, there are three working groups, on wildlife, pollution and fishing. They aim to promote capacity building, information exchange and operational support to suppress crime, to address connections with crossover crimes and to facilitate information and intelligence exchange, networks between members and analytical and operational support. Forest crime has no working group as yet but is addressed through an organized activity entitled Project LEAF, noted above.

Generic international mechanisms are also in place to facilitate general cross-border police and judicial cooperation in law enforcement. For example, the United Nations General Assembly, on the recommendation of the Eighth United Nations Congress on the Prevention of Crime and the Treatment of Offenders, adopted a Model Treaty on Extradition (UNGA resolutions 45/116, annex, and 52/88, annex), a Model Treaty on Mutual Assistance in Criminal Matters (UNGA resolutions 45/117, annex, and 53/112, annex I), a Model Treaty on the Transfer of Proceedings in Criminal Matters (UNGA resolution 45/118, annex) and a Model Treaty on the Transfer of Supervision of Offenders Conditionally Sentenced or Conditionally Released (UNGA resolution 45/119, annex).

These mechanisms are not designed to accommodate new environmental technologies, in relation to which divergent national standards can obstruct international law enforcement cooperation. For example, how might international legal arrangements accommodate mutual recognition or authentication of foreign digital evidence produced through environmental monitoring technologies such as radio frequency identification (RFID), camera feeds, satellite-based position monitoring or video data or the use of DNA evidence on regional population sources?

Mechanisms for deeper cooperation in law enforcement might also be fostered at regional levels. For example, interlinked regional information databases can be (and in some contexts already are) used to monitor vessels at sea to combat transnational marine pollution and to suppress illegal fishing. Port entry prerequisites can be adopted that require blacklisted vessels to discharge regionally agreed criminal penalties prior to being permitted to offload cargo in port or to fish in the region. Pursuit zones across national borders have been created in some regions. Cooperation measures to enhance marine law enforcement have been used in regional seas.

Yet gaps in multilateral law enforcement cooperation remain as cooperation mechanisms could go much further to promote the combination of these new environmental law enforcement technologies with cross-border cooperation.

New approaches

How could the gaps in the international legal and institutional frameworks addressing transnational environmental crime be remedied? Further research to analyze needs and identify opportunities would be helpful, but at this stage it is fair to say that harmonization of national laws and enhanced international law enforcement cooperation are primary issues. They might be promoted by developing specifically applicable international legal frameworks and by building national capacity for international cooperation.

Harmonize national laws

Questions that need exploration in order to harmonize the differences between national approaches include: how to recognize dual criminality (i.e. common offences in each country); how to build common approaches to criminalization of illegal activities by corporate bodies; how to set penalties, whether by administrative sanction, criminal sanction, commensurate with the environmental harm caused, or standardized by the category of offence. Diverse countries would need to adopt a common approach to laws that criminalize environmental harms to enable coordinated enforcement across their borders. Criminal activity is global, and global consensus concerning what comprises criminal activity forms an essential basis for subsequent international cooperation in its suppression. Then, at the international level, cooperative law enforcement mechanisms need to be designed that can function effectively across national borders.

Fisheries

The Port State Measures Agreement (PSM-IUU Agreement) is potentially the most important global legal framework for enforcement of fisheries laws. It provides that the Port State may take specified enforcement measures against a vessel that has engaged in IUU fishing, including denying the use of the port for landing, transhipping, packaging and processing of fish, and denying the use of other port services including refueling and resupply, maintenance and dry docking (PSM-IUU Agreement, Article 18.1(b)).

The PSM-IUU Agreement also explicitly provides that it does 'not prevent a party from taking measures that are in conformity with international law in addition to those specified' (PSM-IUU Agreement, Article 18.3). These additional measures could conceivably include vessel detention and the seizure of catch and/or gear (Sharp 2010). Civil penalties, such as related catch and asset forfeiture, and criminal prosecutions of masters, owners and operators for breaching the publicized conditions of entry into port remain within the power of the Port State. Similarly, criminal penalties such as fines or jail could be imposed.

A protocol to the Agreement, or a declaration or resolution by the parties to it, could seek to harmonize among its parties the adoption of national criminal provisions and to universalize enforcement jurisdiction through law enforcement cooperation. However, as the Agreement has yet to enter into force and has many implementation hurdles to clear, a push to universalize fisheries crime under it is premature at this time.

The IPOA-IUU reflects international consensus that an illegal fishing penalty regime may be based in the criminal justice system or in administrative processes or civil justice systems. Although it stops short of requiring that states criminalize illegal fishing as a serious crime, it offers a basis upon which to build non-legally binding guidelines to harmonize definitions of fisheries crimes.

Non-legally binding norms are easier to agree upon because they are less consequential. Even so, they build consensus as to what later binding norms might look like. Normative frameworks set out in international soft law often form a preparatory basis for the later development of legally binding international standards. Therefore, a resolution and guidelines concerning criminalization of illegal fishing adopted within the framework of the IPOA-IUU may be the more expeditious pathway towards harmonization of laws.

Forests

As there is currently no global legal regime setting out comprehensive standards for forest management, consensus on forest management standards is still needed. These precede global enforcement arrangements against breaches of such standards. Harmonized criminalization might instead be arranged around national standards adopted on a mutual, rather than a global, basis.

For example, the Lacey Act is a legal tool utilized by USA authorities to criminalize the possession and handling of products illegally obtained in foreign jurisdictions (Brack 2007). It sanctions individuals and corporations who deal in any fish, wildlife or wild plant regulated by, *inter alia*, foreign laws or regulations, if that specimen was obtained in violation of such laws or regulations. A subsequent dealing in the specimen is also illegal, including importing, exporting, transporting, selling or receiving, even if that subsequent dealing is by a different person or at a different time from the primary violation of foreign laws or regulations on taking, possessing, transporting or selling the specimen.[16]

Violations of the Lacey Act provisions against unlawful dealing can be prosecuted as serious offences (felonies) or as non-serious offences (misdemeanors), depending upon the degree of criminal intention.[17] The Act also requires an import declaration for plants and plant products, except for plant-based packaging materials used exclusively to import other products.[18] Forfeiture of illegally produced fish or wildlife is permitted 'notwithstanding any culpability requirements'.[19]

The Lacey Act has gained attention in other countries. Australia has adopted similar provisions in relation to trade in illegally harvested foreign timber.[20] Papua New Guinea, Nauru and the Solomon Islands have adopted provisions similar to it within their national fisheries legislation (D'Andrea 2006). The final report of the High Seas Task Force has also recommended that states implement a 'long-arm' approach to enforcement similar to the provisions of the US Lacey Act (High Seas Task Force n.d.).

In the absence of global consensus standards, the Lacey Act might serve as a template for an international regime harmonizing national criminalization of forest crimes to enable enforcement of foreign laws.

Transnational crime prevention

The CTOC serves to harmonize understanding of legal definitions of transnational organized crime and to facilitate law enforcement cooperation. It currently facilitates three protocols concerning some prevalent twenty-first-century transnational crimes – Trafficking in Persons, Smuggling of Migrants, and Illicit Manufacturing of and Trafficking in Firearms. The protocols elaborate detailed standards for harmonized national laws and for international cooperation in relation to their particular subject matters.

The CTOC is the most likely vehicle for formulation of a multilateral treaty to address environmental crime directly. That it could serve this role has been suggested in the CTOC Conference of Parties and by a past Executive Director of UNODC (Costa 2008). This might be by means of a protocol to the CTOC concerning environmental crime that is transnational and organized. The CTOC protocol ultimately formulated could provide common understandings of harms that need to be criminalized under national laws in a harmonized way to facilitate international law enforcement.

A wide range of design options for a CTOC protocol presents itself. For example, the design could utilize selected provisions of multilateral environment agreements. The already established consensus as to common environmental standards to be implemented in the respective areas addressed by those agreements would facilitate harmonization of national laws prescribing criminal offences for breaches of state laws implementing them. Thus, harmonized criminalization of illegal trafficking in hazardous wastes, ozone-depleting substances and other chemical pollutants, threatened flora and fauna, genetically modified organisms and biological resources is facilitated by established agreements setting the principal legal standards in these environmental sectors.[21] A supplementary option is to adopt the model used in the Lacey Act to criminalize selected categories of foreign environmental crimes.

As a foreign offence that forms the basis for subsequent transnational money laundering can be prosecuted only if the prosecuting jurisdiction treats the foreign offence as equivalent to a serious crime under its own domestic laws (i.e. as having dual criminality), selected categories of foreign environmental crimes should be specified as predicate offences for anti-money laundering prosecutions. The criminal treatment of corporate offenders also could be specified, and particular treatments for natural and legal persons could be distinguished.

Some of these proposals may be incompatible with features of jurisprudence in various jurisdictions. Therefore, any legally binding instrument on environmental crimes must allow wide scope for reservations in relation to its harmonization provisions. Some provisions could be specified as optional.[22] In addition, some harmonization measures could be relegated to complementary guidelines, rather than set out in a binding instrument. For example, indicative penalties for specific categories of environmental crime could be set out in guidelines. Additional points of interpretation and guidance on application could also be presented in corresponding guidelines that complement a legally binding instrument – for example, defining environmental crimes in categories as administrative or civil offences, and penal or serious crimes.

Enhanced law enforcement cooperation

Harmonization would provide a basis for enhanced environmental law enforcement cooperation, including the sharing of criminal intelligence by police, designation of national contact officers, cooperative gathering and exchange of information, protocols for prioritization of investigations, production of witnesses, arrest and extradition of accused and recognition of judgments.

Although international instruments already facilitate these generic forms of law enforcement cooperation, they could be supplemented by cooperative provisions to accommodate new technologies relevant to environmental law enforcement.

Optimize legal tools

A new form of law enforcement cooperation that could be facilitated would be mutual recognition of the certification of legality of environmentally sensitive products when they are moved across borders. The legal provenance of such products could be required to be certified and authenticated under a mutually recognized documentation scheme (Brack and Hayman 2002). Such schemes are already in place under the Basel Convention, Montreal Protocol, CITES and chemicals treaties and several regional fisheries regimes. A generic scheme for other environmentally sensitive products nominated by sending or receiving states could be instituted in a transnational environmental crime regime. Initiatives to combat international trade in the products of illegal fishing or illegal logging could be given a multilateral platform through such a scheme.

In addition, the harmonization of national standards for admission of environmental evidence in criminal trials would facilitate the transnational sharing of evidence. Common standards for acceptance as evidence of digital data extracted from technologies used for environmental monitoring – such as emissions gauges, camera feeds, remote earth sensing, radio frequency identification, digital stamping and satellite transponders – would provide a broader basis for international law enforcement cooperation than currently exists.

Additional measures could also address the specific circumstances of regional law enforcement cooperation. Regional arrangements might include cooperative mechanisms to create common environmental law enforcement databases and pursuit zones, and to designate joint investigative teams.

Capacity building

A law enforcement cooperation regime could be supported by a package of capacity-building and technical assistance measures. For example, standard-setting guidelines could be prepared for legislators and a manual on transnational environmental criminal law enforcement for prosecutors and investigators. Technical training could include the provision of technical needs assessment and advisory services, and the organization of training courses for criminal justice and administrative agency personnel. If a new protocol is established, it could provide a platform for such law enforcement cooperation.

Regional environmental law enforcement cooperative arrangements could also be constructed in a variety of forms, including regional treaties or memoranda of understanding that are registered with the secretariat servicing the global regime. The protocol might serve as the overarching framework for these subsidiary regional arrangements, in a way comparable to the model provided by the Convention on Migratory Species.

Further, a study of environmental law enforcement models using selected global, regional and national examples could inform states as to international practices in environmental criminal law enforcement, revealing common and divergent patterns. This information would be helpful for the design of an international cooperative regime. National environmental laws could be surveyed and analyzed according to categories of characteristics, including appointment of specialist environmental crime personnel and resourcing of international contact points for law enforcement cooperation.

Conclusion

In the emerging international criminal law there is little engagement with environmental crime. Genocide, war crimes and crimes against humanity have crystallized as crimes against international law but environmental crimes *per se* have not. Certain transnational crimes – including terrorism, corruption and trafficking in narcotics, arms and people – have become subject to treaties concerning the harmonization of national laws and cooperation in their suppression. However, the international legal harmonization and cooperation needed specifically to suppress transnational environmental crimes has not emerged. The transnational environmental crime area is relatively new to governmental policy-makers and to the academic community. International legal and institutional frameworks have not been designed specifically to address this phenomenon.

In relation to fisheries management, harmonized understandings of fisheries crimes can be built upon the basis of extensive existing international and regional fisheries management standards. State powers in fishing ports could be readily exercised to enforce criminal jurisdiction for transnational fisheries crimes. For forest crimes, there is no adequate set of international management standards, and so the harmonized criminalization of forest offences could be based upon a less standardized bilateral recognition of foreign laws prescribing serious offences in the forest sector.

In contrast, global cooperative efforts to combat crime have produced treaties that require that their parties criminalize specified acts and cooperate in their enforcement. Although none of the mechanisms developed within the international legal frameworks for crime prevention require the proscription of specified acts of environmental harm, they can be incidentally applicable to environmental offences in some circumstances. Primarily, the CTOC could apply, if a crime conducted by an organized transnational criminal syndicate is considered as a serious offence of no less than four years' imprisonment under national law, or entails corruption, money laundering, bribery or obstruction of justice.

To fill gaps in international legal frameworks addressing transnational environmental crime, initiatives to harmonize criminal national laws are essential. This requires the development of international legal mechanisms to harmonize high-priority, selected national environmental laws. The core initiative could be a specifically applicable protocol to the CTOC that draws upon common obligations set out in environmental treaties. In addition, for fisheries, a resolution on fisheries crimes under the IPOA-IUU or PSM-IUU could be adopted. For forests, undertakings for reciprocal enforcement using the Lacey Act model would serve to harmonize national forest crime laws. These harmonization measures could be complemented by coordination and capacity building in law enforcement, including by harmonization of national standards for admission of certain electronic data gathered in natural resources management as evidence in criminal trials.

Notes

1 1955 UNTS 81, entered into force on 1 January 1997. (It is a renewal of a series of agreements under the same name. The previous agreement opened for signature 18 November 1983, 1393 UNTS 67, and entered into force 1 April 1985. The 2006 Agreement has been agreed upon but has not yet taken effect.) It has 59 parties, being 33 'Producing Members' and 26 'Consuming Members'.

2 In 2010, wild capture fisheries amounted to 88.6 million tonnes of fish. The estimated total value of wild capture and aquaculture production for 2010 was US$217.5 billion (FAO 2012).

3 FAO, 'New treaty will leave "fish pirates" without safe haven'. News article (1 September 2009). Available online at www.fao.org/news/story/it/item/29592/icode (accessed 21 January 2014).

4 FAO, *Agreement on Port State Measures to Prevent, Deter and Eliminate Illegal, Unreported and Unregulated Fishing*, Res 12/2009, 36th sess, FAO Doc C 2009/LIM/11-Rev.1 (18–23 November 2009). The PSM-IUU Agreement was approved under art. XIV(1) of the FAO Constitution.

5 EU, Myanmar, Norway, Sri Lanka and Chile. Myanmar and Sri Lanka were not among the original 22 signatories and therefore acceded to the treaty. Accession relates to states or regional economic integration organizations that did not sign the PSM-IUU Agreement when it was open for signature from 22 November 2009. Individual member countries of the EU have neither signed nor ratified the PSM-IUU Agreement as the EU exercises its competences on their behalf under its constitutional agreements, binding the EU Commission and its (currently) 28 EU member countries. An EU exception is France, which has external territories beyond EU jurisdiction and has independently signed and ratified the PSM-IUU Agreement. The lack of individual EU member states ratifying raises the number of non-EU ratifying states required prior to its entry into force.

6 Fisheries treaties and policy instruments have come to distinguish between illegal fishing, unregulated fishing and unreported fishing (IUU fishing). Whereas illegal fishing designates fishing activities in breach of applicable national or international legal standards, unregulated fishing signifies fishing in an area where there are no applicable legal standards, and unreported fishing signifies a failure to report fishing activities to authorities. There is overlap between these categories, as unreported fishing is prohibited under some fisheries laws which makes it illegal fishing. However, if these activities are not prohibited, then they are not illegal.

7 'States should ensure that sanctions for IUU fishing by vessels and, to the greatest extent possible, nationals under its jurisdiction are of sufficient severity to effectively prevent, deter and eliminate IUU fishing and to deprive offenders of the benefits accruing fishing. This may include the adoption of the civil sanction regime based on an administrative penalties scheme. States should ensure the consistent and transparent application of sanctions' (IPOA-IUU para 21).

8 *Article 3. Scope of application*
   1. This Convention shall apply . . . to the prevention, investigation and prosecution of:
      . . .
      (b) Serious crime as defined in article 2 of this Convention;
          Where the offence is transnational in nature and involves an organized criminal group.

   Article 2. Use of terms
          For the purposes of this Convention:
      (a) 'Organized criminal group' shall mean a structured group of three or more persons, existing for a period of time and acting in concert with the aim of committing one or more serious crimes or offences established in accordance with this convention, in order to obtain, directly or indirectly, a financial or other material benefit;
      (b) 'Serious crime' shall mean conduct constituting an offence punishable by a maximum deprivation of liberty of at least four years or a more serious penalty . . .

9 *Article 10. Liability of legal persons*
   1. Each State Party shall adopt such measures as may be necessary, consistent with its legal principles, to establish the liability of legal persons for participation in serious crimes involving an organized criminal group and for the offences established in accordance with articles 5, 6, 8 and 23 of this Convention.
   2. Subject to the legal principles of the State Party, the liability of legal persons may be criminal, civil or administrative.
   3. Such liability shall be without prejudice to the criminal liability of the natural persons who have committed the offences.
   4. Each State Party shall, in particular, ensure that legal persons held liable in accordance with this article are subject to effective, proportionate and dissuasive criminal or non-criminal sanctions, including monetary sanctions.

10 Decision 4/8 Reorganization of the work of the fifth session of the COP to CTOC, Report of the Conference of the Parties to CTOC on its 4th session, Vienna 8–17 October 2008, CTOC/COP/2008/19. Available at www.unodc.org/unodc/en/treaties/CTOC/CTOC-COP.html (accessed 6 February 2014).

11 Signed 17 December 1997 and entered into force on 15 February 1999. Although the OECD has only 30 members, it currently has 38 parties. Available at www.oecd.org/daf/anti-bribery/antibriberyconventionratification.pdf (accessed 6 February 2014).

12 Adopted by the United Nations General Assembly on 31 October 2003 and came into force on 14 December 2005. It currently has 140 signatories and 143 parties. The preamble states that the Parties have adopted the convention because they are:

> Concerned about the seriousness of problems and threats posed by corruption to the stability and security of societies, undermining the institutions and values of democracy, ethical values and justice and jeopardizing sustainable development and the rule of law, . . .
>
> Concerned further about cases of corruption that involve vast quantities of assets, which may constitute a substantial proportion of the resources of States, and that threaten the political stability and sustainable development of those States, [and]
>
> Convinced that corruption is no longer a local matter but a transnational phenomenon that affects all societies and economies, making international cooperation to prevent and control it essential . . .

See: www.unodc.org/unodc/en/treaties/CAC/index.html.

13 Resolution 1/6 International cooperation workshop on technical assistance for the implementation of the United Nations Convention against Corruption.

14 This is illustrated in the literature on the websites of the UNODC and INTERPOL, which each refer to environmental crimes in terms of breaches of multilateral environmental agreements, despite the fact that such instances of non-compliance are not in themselves crimes.

15 INTERPOL was established in 1923 to facilitate cross-border police cooperation. It is a global organization, with 188 member countries, although not part of the United Nations system of organizations. It is based in Lyon, France. See: www.interpol.int.

16 Prior to its amendment in 2008, the Lacey Act applied to wildlife generally but to wild plants only if they were native to the United States and listed in one of the three appendices to CITES or in a federal or state threatened species law. The Farm Bill 2008 ('Food, Conservation, and Energy Act') extended the coverage of wild plants to include products from plants illegally harvested in the country of origin. This means that dealing in products, such as the importation of wood products from illegally logged trees, even if manufactured outside the foreign country where the illegal logging took place, is prohibited under the Lacey Act.

17 16 USC § 3372 (1900). § 3373 provides varying penalties with regard to the requisite knowledge or intent of the individual involved. For a felony, the defendant must have knowingly imported or exported fish or wildlife or plants in violation of an underlying law or regulation, or knowingly engaged in the sale or purchase of them with a market value of over US$350, while knowing that the fish or wildlife or plants were taken, possessed, transported or sold in violation of an underlying law or regulation. A misdemeanor penalty requires that the defendant failed to exercise 'due care' and should have known the specimens were originally illegal. Where a person, in the exercise of due care, should have known that the fish or wildlife were taken in an unlawful manner, that person is liable for a civil penalty of up to US$10,000. A person who knowingly imports or exports fish or wildlife in contravention to the Act, is liable for a fine of up to US$20,000 or five years' imprisonment, or both.

18 Importers must file a declaration upon importation that contains the scientific name of the plant, the value of the importation, the quantity of the plant and the name of the country from which the plant was taken. A provision of the Lacey Act prohibits the making or submitting of any false record of any wildlife imported, exported, transported, sold, purchased or received from any foreign country. See: Anderson, R. (1995) 'The Lacey Act: America's premier weapon in the fight against unlawful wildlife trafficking', *Public Land Law Review*, 16: 27, 53.

19 16 USC § 3374 (1900). Pursuant to this section, the vessels, vehicles, aircraft and other equipment used to contravene the Act may also be subject to forfeiture under specific circumstances.

20 Illegal Logging Prohibition Act (Cth) 2012.

21 As noted above, in the forest sector there is no legally binding, comprehensive or adequately prescriptive set of global standards concerning illegal logging or illicit timber trade for implementation through criminal laws, and therefore the 'long-arm' bilateral enforcement of foreign national law pioneered in the United States' Lacey Act might provide the template for an international regime.

22 Alternatively, a legal instrument could require countries to designate as crimes those activities that comprise transnational environmental crime generically defined by reference to violation of environmental norms or by reference to the causation of specified environmental harms. To do so, it would need to specify those harms or violations of environmental norms as crimes to be proscribed under national laws. This is the approach taken by the Council of Europe Environmental Crime Convention. However, this approach introduces complexities in trying to build new consensus across broader areas of environmental and justice policies and the European Crime Convention seems to have foundered upon them.

References

Baird, R, (2004) 'Illegal, Unreported and Unregulated Fishing: An Analysis of the Legal, Economic and Historical Factors Relevant to Its Development and Persistence' *Melbourne Journal of International Law* 5(2): 299–334.

Brack, D. (2007) *Controlling Illegal Logging: Lessons from the US Lacey Act*, London: Royal Institute of International Affairs.

Brack, D. and Hayman, G. (2002) *International Environmental Crime: The Nature and Control of Environmental Black Markets*, London: Royal Institute of International Affairs.

Cho, B (2001) 'Emergence of an International Environmental Criminal Law?' *Journal of Environmental Law* 19: 11–47.

Commission for Crime Prevention and Criminal Justice: www.unodc.org/unodc/en/wildlife-and-forest-crime/index.html.

Costa, A. M. (2008) 'Raping the Planet', posted on *Costa's Corner* 15 October 2008. Available online at www.antoniomariacosta.com/cc/index.php?option=com_content&view=article&id=76:raping-the-planet&catid=1:unodclatest&Itemid=67 (accessed 22 January 2014).

Council of Europe (2000) *Convention on the Protection of the Environment through Criminal Law – An Explanatory Report*, Strasbourg.

CTOC Conference of Parties (2012), Report on its sixth session, held in Vienna from 15 to 19 October 2012, CTOC/COP/2012/15, 5 November 2012. Available online at www.unodc.org/documents/treaties/organized_crime/COP6/CTOC_COP_2012_15/CTOC_COP_2012_15_E.pdf (accessed 22 January 2014).

D'Andrea, A. (2006) *The 'Genuine Link' Concept in Responsible Fisheries: Legal Aspects and Recent Developments*, Food and Agricultural Organization of the United Nations. Available online at www.fao.org/fileadmin/user_upload/legal/docs/lpo61.pdf (accessed 22 January 2014).

Dupont, A. (2001) *East Asia Imperiled: Transnational Challenges to Security*, Cambridge: Cambridge University Press.

Elliott, L. (2007) 'Transnational Environmental Crime in the Asia Pacific: An "Un(der) Securitized" Security Problem?' *The Pacific Review* 20(4): 499–522.

Environment Investigation Agency (2008) *Environmental Crime – A Threat to Our Future*. Available at www.unodc.org/documents/NGO/EIA_Ecocrime_report_0908_final_draft_low.pdf (accessed 10 February 2014).

FAO (2012). *The State of World Fisheries and Aquaculture 2012*, 4. Available online at www.fao.org/docrep/016/i2727e/i2727e.pdf (accessed 21 January 2014).

Faure, M. and Heine, G. (2005) *Criminal Enforcement for Environmental Law in the European Union*, The Hague: Kluwer Law International.

Gray, M. (1996) 'The International Crime of Ecocide' *California Western International Law Journal* 26: 215–271.

Higgins, P. (2010) *Eradicating Ecocide*, London: Shepheard-Walwyn.

High Seas Task Force, n.d. *Closing the Net: Stopping Illegal Fishing on the High Seas*. Available online at www.imcsnet.org/imcs/docs/hstf_final_report.pdf (accessed 22 January 2014).

International Tropical Timber Organization: www.itto.int.

INTERPOL: www.interpol.int/Crime-areas/Environmental-crime/Environmental-crime.

Jaakko Pöyry Consulting (2005) *Overview of Illegal Logging*. Available online at www.daff.gov.au/__data/assets/pdf_file/0009/37593/illegal_logging_report_16sept05.pdf (accessed 22 January 2014).

Kuemlangan, B. and Press, M. (2010) 'Preventing, Deterring and Eliminating IUU Fishing' *Environmental Policy and Law* 40(6): 262–268.

Michalowski. R. and Bitten, K. (2005) 'Transnational Environmental Crime' in P. Reichel (ed.) *Handbook of Transnational Crime and Justice*, Thousand Oaks, CA: Sage Publications.

MRAG and Fisheries Ecosystems Restoration Research, Fisheries Centre, University of British Columbia (2005) *Final Report: Review of Impacts of Illegal, Unreported and Unregulated Fishing on Developing Countries*. Available online at www.imcsnet.org/imcs/docs/iuu_fishing_synthesis_report_mrag.pdf (accessed 6 February 2014).

Orellana, M. (2005) 'Criminal Punishment for Environmental Damage: Individual and State Responsibility at a Crossroad' *Georgetown International Environmental Law Review* 17: 673–696.

REDD+ (n.d.) *About REDD+*. Available at www.un-redd.org/AboutREDD/tabid/102614/Default.aspx (accessed on 6 February 2014).

Schloenhardt, A. (2008) *The Illegal Trade of Timber and Timber Products in the Asia-Pacific Region*, Australian Institute of Criminology, Research and Public Policy Series, No. 89. Available online at www.aic.gov.au/publications/current%20series/rpp/81–99/rpp89.html (accessed 8 May 2014).

Setiono, B. and Husein, Y. (2005) *Fighting Forest Crime and Promoting Prudent Banking for Sustainable Forest Management*, Occasional Paper No. 44, Bogor: Centre for International Forestry Research. Available online at www.cifor.org/publications/pdf_files/OccPapers/OP-44.pdf (accessed 10 February 2014).

Sharp, A. (2010) *The Effectiveness or Not of the New Port State Measures in the Battle to Control Illegal, Unregulated and Unreported Fishing*, Social Science Research Network. Available online at http://papers.ssrn.com/sol3/papers.cfm?abstract_id=2140528 (accessed 21 January 2014).

Sharp, P. (1999) 'Prospects for Environmental Liability in the International Criminal Court' *Virginia Environmental Law Journal* 18: 217–243.

World Wide Fund – United Kingdom (2003) *Fighting Forest Crime and the Illegal Timber Trade.* Available online at www.wwf.org.uk/filelibrary/pdf/fightingforestcrime.pdf (accessed 22 January 2014).

Index